Daring, Trusting Spirit

Daring, Trusting Spirit

Bonhoeffer's Friend Eberhard Bethge

John W. de Gruchy

Fortress Press
Minneapolis

DARING, TRUSTING SPIRIT
Bonhoeffer's Friend Eberhard Bethge

Cover images: Eberhard Bethge and Dietrich Bonhoeffer, 1938. The text is an extract from "Thoughts on the Day of the Baptism of Dietrich Wilhelm Rüdiger Bethge" written by Bonhoeffer, May 1944. Photos © Chr. Kaiser/Gütersloher Verlagshaus GmbH, Gütersloh, Germany. Cover design: James Korsmo

ISBN 0-8006-3758-5

Manufactured in the Great Britain

09 08 07 06 05 1 2 3 4 5 6 7 8 9 10

Contents

Dedicated to

John Godsey
Theologian, Colleague, Friend

Introduction

Eberhard Bethge is known primarily as the friend, biographer and interpreter of Dietrich Bonhoeffer, the German pastor executed in April 1945 for his resistance against the Nazi regime. The two met in August 1935 when Bethge – 26 years of age, recently dismissed as a student from the seminary in Wittenberg after joining the anti-Nazi Confessing Church – arrived at Bonhoeffer's illegal seminary, Finkenwalde, near the Baltic coastline. By all accounts they became close almost immediately, and the relationship soon overshadowed Bonhoeffer's other friendships. Bethge became Bonhoeffer's right hand, helping to oversee groups of seminarians at Finkenwalde and later in the underground collective pastorates. He travelled with Bonhoeffer and often stayed at the Bonhoeffer family home when he was in Berlin. He was present with Bonhoeffer at secret meetings with members of the German Resistance and even travelled abroad on its behalf. In May 1943 Bethge married Bonhoeffer's niece Renate Schleicher. By then Bonhoeffer was in prison and Bethge himself was an army conscript serving in Italy. During this period, the two friends, who had regularly written to each other when previously separated, conducted a lengthy prison correspondence, one of the most interesting and moving such exchanges ever published. Bethge was eventually arrested by the Gestapo and imprisoned in Berlin from October 1944 until April 1945, when he escaped.

More than anything else, the friendship between Eberhard Bethge and Dietrich Bonhoeffer was a bond between two people who instinctively understood one another from the very beginning. The historical circumstances in which they found themselves gave this closeness a special poignancy. Writing in November 1943 after Bethge had visited him in prison, Bonhoeffer spoke of 'the advantage of having spent almost every day and having experienced almost every event and discussed every thought together for eight years. One needs only a second to know about each other, and now one doesn't really need even that second any more.'[1] For all their differences in personality and background, they shared the same convictions and priorities, and marvelled at how they complemented each other.

It is impossible to ignore the historical context of this friendship. In order to understand and appreciate its significance we must situate it within the social, cultural and familial patterns of that age. The entire Bonhoeffer family was extremely reserved and not given to great expressions of emotion; Germans of that era and class in general were private people. Bethge's magisterial biography of Bonhoeffer reflects this ethos; it is striking for its comprehensive, exhaustive detail and its simultaneous lack of revelation about Bonhoeffer's personality and his private life.[2] Even the love letters to his fiancée Maria von Wedemeyer, the most intimate portrait we have of Bonhoeffer, show great reserve.[3] While Bethge certainly respected these boundaries, he himself was more open and ebullient. His self-description as a mere 'country boy' in the world of the Bonhoeffers may well have been a subconscious need to make room for his own personality in the midst of a very different but strong-willed aristocratic family culture.

Yet in the disastrous wake of Nazism, Bethge became a central figure within that family circle. The execution of four men in the immediate Bonhoeffer family on Hitler's instruction – Dietrich and his brother Klaus, and their brothers-in-law Hans von

---

1. Letter to Eberhard Bethge, 26 November 1943, in Dietrich Bonhoeffer, *Letters and Papers from Prison* (London: SCM Press, 1971), p. 145.

2. Eberhard Bethge, *Dietrich Bonhoeffer: Theologe, Christ, Zeitgenosse* (Munich: Chr. Kaiser Verlag, 1967). References to this work by page number will be to the following edition: Eberhard Bethge, *Dietrich Bonhoeffer: A Biography* (Minneapolis: Fortress Press, 2000)

3. Dietrich Bonhoeffer and Maria von Wedemeyer, *Love Letters from Cell 92* (London: HarperCollins, 1994).

Dohnanyi and Rudiger Schleicher (the father of Eberhard's wife Renate) – devastated the family, including the elderly parents and the one surviving brother, Karl-Friedrich. Bethge emerged as the pragmatic and energetic support, not only for the Bonhoeffer family but also for the widows and children of other executed resistance figures. He helped them settle their financial affairs and dealt with the Allied authorities on their behalf. In the same period Bethge entered the active ministry, serving as a student chaplain and as assistant to Bishop Otto Dibelius in Berlin.

As executor of Bonhoeffer's literary estate, Bethge began publishing selected writings almost immediately after the war: the prison poems in 1946, a commemorative booklet in 1947, and the *Ethics* manuscripts in 1949. That same year, he visited the United States for three months as part of an Allied re-education programme, and used the trip as a chance to contact some of Bonhoeffer's former associates in New York, including Reinhold Niebuhr and Paul Lehmann. Then, in 1953, the year in which he published a selection of Bonhoeffer's prison letters, he followed his friend's footsteps to a German-speaking parish in London, where he served as minister from 1953 to 1961. That might have been the end of it. As a parish minister and young father – by then the Bethges had three children (Dietrich, Gabriele, Sabine) – there wasn't much time for him to write his own recollections or reflect upon the theological aspects of Bonhoeffer's legacy. But through the influence of Lehmann, then teaching at Harvard University's Divinity School, Bethge was invited there to spend a sabbatical year (1957/8) to work more systematically on the Bonhoeffer material.

Bethge, though always a pastor at heart, never returned to the parish ministry. In the decades that followed, his main occupation was editing, publishing and reflecting on the life and legacy of Dietrich Bonhoeffer. The publication of his biography of Bonhoeffer in 1967 was widely acclaimed, with Bethge now acknowledged as the definitive source on Bonhoeffer. Invitations to speak and write from around the world followed. While these invariably related to his stature as the friend and interpreter of Bonhoeffer, it soon became clear that he was a theologian of substance in his own right. Wherever he went he was just as interested in discussing the burning issues that confronted his audiences as he was in talking about Bonhoeffer.

During the years 1961–76, Bethge directed the Rhineland Church Seminary for continuing education, located in Rengsdorf. Drawing upon his experiences under Nazism and the insights gained from Bonhoeffer's approach to theological education, Bethge became an engaged voice in his Church and nation, a strong supporter of the Protestant Church's anti-apartheid movement, and the leading advocate for rethinking Christian attitudes toward Judaism in the light of the Holocaust. Bethge's contribution to these issues is explored in detail in what follows, though for reasons that will become obvious in a moment, more is said about his role in the anti-apartheid movement than about his contribution to Jewish–Christian relations and Holocaust studies. To do full justice to the latter requires a monograph of its own, one that will explore in depth the large amount of material that still needs careful examination and commentary, as well as provide an assessment of Bethge's contribution in the light of the contemporary discussion.

In the 1980s and 1990s, Bethge led and actively helped to edit the German publication of the *Dietrich Bonhoeffer Werke*, a new sixteen-volume critical edition of all of Bonhoeffer's writings.[4] Several of these volumes have provided rich resources for this book, containing as they do all the extant correspondence between the two friends. As Bethge grew older he spoke more and more often at events that commemorated or reflected upon the German resistance, the problems of German history, and the issue of national identity. He used these occasions to challenge his audiences with provocative, often uncomfortable questions. In this regard, Bethge displayed his great skills as a historian,

---

4. Dietrich Bonhoeffer, *Dietrich Bonhoeffer Werke*, ed. Eberhard Bethge *et al.* (Munich: Chr. Kaiser Verlag and Gütersloh: Chr. Kaiser/Gütersloh Verlagshaus, 1989–99). English-language edition: Dietrich Bonhoeffer, *Dietrich Bonhoeffer Works*, general eds Wayne Whitson Floyd Jr, Victoria Barnett and Barbara Wojhoski, 8 vols published thus far (Minneapolis: Fortress Press, 1998–).

theologian and pastor, but he also communicated his compassion for others, his concern for the truth, and his commitment to the cause of justice and peace.

One thesis of this book is that Bethge's role as the definitive Bonhoeffer scholar and the pastoral advocate for a thoughtful, relevant Christianity in his own Church were integrally related. Another thesis, cautiously formulated, is that Bethge's own post-war passions and convictions, together with his experience of other cultures and contexts, shaped his interpretation of Bonhoeffer's legacy. Had another of Bonhoeffer's close friends (say, Franz Hildebrandt) become Bonhoeffer's literary executor and written his biography, in all likelihood we would have a rather different Bonhoeffer today. Indeed, the reactions to the early post-war publications of Bonhoeffer's wartime writings, edited and introduced by Bethge, were quite mixed, not least among some of those who had been Bonhoeffer's students. But Bethge's stature as Bonhoeffer's interpreter was soon recognized. After all, he was the only one to have accompanied Bonhoeffer through the resistance period and his time in prison. Even more, ever since Finkenwalde, he had been intimately involved in his friend's personal life, its joys, struggles and dreams, sharing his hopes for and disappointments in his church and country.

There is no doubt that, after 1945, Bethge's interpretation of his friend's life and thought took Bonhoeffer's theology in the direction he thought it would have gone – admittedly a specula-tive enterprise. What is not speculation is that Bonhoeffer him-self expressed great confidence in Bethge as the one who would most faithfully represent his life and work, naming him his liter-ary executor should he die. He also appreciated Bethge's skill in seeing and writing with simplicity and clarity, and acknowledged his theological insight. Indeed, for five decades after the war, Bethge continued to do theology in the way he learnt so ably from Bonhoeffer: theology as an ongoing conversation with scripture, the church, culture and political reality. In 1989, Heinz Eduard Tödt noted that Bethge's life's work had been something 'very different from the preservation of a legacy'; what Bethge had been engaged in was 'a highly dynamic and thoroughly open

process'.[5] Whenever confronted by a new situation or a challeng-
ing question, he returned to the Bonhoeffer opus and reread,
rethought and revised. But he never simply repeated Bonhoeffer's thought in a way unrelated to historical context. For at
the heart of the task to which he had committed his life was
always Bonhoeffer's own question: 'Who is Jesus Christ, for us,
today?'

In his monumental biography of his friend, Bethge sought to
portray Bonhoeffer as a man who had not been defeated by his
circumstances – a friend who, despite having been caught in a
historical tempest, had done 'what was demanded of him' amidst
the storm, as Bethge wrote in the introduction to the biography.
The same could have been said of Eberhard Bethge himself,
both before and after 1945. The meaning – unspoken, unwritten
– that Bethge gave to his own life is present in his portrayal of
the history of his friend. Yet he could never have written and
interpreted the life of Bonhoeffer had he himself not been
an active witness and participant in the central events of that life:
a daring, trusting spirit, with the gift of 'clear, open and
reverent seeing',[6] who sought to convey the meaning of what he
saw in a way that would create a more just and responsible world.
In narrating the story of Bethge's life we are therefore also
reflecting on the creation of a historical and theological legacy,
about the retrospective construction not just of a life but a
moral universe amidst an often bitter battle waged for several
decades in post-1945 Germany and elsewhere about history and
theology.

Given the nature of the friendship between Bethge and
Bonhoeffer, no biography of Bethge could possibly be written
without constant reference to Bonhoeffer himself. Widely known
and introduced as 'Bonhoeffer's friend', their identities have
been irrevocably linked. So if at times, especially in the first two
chapters, it might appear that the focus is more on Bonhoeffer's
story than on Bethge's, this is only because Bethge's story cannot

5. Heinz Eduard Tödt, 'Eberhard Bethge als Theologe und Zeit-
geschichtsforscher', *Evangelische Theologie* 49:5 (1989), p. 413.
6. Bonhoeffer, *Letters and Papers from Prison*, p. 385.

be told in isolation from Bonhoeffer's, or without reference to those issues and events that were so much a part of their life together from Finkenwalde until Bonhoeffer's death in Flossenbürg concentration camp. As the narrative unfolds, however, so it becomes more and more evident that Bethge's story has its own integrity and value even as Bonhoeffer's friend and interpreter. As such it is a story well worth telling, and equally worth reflecting on. In sum, the truth is that without Bethge we would not know or understand Bonhoeffer in the way we do today. But the reverse is equally true: without Bonhoeffer, Bethge's life, however significant it may have become, would have been very different.

I was privileged to know Eberhard Bethge and spend many hours over the years in his company, and to be in correspondence with him on various issues. But I was not one of his close associates, and therefore not party to details of his life that they might recall. Nonetheless, in telling his story I have sought accuracy in detail, drawing on the various accounts of his life that he has left us as well as his copious notes, lectures and correspondence, and learning much from the memoirs and reflections of many of his closer friends and colleagues. So without pretending that this is *the* definitive 'Bethge Biography', I hope I have done some justice to the subject. The definitive biography may require the passing of more years, and may have to be written by someone quite outside the Bonhoeffer–Bethge circle, someone who comes to the task with fresh eyes and the wisdom of greater hindsight.

Just as Bethge wrote his biography of Bonhoeffer from the perspective of intimate friend and participant with Bonhoeffer in the German church struggle (*Kirchenkampf*) and resistance, as well as from the perspective of the debates and issues that arose in the post-war years, so I have written this account as a South African whose perspective has been influenced by both Bonhoeffer and Bethge in the church struggle against apartheid and in the past decade of democratic freedom. It was precisely as a result of being thus engaged that my friendship with Bethge began and subsequently developed over the years. Of course, my perspective has not, I hope, intruded where it would be inappropriate, but I think Bethge would have been most surprised if I had written his biography in any other way. After all, he always encouraged me to pursue my interest in Bonhoeffer in relation to my own historical context.

When I originally decided to work on this project I was joined by Victoria Barnett as co-author. Unfortunately Vicki eventually had to withdraw in that capacity due to unforeseen circumstances, much to my regret. But she was a great help in the planning of the volume, and contributed much to the writing, translating and editing process. Her research skills, her knowledge of the German church struggle and the Holocaust, evident in her several books and papers, were an indispensable resource. Together we spent time going through Eberhard Bethge's papers at the Bethge home in Wachtberg-Villiprott, benefiting immensely from the memories and insight, as well as the hospitality, of Renate Bethge, who not only made it possible for us to peruse her husband's papers, but also enlightened us on many points of interest as we did so. I hope that Renate will approve the final result, and regard this brief biography as an expression of gratitude to her for all that she has meant to so many of us. I also hope that in due course, Bethge's papers will be properly archived, containing, as they do, such rich material for anyone interested in his life, legacy and times. It should be noted that some of the papers cited in this volume as unpublished may well have been published, but I have not been able to track down the details if that is the case.

Among those who have also helped me along the way, I would like to mention in particular Keith Clements who, *inter alia*, kindly provided a set of tape-recorded interviews he conducted with the Bethges in 1985; Hans Pfeifer, long-time friend of the Bethges and one of Eberhard's close associates; Clifford Green, who read the final draft with great care and made many useful comments; Lyn Holness, my former personal assistant; and Isobel de Gruchy, who shared with me in many visits to the Bethge home and also contributed to improving the text. I would also thank those at both SCM Press and Fortress Press for so readily agreeing to publish the book, and for their help in seeing it through production.

The book is dedicated to John Godsey. John wrote the first

major study in English on the theology of Dietrich Bonhoeffer, and was the first of many doctoral students who benefited from the knowledge and friendship of Eberhard Bethge, preparing the way for the rest of us who followed. Since then, as a professor and now professor emeritus in Washington DC, he has continued to be a wonderful mentor, fine scholar, and good friend to all those involved in the International Bonhoeffer Society and many beyond. He represents what we all seek to espouse, and what Bethge so wonderfully embodied – the true meaning of friendship.

True and lasting friendship is a precious gift. In writing this biography I celebrate one of the great and most remarkable friendships of the twentieth century: a friendship described so poignantly by Bonhoeffer himself in a poem he wrote for Bethge from prison entitled 'The Friend'. At its heart, as recorded in this extract, are the words that have provided the title for this book:

Beside the cornfield that sustains us,
tilled and cared for reverently by men
sweating as they labour at their task,
and, if need be, giving their life's blood –
beside the field that gives their daily bread
men also let the lovely cornflower thrive.
No one has planted, no one watered it;
it grows, defenceless and in freedom,
and in glad confidence of life untroubled
under the open sky.
Beside the staff of life,
taken and fashioned from the heavy earth,
beside our marriage, work, and war,
the free man, too, will live and grow towards the sun.
Not the ripe fruit alone –
blossom is lovely, too.
Does blossom serve only the fruit,
or does fruit only serve the blossom –
who knows?
But both are given to us.

Finest and rarest blossom,
at a happy moment springing
from the freedom of a lightsome, daring, trusting spirit,
is a friend to a friend.[7]

John de Gruchy
January 2005

---

7. Bonhoeffer, *Letters and Papers from Prison*, p. 388.

1

Only a Country Boy

Eberhard Bethge had no memories of his birthplace, the small country village of Warchau in the district of Magdeburg near Brandenburg, nor did he want any. Everyone has heard about Warschau (Warsaw), he once complained, but who has ever heard of Warchau? But it was there, on 18 August 1909, that Elisabeth Bethge, wife of Lutheran pastor Wilhelm Bethge, gave birth to her third son. The first-born, Martin, had died the year before at age five, and Hans, the second son, was by then four years old. Eberhard always thought that Margret and Christoph, his two younger siblings, got a better start in life by being born in Zitz, a larger but still very small village where the family moved in 1911. But, as Eberhard later acknowledged, 'you cannot get rid of your birthplace'.[1] He was a country boy whose early horizons were bounded by Warchau and Zitz. In neither place were you likely to meet anyone exotic; perhaps a few gypsies from time to time, but certainly no Catholics or Jews. Indeed, the young Eberhard only saw pictures of Jews in the large family Bible, and they were normally not complimentary. Zitz was *evangelisch*.[2] There was one church and one cemetery around its tower for everyone, and no one thought it should be different.

---

1. Eberhard Bethge, *In Zitz gab es kein Juden: Erinnerungen aus meinen ersten Vierzig Jahren* (Munich: Chr. Kaiser Verlag, 1989), p. 19.
2. *Evangelisch* or Evangelical refers to the historic Protestant Church in Germany, both Lutheran and Reformed.

Called to be a Pastor

Pastor Bethge was already 48 at the time of Eberhard's birth, twelve years older than his wife Elisabeth. Like most Protestant pastors of that generation, and especially those in the countryside, Wilhelm upheld solid conservative, Protestant and patriotic values that shaped the lives of his family just as they reflected the norms of his parishioners. He was strict and yet warm, conscientious in pursuing his calling yet playful with his children. Together with Elisabeth, pastor Bethge rallied his flock in support of the German war effort and in honouring those who fell at the Eastern and Western Fronts. But he also recognized the pain and suffering that accompanied battle victories and, as Eberhard later indicated, by 1917 anticipated the coming defeat and the disgrace that would follow.[3] Wilhelm Bethge died when Eberhard was only fourteen, but by then he had left a lasting impression upon him. At that young age Eberhard, at his father's funeral, 'made a vow . . . to follow in his footsteps', a decision he never regretted.[4]

Elisabeth was a devoted wife and mother, a pastor's wife of a generation that considered their husband's calling as their own. In particular, she regarded one of her main roles as ensuring the proper development of her children's religious and moral character, not least their sense of modesty and the proper stewardship of money. When Eberhard became a young adult and a university student, she expressed disapproval of what she perceived to be the waste of money that he wanted to spend on a trip down the Danube from Vienna to Constantinople. And, so Eberhard sensed, she was ashamed and disappointed when he spent the Easter holidays with an old school friend in Paris. By contrast, the home was always open to friends of the children, as long as they behaved decently, and, so Eberhard tells us, he probably inherited his love for games from her. But already, as

---

3. Bethge, *In Zitz*, p. 24.
4. Eberhard Bethge, *Friendship and Resistance: Essays on Dietrich Bonhoeffer* (Geneva: WCC, 1995), p. 1.

his visits to Vienna and Paris suggest, Eberhard's own vision of life, though rooted in the Saxon countryside, stretched far beyond. Even though Bethge kept referring to himself as a 'country boy' his vision was already more cosmopolitan than this description suggests.

There were other childhood influences that played a significant role in the early formation of Eberhard Bethge's life and the shaping of his future vocation. One of these was his capacity for making and keeping good friends. In his autobiographical sketch *In Zitz gab es keine Juden* (In Zitz there were no Jews), he devotes a chapter to his closest friends of that time, Karl Körner, Bernard Riemer and his cousin Gerhard Vibrans.[5] His friendship with Riemer continued into adulthood, when Riemer became a pastor in the Confessing Church and was later imprisoned by the Nazis in 1937.[6] Dietrich Bonhoeffer wrote from prison to console Bethge when Riemer died in 1943.[7] But undoubtedly the most significant friendship of those early years was Eberhard's relationship with Gerhard Vibrans, the latter's sister Dorli, and more generally the Vibrans household. The friendship with Gerhard may be traced back to the time when the young Eberhard spent school holidays with the Vibrans family.[8] Eberhard's love of music was greatly stimulated within this environment, though his own ability to read music and play new instruments was largely self-taught.[9]

Like Bethge's own father, Karl Vibrans was a country pastor, in Wegeleben near Halberstadt. His example also influenced Eberhard, as it did his son Gerhard, who later followed the same vocation. The Vibrans household demonstrated what

---

5. Bethge, *In Zitz*, pp. 40–71.

6. See Bethge, *Dietrich Bonhoeffer*, p. 582.

7. Letter to Bethge, 20 November 1943, in Bonhoeffer, *Letters and Papers from Prison*, p. 132.

8. Bethge, *In Zitz*, pp. 63–71. See also the correspondence of Bethge in *So ist es gewesen: Briefe im Kirchenkampf 1933–1942 von Gerhard Vibrans aus seinem Familien-und Freundeskreis und von Dietrich Bonhoeffer*, ed. Gerhard Andersen, Dorothea Andersen, Eberhard Bethge and Elfriede Vibrans (Gütersloh: Chr. Kaiser/Gütersloher Verlagshaus, 1995).

9. Personal conversation with Renate Bethge, March 2003.

Bethge would later refer to as the art of the pastor's home (*Pfarrhauserkunft*).[10] And the fact that Gerhard became part of the Confessing Church in Nazi Germany also tells us something about that parental influence and the values that were imparted in the *Pfarrhaus*. Certainly the two cousins with such similar backgrounds and a shared sense of vocation, as well as a love for music and games, had much in common to reinforce and sustain their friendship during the traumatic years that lay ahead.

Elisabeth Bethge's concern about Eberhard's occasional way-wardness was reinforced by his schoolteachers' reports in Magdeburg, where he attended the Gymnasium from 1920 to 1929. In 1925 his schoolmaster offered a stern evaluation of his student:

> I must reproach Eberhard for taking things too lightly and always making excuses for himself. His instructor, Dr Helms, offered to practise reading Greek three times a week with him and other graduates for no payment . . . Eberhard prefers to spend this time in the craft shop. Since your son has no linguistic gifts whatsoever, I urgently advise you to allow your son to take up a practical trade at Easter . . . It is Eberhard's wish to become a pastor . . . whether Eberhard is up to these demands naturally cannot yet be determined, but I doubt it. I certainly believe that his nature and his attitude are suitable for a pastor . . .[11]

Undeterred, the country boy with a love of handcraft and music set out to become a pastor and theologian.

Unlike some candidates for the Christian ministry there was apparently no sudden conversion experience that determined Bethge's choice of vocation. Rather, as we have already noted, it was the example of his father that made him vow to become a pastor. His knowledge of what it meant to be a pastor was shaped by the traditional rural image of the country parson living in

---

10. Bethge, *In Zitz*, p. 64.

11. Letter from Herr Vondran to Elisabeth Bethge, 21 December 1925, private papers of Eberhard Bethge. See Bethge, *In Zitz*, pp. 36–7.

daily intimate connection with his small flock, preaching to them, baptizing and teaching the catechism to their children, marrying them and sharing in their celebrations, counselling them in times of suffering and need, and burying them at the end. With the manse right opposite the church in Zitz, it was clear to Eberhard that this was no nine-to-five job with clear employment terms of reference, but a lifelong relationship with one's parishioners that knew few time constraints. It was nonetheless one that had security and respect from all social classes, whether landowner, labourer, or burgher. Every candidate for the ministry in the Evangelical Church could be assured of a relatively large house, a reasonably good stipend, an honoured place in the community and, especially in a farming community, the material support of the congregation. While the cultured parents of Berlin's elite, such as the Bonhoeffers, might have been horrified when their sons chose to become ministers, regarding it as a waste of talent,[12] they could be comforted by the fact that at least it was a secure job for their sons at a time of great unemployment and uncertainty. But few, whether in the countryside or the city, could have anticipated the radical challenges and changes that lay around the corner for those called to the ministry in Germany in the 1930s.

Meanwhile several years of intense theological education and training for the ministry lay ahead of Bethge. In company with his cousin Gerhard Vibrans, and following academic tradition in Germany, between 1929 and 1933 he pursued his studies at several universities: Königsberg, Berlin, Vienna and Tübingen, ending up at the theological seminary in Wittenberg, where Martin Luther had launched the Protestant Reformation. It was there that Bethge took his first examinations as a theological candidate for the Magdeburg consistory of the Evangelical or Protestant church of Saxony. Shortly after this he served a required term as an assistant pastor or vicar with the Superintendent in the congregation in Ziesar not far from his birthplace.

---

12. See Bethge, *Dietrich Bonhoeffer*, p. 36.

A Decisive Turn

Adolf Hitler's appointment as Chancellor of the Third Reich on 30 January 1933 was welcomed by many within the traditionally conservative and largely middle-class Protestant provincial churches (*Landeskirchen*). Even if aspects of his rise to power troubled some, many Protestants believed that National Socialism was the only way to counter the spread of Bolshevism, restore law and order as well as the monarchy, combat unemployment, stabilize a chronically ill economy, and recover German dignity after the humiliation of Versailles and the decadence of the Weimar Republic. But even so there was a range of opinions and responses within the church to Hitler as the Führer. Some, albeit a small minority, like the Bonhoeffers in Berlin, immediately sensed danger; many more were uncomfortable about Nazi ideology, demagoguery, and the uniformed riff-raff that began to exert increasingly brutal power. But most were willing to give Hitler the benefit of the doubt, and growing numbers became committed to the Nazi cause with religious passion. Even children of the critical elites became members of the Hitler youth movement (Hitlerjugend).

The German Christian movement (Deutsche Christen) was the Protestant Church group which gave the most zealous support to Hitler. Well-organized and determined to dominate and control the Church, it stridently promoted the unification of the provincial churches into one *Reichkirche* under a *Reichsbischof* of their choice, and in the July 1933 church elections the German Christian candidates had the open support of the Nazi Party. A unified national church appealed to the church leadership, some of whom welcomed many aspects of Nazism, although many were appalled by the theological extremism of the Deutsche Christen.

However, a smaller group within the Protestant Church emerged to oppose the German Christians and soon expanded its critique more generally to Nazi policies. Among these was a circle of pastors in Berlin who, in 1932, had already gathered around Martin Niemöller and Gerhard Jacobi. Highly respected within the Church, Niemöller was the distinguished pastor of Dahlem parish, while Jacobi was pastor of the influential Kaiser Wilhelm Memorial Church. Bonhoeffer, at that time an unsalaried lecturer (*Privatdozent*) at Humboldt University, was associated with this group, though always on its more critical edges.

Another and more widespread organization, though with links to Niemöller's circle, was the Young Reformation Movement. Formed in May 1933, it was dedicated to a recovery of Reformation theology and witness over against Nazi ideology. Eberhard Bethge, his cousin Gerhard Vibrans, and several other theological students from Wittenberg were soon attracted into its ranks. Like the Deutsche Christen, the Young Reformation Movement welcomed the new Germany, regarding it as an opportunity to work for the renewal of the church. But their path to renewal was through a recovery of the 'pure gospel' of the Reformation in opposition to Nazi ideology. This, indeed, was the position adopted by the eminent Swiss Reformed theologian Karl Barth, who was then teaching at the University of Bonn, and who was so influential in Bonhoeffer's own theological development. In his tract for the times entitled *Theologische Existenz heute!*, published in May 1933 and widely circulated and read, Barth wrote: 'I regard the pursuit of theology as the proper attitude to adopt: at any rate it is one befitting Church-politics, and indirectly, even politics.'[13] Significantly, the Nazis confiscated the book, indicating that Barth's kind of theology did, indeed, pose a political threat.

The complex story of the German church struggle (*Kirchenkampf*) defies easy narration and analysis.[14] But some understanding of the issues at stake and the way it unfolded is essential in tracing the formation of Bethge's friendship with Bonhoeffer

---

13. Karl Barth, *Theological Existence To-Day! A Plea for Theological Freedom* (London: Hodder & Stoughton, 1933), pp. 9–10.

14. See Klaus Scholder, *The Churches and the Third Reich: 1918–1934* (London: SCM Press, 1987) and *The Churches and the Third Reich: The Year of Disillusionment 1934, Barmen and Rome* (London: SCM Press, 1988).

and the development of his life and theology. The theological
responses developed during these years (1933–8) not only shaped
Bethge's theology at the time, but profoundly influenced the way
in which he later responded to the church situation in Germany
after World War II, both as an interpreter of Bonhoeffer's legacy
and as a theologian in his own right. So a discussion of these
issues provides the essential background for much that will
concern us later.

The initial issue at stake in the church struggle was the
German Christians' attempt to create a Reich church. Their
opponents won the first round when Friedrich von Bodelschwingh, the widely respected director of the Bethel community for the disabled in Bielefeld, was elected *Reichsbischof* at a
national synod. But his position soon became untenable and he
resigned. Hitler's personal preference, Ludwig Müller, a relatively unknown military chaplain and a long-time member of the
Nazi Party, was then elected to the office on 23 July 1933. To
the dismay of some, the Young Reformation Movement then
withdrew from church politics and devoted itself to preaching
the gospel of the Reformation over against the heresies of the
Deutsche Christen.[15] Despite its opposition to Nazi ideology,
the Young Reformation Movement was unable to transcend the
traditional Lutheran interpretation of the 'two kingdoms' doctrine that kept faith and politics in separate spheres. Only later
under Bonhoeffer's influence would Bethge recognize the
dangers of this doctrine and what he came to call a 'docetic ecclesiology' – a view of the Church as a spiritual community of piety
separate from, rather than embodied in, the world.

In an attempt to address the issues now facing the Church,
Niemöller invited several theologians associated with his circle in
Berlin, including Bonhoeffer and his very close friend Franz
Hildebrandt, to draft a new confession of faith. At Bodel-
schwingh's invitation, the group met on several occasions during
August 1933 at Bethel.[16] The crisis deepened at the Prussian
synod in September, when the German Christians passed a new

---

15. Scholder, *The Churches and the Third Reich: 1918–1934*, p. 453.
16. See Bethge, *Dietrich Bonhoeffer*, pp. 300–4.

church law that included an 'Aryan paragraph', modelled on the Nazi civil service laws, banning those of Jewish descent from the ranks of the clergy, theological faculties, and religious educators. Hildebrandt, being partly of Jewish descent, was personally affected by this decree. In October 1933, in response to these grave new developments, Niemöller established the Pastors' Emergency League to help those affected by the Aryan paragraph. It soon attracted remarkable support throughout the Protestant church and supplanted the Young Reformation Movement.

The first draft of the Bethel Confession, in which Bonhoeffer was directly involved, addressed the theological issues raised by the German Christians and included a section (written by Wilhelm Vischer) on the Aryan paragraph. To Bonhoeffer's dismay, numerous consultants, including Bodelschwingh, watered down the final document in an attempt to make it more conciliatory to the new national spirit that was sweeping through Germany and its churches. Disillusioned but deeply concerned, Bonhoeffer wrote Barth on 9 September 1933, asking whether he thought that a *status confessionis* had now arrived in Germany.

The notion of a *status confessionis* went back to the Reformation and meant that a situation had arisen in the Church that threatened to destroy the integrity of its confession of faith. As such it demanded a restatement of the faith that would inevitably have to distinguish between the 'true' and 'false' Church. For Bonhoeffer, the critical issue was the exclusion of 'non-Aryans' from the Church. Barth agreed that a *status confessionis* was approaching, but was not convinced that those opposed to the Nazification of the Church should take the initiative in dividing the Church on the Jewish issue. Barth preferred that rather than engaging in church politics, they should state their theological position clearly and demand that the church be the church. Disillusioned by the compromises of the Bethel Confession, and perplexed by Barth's caution, Bonhoeffer left shortly thereafter to take up a position in London as the pastor of two German-speaking Lutheran churches, a move that disappointed Barth, who believed that Bonhoeffer was needed in Germany.

In December a large group of Reformed (as distinct from

Lutheran) pastors associated with the Pastors' Emergency
League met in Württemberg, and there commissioned Barth to
draft what became known as the first Barmen Declaration. Then,
in April 1934, concerned pastors and laypeople from around the
country gathered in Ulm and decided to convene a nationwide
confessing synod at Barmen-Wuppertal. The Synod convened
on 29 May, and adopted the Barmen Declaration as its confessional charter. Although the Declaration, also drafted largely
by Karl Barth, did not speak directly to the 'Jewish Question', it
categorically rejected the Nazification of the church. Later Barth
would acknowledge to Bethge that he had been guilty of not
speaking out for the Jews at the time, and that Bonhoeffer 'was
the first and only theologian who really did so'.[17] But at the time
Barth doubted whether even those theologians and church
leaders opposed to the Nazis could have found agreement at
Barmen in 1934 if they were called upon to express solidarity
with the Jews.

Several months later, in October 1934, the Confessing Church
convened again, this time in Dahlem, the suburb of Berlin where
Niemöller was pastor. It was a far more turbulent and divided
synod than Barmen had been, with the more radical members
insisting that the Confessing Church, not the official Reich
Church, was the only legitimate Protestant church in Germany.
In taking this position, the Dahlem Synod represented a high
point in the witness of the Confessing Church for Bonhoeffer and
those who shared his views, and its decision would have a powerful influence on Bethge's own life. To the chagrin of Bonhoeffer
and others, subsequent synods made many compromises for the
sake of church unity in the face of growing pressure from
German Christian church leaders and state officials. Bonhoeffer,
of course, was in London and thus did not participate at either
Barmen or Dahlem, but what he had longed for had now come to
pass. A *status confessionis* had been recognized and the 'true'
Evangelical church had at last taken a stand against the 'false'

---

17. Karl Barth, *Fragments Grave and Gay* (London: Collins, 1971),
p. 119.

church of the Reich. From London, Bonhoeffer led his German-speaking congregation into the ranks of the Confessing Church.

The situation in the official Protestant church became increasingly intolerable for the opponents of the new Reich Church administration. While some of the provincial churches were prepared to work under the new leadership, the struggle for the control of others intensified. The Old Prussian Union Church or Church of the Union, the church of Martin Niemöller, Dietrich Bonhoeffer and Eberhard Bethge centred in Berlin-Brandenburg, took the lead in convening 'confessing synods'. This church, which had been formed in the early nineteenth century to unite Lutherans and Reformed, was the most progressive of the *Landeskirchen*. With its leadership largely located in the capital and its strong Prussian connections, it had a particular national significance and influence. While its sense of patriotism was strong, most of the church opposition to Hitler and Nazism would come from its ranks, whether in the Rhineland or Berlin-Brandenburg itself.

Despite the developing crisis in the church, day-to-day life went on. Yet increasingly Nazism altered the daily patterns of life. At the beginning of April 1934, Bethge was required to attend a month-long military training course in Eckhartshof run by the SA or Sturmabteilung (Nazi storm troopers).[18] This provided him with direct experience of the emerging Nazi military ethos. It is noteworthy that Bethge did not question the need to undergo such training or, if needed, to serve in the army. After all, military training was a normal part of young adulthood for boys in Germany, and very few if any questioned the need for military service to fulfil their duty to the fatherland. Had not Martin Niemöller himself been a submarine officer in the First World War? Patriotism demanded such preparedness and commitment, and Lutheran theology gave it legitimacy. Fortunately there were other, more congenial activities in which Bethge could participate. In July both he and Vibrans attended a short singing holiday course under the leadership of a Jewish cantor named Stier. But even such recreational activities were always

---

18. See *So ist es gewesen*, p. 480.

pursued against the backdrop of the church struggle and the unfolding political landscape.

As momentous as both Barmen and Dahlem were for the church, they were not explicitly acts of political resistance but acts of faith and confession. Nor did they address the Nazi persecution of the Jews. Nonetheless, they had serious consequences for Eberhard Bethge and fourteen of his fellow theological students in Wittenberg, who courageously took the risk of publicly identifying with the Confessing Church. Mindful of Luther's own fateful step in nailing his 'ninety-five theses' to the Wittenberg Castle Church door in 1517, fifteen candidates for the ministry wrote a terse letter to the secretary of the *Reichsbishop* on 28 October 1934, informing him that they had shifted their allegiance to the Council of Brethren of the Confessing Church.[19] At the insistence of the Reich Church authorities in Berlin they were immediately expelled from the seminary and thus lost the possibility of sitting their second theological examination, which was necessary for ordination.

They now found themselves both locked out of the former Augustinian monastery where Luther had lived and excluded from the security of the official church. But at least they were free to identify fully with the Confessing Church. Bethge might not have had a conversion experience or a dramatic call to ministry, but by identifying with the Confessing Church and especially the decision at Dahlem, he and his companions had made a choice that now determined their future. Reflecting back on that decision Bethge graphically described its immediate consequences:

And now we stood, shut out by the consistory and its coffers for the first time and, as it soon developed, often from the parsonages as well, indeed even from the church buildings. And for the first time the (rather young) men in the councils of brethren felt the burden of the unusual worry about the unemployable 'illegals', the 'young colleagues'.[20]

---

19. *So ist es gewesen*, p. 108.
20. Bethge, *In Zitz*, p. 84.

Yet, as Bethge later recalled, the fifteen seminarians were in high spirits. Months of agonizing over a decision were behind them. And their action even gave a 'remarkable boost for the young Confessing Church. Our simple changing of the conditions of our existence also changed all the other levels of our spiritual life, giving new meaning and depth to community, prayer and preaching for a long time to come. Truer existence made truer, indeed, the presentation of the gospel.'[21]

Bethge's life and ministry had taken a decisive turn. At that time, of course, neither he nor the other 'Dahlemites', as the young 'illegal' pastors who would be ordained under the Dahlem emergency law came to be known, knew exactly what the consequences of their decision would be in the long term. How serious these were only emerged later, when even the Confessing Church succumbed to pressure from the Reich Church to require clergy to take the oath of allegiance to Hitler, and the 'illegal' pastors were encouraged to become 'legal' and thus enjoy the benefits of their office.[22] But for now at any rate Bethge was able to pursue his calling and serve his pastoral apprenticeship. Thus, in October 1934, he started his ministry as vicar in the confessing congregation at Lagendorf (Altmark) under the senior pastor Paul Henheik. At the same time his cousin Gerhard Vibrans began his term as vicar in Annarode. Unlike in the English-speaking world, where 'vicar' usually refers to the parish priest, in the German Protestant Church the *Vikariat* was a post-academic year of practical ministry. This meant Bethge still had to take his final theological examination, something that required returning to a seminary. But where would he now be sent to complete his training to be a pastor in the Confessing Church? The Reich Church government had already closed down all the preachers' seminaries run by the Old Prussian Union Church because of their identification with the Confessing Church.

21. Eberhard Bethge, 'The Confessing Church, Then and Now: The Barmen Declaration, 1934 and 1984', in *The Barmen Confession: Papers from the Seattle Assembly*, ed. Hubert G. Locke (Lewiston/Quenston, Canada: Edwin Mellen Press, 1986), pp. 201–2.
22. Bethge, *Dietrich Bonhoeffer*, pp. 607–9.

2

Beginnings of a Friendship

Although Bethge's future training for the ministry had now become problematic, in 1934 the Council of Brethren of the Old Prussian Union Church had established five 'illegal' seminaries to replace those closed down by the Reich Church government. Appointing the directors of these seminaries was a critical task for the Council. They required well-trained theologians who were committed to the witness of the Confessing Church and who could provide training in practical and pastoral theology. Bonhoeffer, although young and relatively unknown, was an ideal candidate. So he was invited to return to Germany from London in order to become the director of the seminary to be located in Pomerania. He took up his new responsibilities in April 1935.

Meanwhile the Council of Brethren of the Confessing Church in Saxony decided to send Bethge and several other Saxonians to this seminary to complete their training for the ministry. This decision was strongly advocated by Wolfgang Staemmler, the director of ordinands, whose friendship and support, as well as integrity and courage as a Confessing Church pastor, were deeply appreciated by Bethge.[1] To Bethge's delight, Bonhoeffer would later strike up a friendship with Staemmler, in whom, in Bethge's words, he 'found a man with a rare facility for meeting him on his own ground, someone who also possessed biblical insight and was willing to translate what he heard into concrete action'.[2] In 1940 Staemmler would be imprisoned for one year

---

1. Bethge, *Dietrich Bonhoeffer*, pp. 495–8.
2. Bethge, *Dietrich Bonhoeffer*, p. 440.

for speaking in public despite having been forbidden by the Gestapo to do so.

Finkenwalde

Bethge was one of a group of 23 candidates who arrived at Zingst near the Baltic coast and settled into the isolated farmhouse that had been chosen as the temporary location of the seminary.[3] The first session began on 26 April and lasted until 16 October. Amongst Bethge's earliest memories were the Spartan conditions, specifically the 'unheatable thatched roof huts on the Baltic sea'.[4] But it was 'an ideal refuge' for an illegal seminary trying to avoid the attention of the Gestapo, and had many outdoor attractions in good weather.[5] Very soon after, however, the seminary relocated to a disused teachers' training school in the small town of Finkenwalde not far from Stettin. This provided more adequate accommodation, with its classrooms and halls, but it was still basic and in need of renovation and furnishing.[6] One of a later group of candidates, Wolf-Dieter Zimmermann, recalls how even a year later, all 25 of them still 'slept in one big room crowded with beds'.[7] But at least there was a large garden in the back yard, and whenever the weather permitted they could walk alongside the river, and sometimes Bonhoeffer would take them to the sea coast for relaxation, games and seminars on the beach.

More than half of the first group of ordinands, including Albrecht Schönherr, Winfried Maechler and Joachim Kanitz,

---

3. During the short two-year life-span of the Preachers' Seminary (1935–7), 149 candidates attended the five courses. See the lists of all the candidates in Dietrich Bonhoeffer, *Illegale Theologenausbildung: Finkenwalde 1935–1937* (hereafter *Finkenwalde*), Dietrich Bonhoeffer Werke, vol. 14 (Gütersloh: Chr. Kaiser/Gütersloher Verlagshaus, 1996), pp. 1050–3.

4. Bethge, *Friendship and Resistance*, p. 23.

5. Bethge, *Dietrich Bonhoeffer*, p. 425.

6. Keith W. Clements, *What Freedom? The Persistent Challenge of Dietrich Bonhoeffer* (Bristol: Bristol Baptist College, 1990), p. 22.

7. *I Knew Dietrich Bonhoeffer: Reminiscences by his Friends*, ed. Wolf-Dieter Zimmermann and Ronald Gregor Smith (London: Collins, 1966), p. 107.

knew Bonhoeffer from their student days in Berlin, when Bonhoeffer had taught them at the university in 1932. Not only were they already on good terms with him, but they knew his ability as a theologian and were aware of his growing stature within the Confessing Church and the ecumenical world. Bethge and Vibrans, on the other hand, joined the group as outsiders from the countryside of Saxony. They had never heard of Bonhoeffer.[8] Indeed, Bonhoeffer was remarkably young to be in such a position of leadership and authority, only three years older than Bethge himself. Bethge would later recall that at their first meeting he couldn't make out which one was Bonhoeffer, and when he did 'he looked so "sporty"'.[9] Yet there was no doubt about who was in charge. Bonhoeffer had a very strong personality; in fact, he was acutely aware of this and of its dangers. According to Schönherr, 'Bonhoeffer detested binding men to himself', but 'perhaps for that very reason so many were drawn to him'.[10] Bonhoeffer would later express his concern about 'personality cults' in his book *Life Together*.[11]

In company and comparison with the theologically sophisticated Berlin students, Bethge really did feel his 'country boy' status rather acutely, and was initially treated by some of the 'insiders' with some condescension. Years later in his biography of Bonhoeffer, he wrote drily:

> For the newcomers the first classes in Zingst were a breathtaking surprise. They suddenly realized that they were not there simply to learn new techniques of preaching and instruction, but would be initiated into something that would radically change the prerequisites for those activities.[12]

But as a young radical in the intensifying church struggle and one of the first 'illegals' in the Confessing Church, Bethge was hardly

---

8. Bethge, *Friendship and Resistance*, p. 4.

9. Clements, *What Freedom?*, p. 21.

10. *I Knew Dietrich Bonhoeffer*, p. 126.

11. Dietrich Bonhoeffer, *Life Together; Prayerbook of the Bible*, Dietrich Bonhoeffer Works, vol. 5 (Minneapolis: Fortress Press, 1996), p. 106.

12. Bethge, *Dietrich Bonhoeffer*, p. 450.

a newcomer to the theological and political issues that would be the focus of the Finkenwalde seminarians. Both by virtue of personality and life experience, he had an acumen and solidity that made him stand out.

Bethge and Bonhoeffer quickly came together through their mutual love of music. As Renate Bethge would later comment, when Bonhoeffer and his close friend Franz Hildebrandt met they invariably talked theology, but when Bonhoeffer and Bethge met they invariably made music, Dietrich playing the piano to accompany Bethge's singing.[13] This undoubtedly helped to cement their friendship. But they also did talk a great deal of theology and Bonhoeffer soon recognized Bethge's exegetical skills, especially after he preached an excellent first sermon at the seminary on Isaiah 53. Six years later Bethge would still recall this moment in their relationship, and how ever since then Bonhoeffer had sought to encourage him and build up his confidence.[14] At the same time the relationship was by no means one-way. The recollections of the other students suggest that Bonhoeffer quickly sensed that Bethge had much to offer him. As his cousin Gerhard Vibrans commented in a letter to his parents, Eberhard's sermon on Isaiah 53 was brilliant and he was clearly one of the real 'theologians' at the seminary.[15]

At the same time, the increasingly close relationship between Bonhoeffer and Bethge was resented by some at Finkenwalde, who viewed it as disruptive to community life. One student from the Rhineland even spoke of Bethge as the 'representative of the Führer',[16] the latter a caustic reference to Bonhoeffer. Even Vibrans, fearing that the relationship would undermine his own long-standing friendship with his cousin, was somewhat disconcerted by the fact that Bethge had become the 'chief's favourite' (*Nun ist er ausgeprochener Liebling des Chefs*).[17] There

---

13. Personal conversation with the author, March 2003.

14. Letter to Bonhoeffer, February 1941, in Dietrich Bonhoeffer, *Konspiration und Haft 1940–1945*, Dietrich Bonhoeffer Werke, vol. 16 (Gütersloh: Chr. Kaiser/Gütersloher Verlagshaus, 1996), pp. 122–3.

15. *So ist es gewesen*, p. 178.

16. Quoted in *I Knew Dietrich Bonhoeffer*, p. 132.

17. *So ist es gewesen*, p. 178.

was undoubtedly some tension and jealousy in the community in
regard to their relationship, as Bethge later acknowledged.[18]
Sensitivity to these feelings was perhaps a reason why Bonhoeffer
insisted that no one was 'to speak about a fellow ordinand in his
absence or, if this should happen, to tell him about it afterwards'.[19]

Prior to Finkenwalde, Bonhoeffer had already formed several
close particular friendships. Among them was the Berlin pastor
Walter Dress, who had studied with him in Tübingen (and who
married Bonhoeffer's sister Susanne). Another was Franz Hildebrandt, whose friendship began when the two were students of
Adolf von Harnack in Berlin. Bonhoeffer had also had a short but
significant friendship with Elisabeth Zinn, a distant cousin and
fellow theological student.[20] And then, during his study year at
Union Theological Seminary in New York (1930/1), Bonhoeffer
had formed several friendships that were significant in shaping
the future of his life, notably with French Protestant pastor
Jean Lasserre, doctoral student Paul Lehmann, and Franklin
Fisher, an African American who introduced Bonhoeffer to the
Abyssinian Baptist Church in Harlem. But now began a friendship that became the most significant of all. And it was all the
more remarkable for being between the self-confessed 'country
boy' from Warchau in the province of Saxony, and the well-
travelled, sophisticated theologian from Berlin's intellectual
aristocracy.

Bethge had only been at Finkewalde for a week when, on
Labour Day, 1 May 1935, Hitler announced the reintroduction
of military conscription, which became effective on 16 March
1936. Some of the seminarians saw this as an opportunity for
them to declare their patriotism and to show that members of the
Confessing Church were good Germans even if they were not
good Nazis. As Bethge recalls, 'we were all certainly Prussian
Lutheran theologians, most of us the sons of pietistic, nationally

---

18. Bethge, *Friendship and Resistance*, p. 80.

19. Bonhoeffer, *Life Together*, p. 94, n. 3.

20. Bethge, *Friendship and Resistance*, pp. 85–6; Bethge, *Dietrich
Bonhoeffer*, pp. 137–8.

conscious parsonages'.[21] To their consternation, 'Herr Direktor Bonhoeffer' had other ideas about the subject, and did not share their enthusiasm for such patriotism. This came as no surprise to those from Berlin, but for those from elsewhere who had expected their director to be a good Lutheran, steeped in Reformation theology, the fact that he could have pacifist inclinations was unimaginable, indeed absolutely shocking.[22] It was nothing less than an expression of resistance to the authority and even legitimacy of the state. As 'young Lutherans in 1934', Bethge later wrote, 'we were totally unprepared for something like political resistance'.[23]

Whatever Bethge had learnt at university or at the seminary in Wittenberg, it was at Finkenwalde, under the influence of Bonhoeffer, that his theology began to engage critically with the Lutheran tradition, and especially with the separation of faith and politics as seemingly decreed by the doctrine of the 'two kingdoms'. In his calm and reasoned manner, Bonhoeffer got Bethge and the other seminarians to think differently about such issues, helping them to see how often Lutheran doctrine and the traditional interpretation of Romans 13 had been falsely distorted with frightful consequences.[24] Indeed, faithfulness to that distorted tradition had been the reason why those belonging to the Young Reformation Movement, including Bethge, had initially decided to avoid all political engagement. What mattered to them were the 'pure gospel' and the need for the 'church to be the church'. In contrast, Bonhoeffer was concerned about the gospel and the church not in isolation from political and social reality but through engagement with it.

These political and social realities confronted the German populace and its churches with new challenges almost daily. On 15 September 1935, Hitler announced new laws affecting 'non-Aryans' at a Nazi Party rally in Nuremberg, laws even more rigid than those already in existence. How would the Confessing

---

21. Bethge, *In Zitz*, pp. 93–4.
22. Bethge, *In Zitz*, p. 94.
23. Bethge, *Friendship and Resistance*, p. 19.
24. Bethge, *In Zitz*, p. 95.

Church respond? An urgent phone call from Hildebrandt, then serving as assistant to Niemöller in Dahlem, led Bonhoeffer to take the seminarians with him to the Steglitz-Berlin Confessing Synod that was being held from 23 to 26 September, and where the issues were to be debated.[25] By this time divisions within the Confessing Church had become particularly evident. Some delegates urged a more moderate stance on relations with the official Reich Church and a watering-down of the strong stand taken at the 1934 Dahlem Synod. But what was particularly disturbing for Bonhoeffer and the Finkenwaldians was the debate about the Nuremberg Laws. This revealed a growing division between those who believed that, while the church could reject the Aryan clause within its own life, it could not speak on its wider political implications, and others who refused to accept such a 'two kingdoms' approach. Marga Meusel, a Protestant deaconess in Berlin who had become active in helping Jews, had submitted a memorandum to church leaders calling for a clear statement of solidarity not only for Christians of Jewish descent, but also for all Jews in Germany. Meusel's memorandum did not even make it onto the Steglitz agenda; Confessing Church conservatives threatened to leave if the issue of Nazi anti-Jewish policy was addressed.[26] A 'compromise' resolution was even submitted that would have given implicit church affirmation to the Nuremberg Laws. Bonhoeffer and his seminarians, Bethge amongst them, disrupted the synod, heckling from the gallery. The synod rejected the compromise resolution but refused to consider Meusel's memorandum, much less publicly condemn the Nuremberg Laws.

The divisions in the Confessing synod in Steglitz revealed themselves again at what turned out to be the last of the national Confessing synods, held in Bad Oeynhausen from 17 to 22 February 1936. Instead of becoming more concrete in its

---

25. Bethge, *Dietrich Bonhoeffer*, pp. 486–90.

26. See Victoria Barnett, *For the Soul of the People* (New York: Oxford University Press, 1992), pp. 132–3; and Wolfgang Gerlach, *And the Witnesses were Silent* (Lincoln, Nebr.: University of Nebraska Press, 2000), pp. 84–6.

confession by speaking out against the persecution of the Jews, the Confessing Church was more concerned with maintaining church unity and professing its patriotism. But Bonhoeffer, as Bethge would recall, 'quickly made us understand that top-level declarations against the Nazification of doctrine and practice, no matter how breathtaking, were not enough and that much remained to be done'.[27] While Steglitz and the other synods had 'an excellent language to speak *against* Nazification, they had no language to speak *for* its victims'.[28] Mere confession meant complicity: 'We were resisting by way of confession, but we were not confessing by way of resistance'.[29] 'The church', Bethge wrote, 'was trying to derive its inner legitimacy from the struggle for its legal status, instead of regaining its legal status through its legitimacy' by speaking up for the victims and the voiceless.[30]

Soon after the Steglitz synod, in the middle of October, the first session at Finkenwalde was concluded. Bethge had now completed his theological training. In March 1936, he took his second theological examination for the Council of Brethren and, together with Vibrans and Hulda Trebesius, all seminarians from Saxony, was ordained by Staemmler and Bonhoeffer in the town of Stendal.[31] It was, for Bethge, an 'unforgettable confirmation' of his calling.[32] But in the aftermath of Steglitz, it was clear to him that he was entering a different form of ministry than anything he had imagined. Even as the church delegates were meeting in Steglitz, the government's Ministry for Church Affairs in Berlin promulgated new regulations for the administration of church finances that directly affected the independence of the confessing congregations and their ability to pay the stipends of 'illegal' pastors. This was of considerable concern to the seminarians whose ordination was imminent, as well as those recently ordained such as Bethge and Vibrans.

---

27. Bethge, *Friendship and Resistance*, p. 23.
28. Bethge, *Friendship and Resistance*, p. 24.
29. Bethge, *Friendship and Resistance*, p. 24.
30. Bethge, *Dietrich Bonhoeffer*, p. 490.
31. Bethge, *Dietrich Bonhoeffer*, p. 517.
32. See Bethge's letter to Präses Brandt, quoted in Manfred Kock, 'Funeral Eulogy', *Bonhoeffer Rundbrief* 62 (June 2000), p. 10.

The House of Brethren

At this time Bonhoeffer was still teaching once a week at Humboldt University in Berlin and was involved in other duties on behalf of the Confessing Church that took him away from Finkenwalde. His theological and exegetical output continued to be remarkably extensive, to say nothing of his sermons and addresses.[33] In particular, Bonhoeffer had the opportunity to reflect further on the Sermon on the Mount, a subject that had taken on a radically fresh, existential significance for him during his year of study abroad at the Union Theological Seminary in New York during 1930/1. Many of his homilies and lectures at Finkenwalde, especially during the fourth and fifth sessions (October 1936 to September 1937), were focused on this theme. By the time the seminary was forced to close by the Gestapo in September 1937, Bonhoeffer had completed the manuscript for his book *Nachfolge* (Discipleship), which was published in November.[34]

Bethge attended the majority of these lectures and homilies during the five sessions held at Finkenwalde, only missing out when on a few occasions he was away from the seminary during term time. Much later in life he recalled how he found Bonhoeffer's lectures on preaching 'extremely practical and full of useful advice';[35] how those on the ministry and the church 'dealt with the burning questions of the time' with each article of dogma being examined in relation to the issues at the heart of the church struggle.[36] Bonhoeffer's lectures on the confessional writings of the Reformation were critical of their abuse within

---

33. For the full details see Bonhoeffer, *Finkenwalde*, pp. 305–980, 1054–64.

34. For Bethge's account, see *Dietrich Bonhoeffer*, pp. 450–60. *Nachfolge* was the first of Bonhoeffer's books to be published in English, in an abbreviated edition in 1948, when it was given the title *The Cost of Discipleship*: see Dietrich Bonhoeffer, *Discipleship*, Dietrich Bonhoeffer Works, vol. 4 (Minneapolis: Fortress Press, 2001), pp. 29–30.

35. Bethge, *Dietrich Bonhoeffer*, p. 443.

36. Bethge, *Dietrich Bonhoeffer*, p. 444.

the Lutheran tradition, expounded in an ecumenical spirit, and restated with fresh insight and relevance. In fact, there are many other comments scattered through Bethge's correspondence of that period which indicate the extent to which Bonhoeffer's theological insight, as well as his personality, had decisively begun to shape his friend's life and thought. Whatever Bethge had learnt from his previous theological teachers, Bonhoeffer was his mentor in doing theology in the context of the *Kirchenkampf*.

The community created at Finkenwalde, especially what came to be called the 'House of Brethren', also profoundly influenced Bethge. Prior to his return to Germany in 1935, Bonhoeffer had thought much about theological formation and had examined various models of Christian community and seminary training within the British context.[37] He was particularly attracted to the Community of the Resurrection at Mirfield and the Society of the Sacred Mission at Kelham, where students for the Anglican priesthood studied within the framework of a monastic tradition of liturgical and spiritual formation. But he also visited several Protestant seminaries, including the Quaker college, part of Selly Oak Colleges in Birmingham. Bonhoeffer's thinking about intentional Christian community life, however, had been gestating for some time. His visit to Rome as a student during the 1920s had awakened a sense of the church as a liturgical community, engaged in daily worship, that was absent in his own German church context, and he had more recently experimented with retreats for his students in Berlin. In the process he had become convinced that Protestants had to recover what had been preserved within the Catholic monastic tradition, without necessarily establishing celibate communities – though the latter might be necessary under certain circumstances.

So when the opportunity presented itself at Finkenwalde, Bonhoeffer sought to establish a disciplined common life of worship, study and work for those in his charge. While some of his former Berlin students might have anticipated what was awaiting them, others were surprised if not alarmed by what Bonhoeffer required of them, and some opposed the attempt

---

37. See 'Introduction' to Bonhoeffer, *Life Together*, pp. 11–13.

altogether. Like Finkenwalde's critics elsewhere, these students initially regarded it as *unevangelisch* and contrary to what was expected of Protestant pastors. According to Wolf-Dieter Zimmermann, it was 'a burden difficult to bear, a discipline to which we did not like to submit. We made jokes about it, mocked at this cult and behaved like stubborn asses.'[38] Not only did Bonhoeffer encourage a radical discipleship of pacifism and resistance that seemed dangerously Anabaptist and fanatical, but the liturgical life and spiritual discipline were suspiciously Catholic. Yet, according to Bethge, 'Finkenwalde attracted more than it repelled, drawing visitors who knew that they would hear questions discussed there which had too long remained unasked.'[39]

Among the frequent visitors was Ruth von Kleist, a strong supporter of the Confessing Church and the seminary, who brought her grandchildren Ruth-Alice and Maria von Wede- meyer to services in the chapel. Maria, who was very much younger than Bonhoeffer, would later become his fiancée. But no one had any reason to anticipate such future developments, though Bonhoeffer and Bethge now began to spend holidays together at Ruth von Kleist's family estate of Klein-Krössin near Kieckow.[40] Her grasp of church affairs and developments in theology was remarkable, as can be seen from a letter she wrote to Bethge in 1938 in which she discussed Bonhoeffer's lectures on discipleship and some of Karl Barth's writings.[41] Her home also became the meeting place for gatherings of the Confessing Church pastors in the Stettin area.

Whatever other visitors might have thought about what was going on at Finkenwalde, the seminarians themselves were

---

38. *I Knew Dietrich Bonhoeffer*, pp. 110–11.
39. Bethge, *Dietrich Bonhoeffer*, p. 433.
40. Bethge, *Dietrich Bonhoeffer*, pp. 438–9.
41. Dietrich Bonhoeffer, *Illegale Theologenausbildung: Sammelvikariate 1937–1940* (hereafter *Sammelvikariate*), Dietrich Bonhoeffer Werke, vol. 15 (Munich: Chr. Kaiser Verlag, 1998), pp. 68–70. See Mary Bosanquet, *The Life and Death of Dietrich Bonhoeffer* (London: Hodder & Stoughton, 1968), p. 184.

increasingly aware that the times in which they were living required changes in the ministry, and 'contrary to the general earlier reluctance to try new things, the seminaries appeared to be a good place for such an attempt'.[42] For Bonhoeffer, this did not mean 'fleeing into psychological and liturgical forms of inwardness',[43] but listening intently and intensely to the Word of God in order to discern what obedient discipleship in the world demanded. As Schönherr later described daily life at the seminary, 'God's Word was to be the first word spoken each day. The candidates committed themselves to silence until the worship that started their day together.'[44]

There was, nonetheless, more to life at Finkenwalde than theology, prayer and political discussion. Music, literature, games were all part of the weekly schedule, something Bethge relished. Later, writing from prison, Bonhoeffer would ask the question: 'Who is there, for instance, in our times, who can devote himself with an easy mind to music, friendship, games, or happiness? Surely not the "ethical" man, but only the Christian.'[45] He must have thought back to such times at Finkenwalde, and perhaps especially of his friend Bethge, when that had been such a rich part of their shared experience. In the midst of the church struggle and the political upheavals, which included arrests, conscription and death, the Finkenwaldians experienced life together as a sphere of freedom in which they could enjoy the polyphony of life without losing their core commitment to discipleship and witness.

While Bonhoeffer introduced those in his charge to such an uncustomary disciplined life in community, they were only there for one semester before being sent off to serve Confessing congregations or being conscripted into the military. So in order to give some structured continuity to his project and introduce new students to the ethos of Finkenwalde, Bonhoeffer obtained permission from the Council of Brethren in Berlin to form an

---

42. Bethge, *Dietrich Bonhoeffer*, p. 462.
43. See 'Editor's Afterword' to Bonhoeffer, *Life Together*, p. 122.
44. Bonhoeffer, *Life Together*, p. 123.
45. Bonhoeffer, *Letters and Papers from Prison*, p. 193.

'Evangelical House of Brethren'. This was to consist of a few seminarians who would spend a longer period at Finkenwalde, sharing a common life together. In his letter to the Council, Bonhoeffer made it clear that the goal he had in mind was 'not cloistered isolation, but the most intense concentration for ministry outside the seminary', by which he meant involvement in the life of the Confessing congregations within the context of the church struggle.[46] Nevertheless, suspicions of what was happening at Finkenwalde were strengthened by this development, and continued to surface in the wider church.

Six candidates were given permission to become part of the House, one of whom was Bethge himself. Together with Bonhoeffer they signed the proposal that brought the House of Brethren into being on 6 September 1935. Bethge recognized the value of what Bonhoeffer sought to do and wrote at length on behalf of Finkenwalde to the Council of Brethren in Saxony in support of the House and to explain and support the practice of meditation as introduced by Bonhoeffer.[47] The Council clearly came to recognize the importance of what was happening at Finkenwalde, and set Bethge free to work for it.[48] He was one of the very few members of the House of Brethren who remained as part of the group throughout the four sessions it lasted. Two of these were later killed during the war, and those who survived – Joachim Kanitz, Winfried Maechler, Albrecht Schönherr, and Bethge – were important in keeping the Bonhoeffer legacy alive after 1945. But it was Bethge who was put in charge of the financial accounts, given responsibility for some of the tutorials, homilies and lectures, and who acted on behalf of Bonhoeffer during his frequent absences.[49] He was especially regarded as the seminary expert in liturgy, church music, and the interpretation

---

46. Letter to the Council of the Church of the Old Prussian Union, 6 September 1935; English translation in Dietrich Bonhoeffer, *The Way to Freedom* (London: Collins, 1966), p. 30.

47. See Dietrich Bonhoeffer, *Gesammelte Schriften*, vol. 2 (Munich: Chr. Kaiser Verlag, 1959), pp. 478ff.

48. Bonhoeffer, *Finkenwalde*, p. 255.

49. Bethge, *Dietrich Bonhoeffer*, pp. 467–8.

of hymns.[50] Thus, the later interpreter of Bonhoeffer was already becoming well practised in that art. But perhaps more significant was the growing level of intimacy in their relationship, something indicated by the fact that Bonhoeffer asked Bethge to become his confessor, a practice he encouraged within the House of Brethren.

---

50. Bonhoeffer, *Finkenwalde*, p. 209, n. 16.

3

Entering a New World

Bonhoeffer gave his last lecture in Berlin on 14 February 1936, having been forced by the Reich Church authorities to choose between Finkenwalde and the university.[1] But he continued to travel to Berlin regularly to visit his family and to consult with the Council of Brethren of the Old Prussian Union. Bethge began to accompany him on these visits and gradually became part of the Bonhoeffer family circle. He had first been introduced to the Bonhoeffer family earlier when, at Christmas 1935, Bonhoeffer took him home from Finkenwalde.[2] In entering this circle, Bethge the 'country boy' had, in his own words, entered 'a new world' of both Berlin culture and the embryonic resistance movement.[3] The implications of this new relationship were something that he could not fully appreciate at the time. But he certainly discovered within the Bonhoeffer household a remarkably enriching cultural and intellectual life that often found expression during meal times and around the piano.

A Growing Intimacy

Bethge went with Bonhoeffer on other journeys in Germany and beyond. One of these visits, which included several of the Finkenwaldians, was to Sweden, from 1 to 10 March 1936. The visit was requested by the seminarians who, having heard

---

1. Bethge, *Dietrich Bonhoeffer*, pp. 515–16.
2. Bethge, *Friendship and Resistance*, p. 72; Bethge, *In Zitz*, p. 103.
3. Bethge, *In Zitz*, p. 102.

Bonhoeffer's accounts of his travels and various ecumenical encounters, wanted to share in similar experiences. But there was also the need to inform the ecumenical church about what was happening in the church struggle. In addition to giving theological lectures and introducing his students to Swedish church leaders, Bonhoeffer spoke publicly about the German church struggle and the controversies within German Protestantism, drawing the wrath of Bishop Theodor Heckel, the Reich Church official who dealt with foreign matters.

The Olympic Games opened in Berlin on 1 August 1936. Hitler hoped to use them as a showcase for Nazi Germany; the Reich Church authorities hoped to demonstrate that Germany remained Christian in character. Despite their antipathy towards Bonhoeffer, the Reich Church authorities even invited him to be one of the main preachers in the huge tent that had been erected near the Olympic stadium for worship services. Bonhoeffer saw through this propaganda stunt and declined the invitation, but he did agree to participate in alternative 'Confessing' services arranged by the Council of Brethren.[4] This was, for him, a great opportunity to speak about the witness of the Confessing Church and about Finkenwalde, as he told Bethge in a letter at the time.[5] Bonhoeffer's involvement and input was condemned by the Reich Church authorities as one-sided. This, together with the controversy that had erupted after the visit of the Finkenwaldians to Sweden, provided the Reich Church authorities with reasons to terminate on 5 August Bonhoeffer's right to teach at Berlin University.

The correspondence and frequent telephone calls between Bethge and Bonhoeffer, at the time of the Olympics, the one in Finkenwalde, the other in Berlin, well illustrates the intimate relationship that had developed between the two friends, and the extent to which Dietrich now relied on Eberhard.[6] 'I now sense in such matters how self-evident it has become to me to discuss important matters with you,' Bonhoeffer wrote to Bethge in

---

4. Bethge, *Dietrich Bonhoeffer*, pp. 538–9.
5. Bonhoeffer, *Finkenwalde*, pp. 208–11.
6. See Bonhoeffer, *Finkenwalde*, pp. 188–222.

August 1936.[7] And he often concluded his letters with the words: 'pray for me, as I do for you'.[8] Much of the correspondence that summer focused, however, on Bonhoeffer's plans for the two of them to take a holiday together.[9] Bonhoeffer had become a demanding friend, and the correspondence illustrates how the growing friendship with Bethge was altering his other relationships.

Plans for that summer had originally included a trip with Gerhard Vibrans to Flensburg[10] – a trip that Bonhoeffer abruptly cancelled in July when he invited Bethge to travel with him to Switzerland,[11] planning to combine that with the upcoming ecumenical meeting in Chamby. Bonhoeffer was asked to attend Chamby by the Provisional Administration of the Confessing Church because the status of the Confessing Church as representative of the Evangelical Church in Germany was on the agenda, something adamantly opposed by the Reich Church. Somewhat reluctantly Bonhoeffer agreed to be there.[12] But the conference confirmed what Bonhoeffer had feared. With a few exceptions the ecumenical leaders preferred not to take sides and insisted that they would accept delegates from all sides of the church struggle, thus ending up with half-hearted resolutions that did little to clarify the church situation in Germany.[13] Uncharacteristically Bonhoeffer was silent for much of the conference, lacking enthusiasm for what was being debated, as well as exhausted and distressed by events back home. Resigned to the ineffectiveness of the ecumenical movement in dealing with the issues, Bonhoeffer and Bethge journeyed together for a brief holiday in Rome at the conclusion of the conference on 25 August. Shortage of funds made it necessary, however, for them

---

7. Bonhoeffer, *Finkenwalde*, p. 215.

8. Bonhoeffer, *Finkenwalde*, p. 190.

9. For example, in Bonhoeffer's letter of 28 June 1936, in Bonhoeffer, *Finkenwalde*, p. 206.

10. Bonhoeffer, *Finkenwalde*, p. 205, n. 8.

11. Bonhoeffer, *Finkenwalde*, pp. 204–5.

12. Bethge, *Dietrich Bonhoeffer*, p. 550.

13. Bethge, *Dietrich Bonhoeffer*, p. 554.

to return to Germany sooner than hoped, arriving back in Finkenwalde on 13 September.

Although Chamby had altered their earlier holiday plans, the correspondence between Bonhoeffer, Bethge and Vibrans prior to going there had sparked off a rather complicated and increasingly intense exchange among the three friends. Bethge had spontaneously invited Vibrans as well as his own brother Hans to join them, and informed Bonhoeffer accordingly.[14] Bonhoeffer sent a rather irritable reply:

> Just had a call from Gerhard in Berlin. Hans wants at your request to come along to Switzerland. I was very perplexed and could not really respond. Naturally, if you would like it, your brother should come along. But it was something of a surprise to me . . . Do you believe it is good for the four of us to travel? Perhaps. But it is naturally somewhat noisier. But I do not wish to stand in the way in any sense.[15]

As it happened, only Vibrans joined them, but the atmosphere among the three during the trip itself was apparently so tense that Bonhoeffer later wrote to Vibrans to apologize.[16] He was particularly distressed by an apparent breakdown in the relationships between himself, Bethge and Vibrans that made Vibrans feel an outsider. Among other things, the letter indicated that Bethge could hold his own against the strong-willed Bonhoeffer:

> I spoke with Eberhard about what you said to me. He thought you were right. Initially that hurt me very much. But I have now gotten over it . . . I must now have the feeling that [what I said] has been misunderstood. I believe, by the way, that you misunderstood it less than did Eberhard. But that's how it is. Result: I have talked about everything with Eberhard and we are done with it. I now request of you that you get back

---

14. Bonhoeffer, *Finkenwalde*, p. 223.
15. Bonhoeffer, *Finkenwalde*, p. 223.
16. Letter to Gerhard Vibrans, 24 August 1936, in Bonhoeffer, *Finkenwalde*, pp. 227–9.

together with me and with us. It would be unbearable to me if
something serious came and remained between us . . .[17]

Vibrans immediately responded, acknowledging his own fault in
the matter and then, in a few revealing sentences, his acceptance
of the very special relationship which existed between Dietrich
and Eberhard. He had learned to overcome any envy, and was
grateful that he was in fact connected with both in friendship not
only in the past, but also, as a result of the past, in the present as
well.[18]

Vibrans himself had returned to his pastoral responsibilities in
Rosian, and the misunderstandings of the Chamby journey were
apparently soon forgotten. Vibrans remained in his pastorate
until it became impossible for 'illegal' pastors to avoid conscription. In May 1940 he was drafted into the army, serving in
France, then the Balkans and finally on the Russian front, where
his unit was involved in the invasion in June 1941. He was killed
in action on 3 February 1942. Throughout this period Vibrans
remained Bethge's close friend, as well as a friend of Bonhoeffer
and others from his Finkenwalde days.[19] Bethge preached at his
memorial service in Rosian on 22 March 1942, reminding those
gathered not only of Gerhard's life and witness as a Christian and
pastor of the Confessing Church, but of his love of music and
especially poetry, and his longing for community, friendship and
love.[20] Thus, sadly, Bethge's friendship with his cousin, which
had begun in boyhood and had lasted for so many years, came
to an end. After the war, Vibrans' widow, Elisabeth, married
Christoph Bethge, Eberhard's younger brother.

In that first summer of their friendship, Bonhoeffer and
Bethge were also working out their professional relationship. As

---

17. Letter to Vibrans, 24 August 1936, in Bonhoeffer, *Finkenwalde*,
pp. 228–9.

18. *So ist es gewesen*, p. 287.

19. See the correspondence during the war years in *So ist es gewesen*,
pp. 400, 403, 411, 425, 427, and Bonhoeffer's letter to his parents after his
death: *So ist es gewesen*, p. 437.

20. *So ist es gewesen*, p. 442.

Bonhoeffer prepared to leave for the Berlin Olympics, Wolfgang Staemmler asked Bethge to travel to Saxony and resolve a bitter struggle between the Confessing congregation in Helbra and its German Christian-led church council. Bethge's reply indicates how strongly he had begun to feel his own responsibilities in Finkenwalde:

> Please understand, esteemed superintendent, that I now have the feeling of being taken away from my work here and our plans here under entirely different conditions than those under which I automatically expressed my readiness to help . . . Now the situation has essentially changed . . . it is not a matter of me personally, but of the right course for Helbra and for the House of Brethren . . .[21]

Had he come under pressure from Bonhoeffer? Bonhoeffer attached great importance to the role played by the members of the House of Brethren, especially while he was away, and was alarmed by the prospect of Bethge's absence.[22] Yet Bethge, too, had developed a strong commitment to the work at Finkenwalde, and his reply illustrates how, less than a year after his arrival, he had gone from being a student to a leader, second only in importance to Bonhoeffer himself: 'Here in Finkenwalde, however, the commitment to my work has been joined by a deep love for this work.'[23] These developments were a sign both of the growing friendship between the two men and of Bethge's own growing stature in the seminary. He did indeed feel a deep commitment to and love for the work, but as Staemmler's invitation to mediate in Helbra indicated, others recognized Bethge's capabilities and needed him as well.

This early correspondence between the two friends shows how Bethge's steady personality stood in contrast to Bonhoeffer's occasional depression – one of the few characteristics of

---

21. Bonhoeffer, *Finkenwalde*, pp. 183–4.

22. Bethge, *Dietrich Bonhoeffer*, p. 541; Bonhoeffer, *Finkenwalde*, pp. 188–9.

23. Bonhoeffer, *Finkenwalde*, p. 184.

Bonhoeffer's personality that Bethge did comment on in the later biography. The situation was particularly bad for Bonhoeffer in early 1936: 'There were days', Bethge writes, when Bonhoeffer 'was overcome by what he later called his "accidie, tristia, with all its menacing consequences".'[24] Only Bethge knew about these bouts of depression. They were not occasioned by feelings of deprivation or by vain desire, but beset Bonhoeffer precisely when he realized how strongly others believed in the success of his path and placed great faith in his leadership, with the result that his intellect, as Bethge observed, gained 'an evil ascendancy over faith. Then, in private confession, he would seek and find a renewed innocence and sense of vocation.'[25]

Bonhoeffer was also moody and anxious about his friendship with Bethge. In July 1936 he wrote to Bethge about the mis-understanding with Vibrans: 'I know that I must ask you once again not to hold this against me. I should not have become so agitated about such a small matter.'[26] Bonhoeffer himself reflected on this. He was learning something new about the art of friendship: he needed to remember, as he wrote Vibrans, 'that we are no longer students, and that each of us brings more charac-teristics along than he realizes and wants to'.[27] But whatever the demands of their friendship, none of this distracted either Bethge or Bonhoeffer from the larger issues facing the church and the nation, or from their own responsibilities within Finkenwalde and the Confessing Church.

The fifth session at Finkenwalde ended on 11 September 1937. The two friends spent the next two months at Marien-burger Allee 43 with Bonhoeffer's parents and took a holiday together during October in southern Germany. This pattern of vacationing together at the conclusion of the Finkenwalde sessions was now firmly established, and it would continue for the next few years in the new context for the seminary, the

---

24. Bonhoeffer, *Letters and Papers from Prison*, p. 129; see Bethge, *Dietrich Bonhoeffer*, p. 833.

25. Bethge, *Dietrich Bonhoeffer*, p. 506.

26. Bonhoeffer, *Finkenwalde*, p. 190.

27. Bonhoeffer, *Finkenwalde*, p. 229.

'collective pastorates' in Köslin and Gross-Schlönwitz. These secret seminary classes were offered on a rotating basis, meeting on private estates in rural Prussia after the 1937 Himmler Decree forced the closure of all the Confessing Church seminaries. Most of those attending the collective pastorate classes were already serving Confessing parishes in the surrounding countryside.

The Collective Pastorates

In June 1937 the Gestapo began arresting leaders of the Confessing Church in Berlin. On 1 July, Bethge and Bonhoeffer went to the capital to attend the trial of Wilhelm Niesel. On arriving at the Dahlem manse of Martin Niemöller they were told by Franz Hildebrandt that Niemöller had already been arrested. Shortly thereafter the Gestapo returned and surrounded the house. Bonhoeffer, Bethge and Hildebrandt tried to escape but were caught in the net and had to watch the Gestapo search Niemöller's house for seven hours.[28] Hildebrandt, who was considered 'non-Aryan' under Nazi law, fearing that his own arrest was imminent, decided to emigrate to England, where he had spent time with Bonhoeffer in 1933. Meanwhile Bethge returned with Bonhoeffer unhindered to Finkenwalde. Some of those who protested Niemöller's arrest were themselves arrested. By the end of 1937 many members of the Confessing Church had been imprisoned, even if only briefly.

During this time Bonhoeffer, Bethge and the House of Brethren struggled to keep the ethos of Finkenwalde alive in the even more clandestine collective pastorates that began in December in two neighbouring deaneries in a remote part of Pomerania. The seminarians lived and studied together but in order to mislead the police, to whom they had to report regularly, they appeared to be pastors of congregations.[29] Bonhoeffer himself spent the first part of each week teaching in Köslin, halfway between Stettin and Danzig, and for the rest of the week in

---

28. Bethge, *Dietrich Bonhoeffer*, p. 579.
29. Bethge, *Dietrich Bonhoeffer*, pp. 587–91.

Gross-Schlönwitz, where Bethge acted as his assistant and the supervisor of studies.[30] In some respects, Bethge tells us, the daily regime of work and meditation, homiletics and exegesis 'was carried on in the small undistracted circle of the collective pastorates almost more intensely than in the spacious house in Finkenwalde'.[31]

The House of Brethren, however, found it very difficult to continue its corporate existence and assist with the work of the collective pastorates under these new and trying circumstances. Bonhoeffer, for one, was very unsettled, living a nomadic life, and always uncertain about the future. Although arrest was a distinct possibility at any time, more immediately Bethge and Bonhoeffer, along with all the seminarians, began to worry about conscription to the military. Meanwhile the surrounding countryside of Pomerania, bordering on Poland, was becoming a huge military camp in preparation for war. This, together with the increasing surveillance of the Gestapo, made it necessary for the collective pastorates to move from Gross-Schlönwitz to Sigurdshof, a farmhouse deep in the forests of the von Kleist estate. In this relatively peaceful setting it was still possible to prepare the new ordinands for ministry. But those involved recognized how inadequate this was for the challenges that awaited them.[32]

In January 1938 the Gestapo banned Bonhoeffer from entering Berlin. Fortunately, through the influence of his father he was given permission to visit as long as he did not speak at or attend meetings.[33] In fact he now visited Berlin even more frequently, often in the company of Bethge, to stay with his parents, in whose home at Marienburger Allee 43 he met with friends in the Confessing Church and the resistance. There were at the time several resistance groups in the country. The one closely associated with the Bonhoeffer family had its centre in the Abwehr or Military Intelligence, and included Bonhoeffer's

---

30. Bethge, *Friendship and Resistance*, p. 60.

31. Bethge, *Dietrich Bonhoeffer*, p. 592.

32. See the comments of Hellmut Traub in *I Knew Dietrich Bonhoeffer*, p. 158.

33. Bethge, *Dietrich Bonhoeffer*, p. 598.

brother-in-law, the lawyer Hans von Dohnanyi. Bonhoeffer first
met with the military leaders of the resistance, Admiral Canaris
and Generals Hans Oster and Ludwig Beck, that February in
Berlin.

Bethge was aware from early on that members of the
Bonhoeffer family, including Dietrich, were seriously discussing
the need to stop Hitler from plunging Germany into war. On the
very first occasion that Bethge visited the Bonhoeffer home in
1935 he was left alone to talk to Christine von Dohnanyi while
her husband, Hans, and Dietrich had private discussions, presumably on the subject of the resistance.[34] By the beginning of
1938, Bethge was even more aware that his friendship with
Bonhoeffer had begun to lead him into the shadowy world of
political intrigue, something that would not be easily understood
or accepted by the Confessing Church and his fellow pastors.
The Austrian Anschluss came in March that year, an ominous
sign of worse things to come.

At the end of March the first session of the collective pastorates concluded. Shortly thereafter, Bethge joined Bonhoeffer
in a visit to the von Kleist family home in Kieckow for the
confirmation of two of the grandchildren, whom Bonhoeffer had
prepared for the occasion. Bonhoeffer preached the sermon.[35]
Bethge was now not only a very welcome addition to the Bonhoeffer family circle in Berlin, but also of the von Kleist family
in Stettin. After the confirmation the two friends went together
on holiday at Friedrichsbrunn, the Bonhoeffer holiday home,
returning for the start of the second course at Gross-Schlönwitz
at the end of April.

This was an exceedingly difficult time for all those young pastors who had been ordained under the emergency regulations of
the Dahlem Synod and who served under the authority of the
Councils of Brethren of the Confessing Church.[36] This included
Bethge and all those who had been trained at Finkenwalde and in
the collective pastorates. The temptation to become 'legal' was

34. Bethge, *In Zitz*, p. 103.
35. Bonhoeffer, *Sammelvikariate*, pp. 476–8.
36. Bethge, *Dietrich Bonhoeffer*, pp. 608–9.

great, not only for the security of a salary and manse, but also for the opportunity to fulfil their pastoral calling in a congregation. For by that time the 'Dahlemites' were being forced out of congregations by various Reich Church regulations and drafted into the military. Added to the temptation to become 'legal' was the fact that many within the Confessing Church had that status by virtue of their earlier ordination. Bonhoeffer fought tooth and nail on behalf of the 'illegals', insisting that they were called to be preachers of the Word above all else, and that they should stand fast not only by the Barmen Declaration but also by the equally important decisions of the Dahlem Synod.

The whole matter was brought to a head by a command from the authorities of the Reich Church that all pastors take a special oath of allegiance to Hitler in celebration of his fiftieth birthday on 20 April. This was as unthinkable for Bethge as it was for Bonhoeffer and others who held strongly to their convictions, but it was tempting for those who were concerned about their future security as pastors and the welfare of their families. Together, Bonhoeffer and Bethge attended many almost 'unendurable meetings' of pastors during those awful weeks, trying to convince them to remain firm. But, Bethge tells us, Bonhoeffer's 'arguments did not prevail. They were viewed as coming from someone who was not affected'.[37] In the end, the whole issue of the oath of allegiance turned into an embarrassing debacle for the Confessing Church, with Hitler indicating that he was not really interested in whether or not pastors took the oath. This was, for Bethge, the low point of the church struggle.[38]

In June Bonhoeffer and Bethge took 45 young pastors who had studied at Finkenwalde on a farewell retreat to Zingst, commissioning them to care for one another. This is the origin of Bonhoeffer's short book on *Temptation*, the subject of his meditations on that occasion and one of considerable existential significance for those 'illegal' Dahlemites as they struggled to resist the pressures placed upon them. Once again, the two friends found time to take a brief holiday in July on the Baltic

37. Bethge, *Dietrich Bonhoeffer*, p. 601.
38. Bethge, *Dietrich Bonhoeffer*, pp. 596–607.

coast before bringing the second session to an end in August. 'By this time,' writes Mary Bosanquet, 'the two had become almost perfectly complementary to each other, and while Bethge's spirit was quickened by Bonhoeffer's fire, he could himself provide, through his own particular quality of quiet steadfastness, that shadow of a great rock in a weary land which met a fundamental need in Bonhoeffer's more dynamic nature.'[39]

On 9 September, with even more serious non-Aryan legislation looming, Gerhard and Sabine Leibholz, Bonhoeffer's brother-in-law and twin sister, finally emigrated to England. Bonhoeffer and Bethge went to Göttingen to help them leave, and accompanied them to Giessen. They then returned to the Leibholz home, where they stayed until 10 October. Bethge spent much of this time reading Karl Barth's *Church Dogmatics* I/2, while Bonhoeffer wrote his book on Christian community entitled *Life Together* (*Gemeinsames Leben*), based on his experience at Finkenwalde and especially the House of Brethren. But they had some 'delightful breaks' from this routine, Bethge later recalled, playing tennis for an hour each day, and attending the Music Festival in Kassel.[40] Within a year of its publication early in 1939, *Life Together* had already gone through a fourth printing and has subsequently become one of the classic Christian texts of the twentieth century. Christian discipleship and confession in the world, a theme that was much on Bonhoeffer's mind at the time, could not be separated from what he would later refer to, in his prison correspondence with Bethge, as the 'secret discipline' (*disciplina arcana*).[41] That is, the practice of meditation on the Word and prayer, of confession and absolution, of silence and sacramental worship, within a community of faith and obedience, was essential for empowering the struggle for justice in the world.

The night of 9 November 1938, 'Crystal Night' (*Kristallnacht*),

---

39. Bosanquet, *The Life and Death of Dietrich Bonhoeffer*, p. 197.

40. Eberhard Bethge, 'Afterword' to the 1979 edition of *Gemeinsames Leben* (Munich: Chr. Kaiser Verlag); translation in *International Bonhoeffer Society Newsletter: English Language Section*, 56 (1994), pp. 10–14.

41. Bonhoeffer, *Letters and Papers from Prison*, pp. 281, 286, 300.

was a critical turning point in the Nazi persecution of the Jews. On that night Nazi thugs went on the rampage through the Reich destroying synagogues and plundering Jewish shops and businesses. About 35,000 Jews were arrested and deported. From now on there would be no turning back from the attempt to eliminate all Jews from the face of Europe. Those serving in the collective pastorates were somewhat cut off from events, not least because there was no Jewish presence in the area of Gross-Schlönwitz. Only gradually were they able to get information about what had happened.[42] That weekend Bethge accompanied Bonhoeffer to Berlin, and then, at Bonhoeffer's request, went on to Göttingen to check if the Leibholz house had been affected by the pogrom there.[43] But they found everything in order.

The winter session at Gross-Schlönwitz ended on 8 March 1939 and two days later Bethge and Bonhoeffer went together to London.[44] This was Bethge's first visit to Britain. It provided a wonderful opportunity to meet Bishop George Bell, Bonhoeffer's great supporter within the hierarchy of the Church of England, as well as other key people in politics and the ecumenical movement. Bethge's later accounts of Bonhoeffer's visits virtually excluded himself from the record of the visit. But he was there, and presumably was party to many of the meetings and discussions. This was also an opportunity to visit the Leibholzes, now in exile, with whom they discussed not only Bonhoeffer's possible emigration, but also that of Bethge himself, to England.[45] As it happened, it was only Bonhoeffer who left Germany, having accepted an invitation to the United States on receiving his military call-up papers in May.[46] Passing through London yet again, he arrived in New York on 12 June.

In Bonhoeffer's absence Bethge assumed many additional responsibilities, not only for the collective pastorates and related

---

42. Bethge, *Friendship and Resistance*, p. 61.
43. Bethge, *Friendship and Resistance*, p. 61.
44. Bethge, *Dietrich Bonhoeffer*, p. 638.
45. See Bonhoeffer, *Sammelvikariate*, p. 180, n. 4.
46. See the account of the agonizing process of making these decisions in Bethge, *Dietrich Bonhoeffer*, pp. 634–8.

concerns, but also in dealing with the leadership of the Confessing Church and Bonhoeffer's own personal affairs.[47] He kept
in touch with Bonhoeffer's parents, to whom in a letter of June
1939 he expressed his deep gratitude for so often welcoming him
into their home and providing him with hospitality.[48] He wrote:
'I would like to take Dietrich's departure as the occasion to give
special thanks to you for offering me so often the privileges of a
guest in your family.'[49] Bethge also shared with them how much
Dietrich's friendship had meant, and how much he had learnt
from him, as well as how much they themselves had helped him,
not least through their influence on their son during the past few
years.[50] 'Above all,' he wrote, 'I will not forget the experiences of
the past half year.'[51] And he continued later: 'I can only say that
in your home I have been able to reach decisive and committed
viewpoints and clarity in this matter, for which I am and will
remain particularly grateful.'[52]

Almost as soon as he arrived in America, Bonhoeffer decided
that he had made a mistake and made plans to return home.[53] He
was haunted by guilt at having abandoned the struggle against
Nazism and, perhaps even more importantly, having abandoned
his 'brothers' in that fight. Beset by loneliness, his thoughts were
constantly of Bethge and their seminarians; he calculated when
they would be in prayer and tried to make his prayers in New
York coincide with theirs.[54] He and his brother Karl-Friedrich,
who was visiting there at the time, left New York for Germany
via London on 7 July.

Bethge was overjoyed by the prospect of Bonhoeffer's return,

---

47. See the letters from Bethge to Bonhoeffer of 12 June 1939 and 23
June 1939, in Bonhoeffer, *Sammelvikariate*, pp. 183–5, 195–8.

48. Bonhoeffer, *Sammelvikariate*, p. 185.

49. Bonhoeffer, *Sammelvikariate*, p. 185.

50. Bonhoeffer, *Sammelvikariate*, p. 185.

51. Bonhoeffer, *Sammelvikariate*, p. 185.

52. Bonhoeffer, *Sammelvikariate*, p. 186.

53. See Bethge, *Dietrich Bonhoeffer*, pp. 648–62; as well as Bonhoeffer's
journal from his weeks in New York, in *Sammelvikariate*, pp. 217–41.

54. *Sammelvikariate*, p. 219.

as he told him in a letter sent to London on hearing the news.[55] A flurry of correspondence ensued between the two friends as they planned their reunion.[56] Bethge also mentioned that he was practising hard in order to beat him at tennis at the first opportunity![57] Bonhoeffer felt it might be better for them to meet in Stettin rather than Berlin in order to have more time together, but there was no holding Bethge back once the term ended on 25 August. Two days later he joined Bonhoeffer's train at Hanover.[58] The three-hour journey together to Berlin enabled them to catch up on all the news before arriving in Berlin on 27 August, where they went straight to Bonhoeffer's parents' home at Marienburger Allee 43.

The German invasion of Poland on 1 September 1939, and the declaration of war on Germany by Britain and France two days later, brought considerable changes to the situation in eastern Pomerania, where the collective pastorates were located, and for the Confessing Church as a whole.[59] During September and October, Bonhoeffer and Bethge stayed together in Berlin at Marienburger Allee 43, sharing Bonhoeffer's room. Fortunately, Bethge notes, they 'were both late sleepers!'[60] But then they returned to Stettin and to the collective pastorates. While it was no longer possible to continue the courses at Köslin, a new semester began at Sigurdshof at the end of October. 'Surprisingly,' writes Bethge, 'there were still a few ordinands who had passed their examinations with the Confessing church and awaited their final training.'[61] Despite primitive conditions and a severe winter, the course was duly completed on 15 March 1940. But then, after very little interference thus far from the Gestapo, the seminary at Sigurdshof was finally forced to close on 18 March.

---

55. Bonhoeffer, *Sammelvikariate*, pp. 241–3.
56. Bonhoeffer, *Sammelvikariate*, pp. 244–5.
57. Bonhoeffer, *Sammelvikariate*, pp. 246–7.
58. Tape-recorded interview with Keith Clements, 1985, tape 2.
59. Bethge, *Dietrich Bonhoeffer*, p. 664.
60. Bethge, *Friendship and Resistance*, p. 73.
61. Bethge, *Dietrich Bonhoeffer*, p. 666.

So ended the first five years of Bethge's friendship with Bonhoeffer, establishing a pattern that would continue, develop and deepen over the next five fateful years. Each had contributed to the relationship out of their very different personalities, backgrounds and skills. But in the mix something remarkable had emerged that linked them together in a way that was to endure even beyond Bonhoeffer's early death. Just as war had robbed Bethge of his boyhood friend Gerhard Vibrans, so it would rob him of his friend from Finkenwalde, to whom he had become both intimate companion and 'father confessor'. But the five years remaining to them when they left the collective pastorates behind would determine Bethge's life in ways that he could not have anticipated.

4

Sharing a Double Life

Following the closure of the collective pastorates in March 1940, Bonhoeffer and Bethge continued their ministry together, visiting and preaching in the Confessing Church congregations of East Prussia. The full extent of this programme may be judged from the detailed list Bonhoeffer kept of their engagements.[1] One event from this period stood out in Bethge's later memory. He would often recall how that June in Memel, a town now located in Lithuania but then a naval seaport in Germany, he and Bonhoeffer were sitting at an open-air café enjoying the sun when

> suddenly the fanfare boomed out of the café's loudspeaker, signalling a special announcement: the message that France had surrendered. The people around the tables could hardly contain themselves; they jumped up, and some even climbed on the chairs. With outstretched arms they sang '*Deutschland, Deutschland über alles*' and the Horst Wessel song. We had stood up, too. Bonhoeffer raised his arm in the regulation Hitler salute, while I stood there dazed. 'Raise your arm! Are you crazy?' he whispered to me, and later: 'We shall have to run risks for very different things now, but not for that salute!'[2]

Bethge was paralysed![3] Everything that he had learned from

---

1. Bonhoeffer, *Konspiration und Haft*, pp. 37–43; see also Bethge, *Dietrich Bonhoeffer*, pp. 969.
2. Bethge, *Dietrich Bonhoeffer*, p. 681.
3. As he states in his interview with Clements, tape 2.

Bonhoeffer about confessing the faith and standing firmly and openly for the truth now had to be rethought in relation to the unexpected defeat of France and its serious implications for the resistance. The likelihood of generals joining in the effort to remove Hitler from power was now remote. So those in the resistance had to enter more deeply into the shadowy underworld of conspiracy, increasingly convinced that the removal of Hitler was necessary to end the war.[4] 'The use of camouflage', Bethge would later write, 'became a moral duty.'[5] Bonhoeffer even made statements within circles of the Confessing Church which were, to say the least, ambiguous, suggesting to some that he had capitulated before the 'facts of history' which seemed to be leading to a victorious Third Reich.[6]

First Steps into Resistance

Bethge and the other Finkenwaldians had been taken by surprise when Bonhoeffer declared his pacifist rejection of German militarization. Now, in what appeared to some an apparent reversal of Bonhoeffer's position that would make him a controversial figure within his church after 1945, Bonhoeffer and the other conspirators began to plan a coup that included tyrannicide. It was an issue that divided the different circles of the conspiracy itself. Hans-Bernd von Haeften, a legation official who was also a member of the Confessing Church, was firmly opposed to assassination on religious grounds. Another leading conspirator, Helmut von Moltke, initially argued that Hitler and other Nazi leaders should remain alive to stand trial. He also feared that the use of violent means to remove Nazi leaders could undermine the moral standing of any government that followed.[7] According to

---

4. On Bonhoeffer's views regarding tyrannicide, see 'Introduction' to Dietrich Bonhoeffer, *Ethics*, Dietrich Bonhoeffer Works, vol. 6 (Minneapolis: Fortress Press, 2004), pp. 11–14.

5. Bethge, *Dietrich Bonhoeffer*, p. 628.

6. Bethge, *Dietrich Bonhoeffer*, pp. 681–84.

7. See Peter Hoffmann, *The History of the German Resistance 1933–1945*

Bethge, however, Dietrich Bonhoeffer and other family members never questioned the necessity of removing Hitler from power, and it became clear quite early that this meant his assassination.[8]

Discussion of the moral questions and personal risk also began early, but only developed gradually. Bethge later recalled a visit to the von Dohnanyi home in Sakrow in 1940, soon after the war began:

> We were just sitting together at the fireside, and Hans von Dohnanyi, who had certain elements of piety even then, asked Dietrich, 'What about Jesus' saying, "Whoever takes up the sword will perish by the sword?".'[9]

Bonhoeffer's response, as Bethge recalls it, was unequivocal. 'Yes, that's true,' he responded, and went on to say that Jesus' word was still valid: 'The time needs exactly those people who do that, and let Jesus' saying be true. We take the sword and are prepared to perish by it.' This meant accepting the guilt that such a deed implied as well as its consequences. Such Christians were no longer simply engaged in a struggle for the 'true church', the struggle of confessing Christ concretely within the community of faith, but involved in treasonable action against the state. There was no middle path, and no one could be a part-time conspirator.[10] Thus far the risks taken had been serious enough, but the terrain on which they had fought and the weapons they had used were church and theology; now, with 'little ground under their feet', they had to learn 'the arts of equivocation and

---

(Cambridge, Mass.: MIT Press, 1977), pp. 371–2. Moltke also feared a backlash among the German population similar to the post-World War I 'Dolchstoss legends' – that Germany had been 'stabbed in the back' by Jews, liberals and others.

8. Interview with Victoria Barnett, 12 November 1985. Klaus Bonhoeffer's widow Emmi confirmed this in a separate interview with Barnett, 16 May 1986. See also Barnett, *For the Soul of the People*, pp. 181–4.

9. Clements, *What Freedom?*, p. 37.

10. Interview with Clements, tape 2.

pretence' in order to take even greater risks with much greater consequences.[11] This meant duplicity even among friends. On one occasion, although he did not know it at the time, Bethge carried in his car the explosives that were to be used for one of the assassination attempts – the reasoning being that, if he were to be arrested, his chances under interrogation would be better if he could genuinely profess innocence.

At the time Bethge had little sense of what the conspiracy might eventually mean for Bonhoeffer or himself.[12] That awareness grew over the ensuing months as they discussed events together, and as Bethge entered ever deeper into the family circle as well as that of the conspirators. Indeed, by virtue of his close relationship with Bonhoeffer, Bethge was inevitably drawn into the resistance even if he was not part of the inner circle. Even though he often described himself later as 'a marginal figure in the whole thing',[13] his role was hardly marginal. Rather we may best describe him as a participant-witness. And although Bonhoeffer is sometimes portrayed as pastor to the conspiracy, in some respects Bethge fulfilled that role as well, not least in acting as a sounding board for Bonhoeffer as he wrestled with the issues both theologically and also personally.

In the early days of the war, however, the energies of both Bethge and Bonhoeffer were devoted more to their ministry in the besieged Confessing Church than to the resistance. However, Bonhoeffer's personal situation in the church took a turn for the worse as a result of a conference that he and Bethge arranged for their former students and held in Blöstau in July 1940.[14] Despite protests of innocence from Bonhoeffer that he had done nothing wrong, on 9 September the Gestapo informed him that he could no longer speak in public.[15] This meant that his public ministry

---

11. See Bonhoeffer's reflections, 'After Ten Years: A Reckoning Made at New Year 1943', in Bonhoeffer, *Letters and Papers from Prison*, pp. 3, 16.

12. Interview with Clements, tape 2.

13. Clements, *What Freedom?*, p. 46.

14. Bethge, *Dietrich Bonhoeffer*, p. 697.

15. See Bonhoeffer's letter of protest to the State Police in Köslin, 15 September 1940 in Bonhoeffer, *Konspiration und Haft*, pp. 61–4.

had effectively come to an end. The Confessing Church considered placing him in the small country parish of Altmark.
Bethge went to Jena to discuss this with Staemmler, who agreed
that this was not the right appointment. Formally, at least,
Bonhoeffer was to continue as director of theological training
within the Confessing Church.[16] But Bonhoeffer's focus was
clearly shifting to his role in the resistance – linked for him (and
for Bethge) to a position that would keep him out of the military.
Here the Bonhoeffer family connections became important, and
in particular his relationship with his brother-in-law Hans
von Dohnanyi, who was in the Abwehr office under Canaris.
Bethge was party to the conversations between Bonhoeffer, von
Dohnanyi, Oster and Hans Gisevius, a lawyer working for the
Abwehr (Military Intelligence), at which these issues were
discussed and a plan of action agreed upon.[17]

Von Dohnanyi was a key figure in the resistance, someone who
had great respect for Bonhoeffer's strong sense of reality and 'an
unusual capacity to help other people arrive at decisions'.[18]
During the church struggle he had occasionally passed on timely
information to Bonhoeffer; now he was in the process of gathering information about Nazi crimes in a 'chronicle of shame',
intended as documentation for the prosecution of Hitler and the
Nazi leadership after a coup. And it was von Dohnanyi who now
made it possible for Bonhoeffer to work for the Abwehr, ostensibly on the grounds that his ecumenical contacts outside of
Germany would be useful in providing information for the
German war effort. But in effect, Bonhoeffer became a double
agent engaged in assisting the resistance, which had its centre in
the Abwehr headed by Admiral Canaris and, in Berlin, by Oster.

---

16. See Bonhoeffer's letter to Bethge, 16 November 1940, in Bonhoeffer,
Konspiration und Haft, p. 69; and also Bethge, *Dietrich Bonhoeffer*, p. 699.

17. Bethge, *Dietrich Bonhoeffer*, p. 698.

18. Bethge, *Dietrich Bonhoeffer*, p. 625. The most complete history of
Dohnanyi's resistance is in Winfried Meyer, *Verschwörer im KZ: Hans von
Dohnanyi und die Häftlinge des 20. Juli 1944 im KZ Sachsenhausen* (Berlin:
Edition Hentrich, 1998).

Von Dohnanyi and Oster decided that the best place for Bonhoeffer to be located was in Munich.[19]

The ban on Bonhoeffer speaking in public, as well as his travels on behalf of the resistance, meant that Bethge was largely alone in continuing the ministry that they had jointly pursued since the closing of Finkenwalde. Yet the constant threat of conscription confronted Bethge with the same dilemmas Bonhoeffer had faced, prompting the Confessing Church leaders in Berlin to find a solution. So it was that in September 1940 Bethge began work as an 'inspector of missions' for the Gossner Mission Society in Berlin, an appointment confirmed by the church authorities in November.

Despite everything else he was doing, Bonhoeffer's long-standing passion to write a book on Christian ethics remained compelling. He started on this project early in October 1940 while staying with Maria von Wedemeyer's grandmother at Klein-Krössin. But from November 1940 to February 1941 he managed to take a longer break from his other activities to concentrate on writing draft manuscripts of the *Ethics* while a guest at the Benedictine monastery in Ettal, Bavaria. The months spent there comprised the longest period of time that Bonhoeffer had during the war years to concentrate on his theological work in a settled environment. But it was also a time during which he wrote copious letters to Bethge, who played his accustomed role as sounding board for Bonhoeffer's ideas.[20]

Many of the themes discussed between the two friends were influenced by Bonhoeffer's exposure to Catholic moral teaching, notably on natural law.[21] Later, when Bonhoeffer was in prison, the conversation would continue in much the same way as he struggled to come to terms with the meaning of 'Jesus Christ, for

---

19. Bethge, *Dietrich Bonhoeffer*, p. 700.

20. See, for example, Bonhoeffer's letter from Ettal on 27 November 1940, in which he discussed the relationship between the 'ultimate and the penultimate'. Bonhoeffer, *Konspiration und Haft*, p. 79; Or Bethge's letter to Bonhoeffer of 14 February 1941, in which he commented on Bonhoeffer's thoughts on suicide: Bonhoeffer, *Konspiration und Haft*, p. 143.

21. See Bonhoeffer, *Ethics*, pp. 171–218.

us, today'. In other words, the more famous letters written later to Bethge from prison were part of an ongoing conversation about theological issues that had been in process for some time. And even though Bonhoeffer later began to break fresh ground, Bethge was then in a position to understand better than anyone else what was in his friend's mind when he wrote about 'non-religious Christianity' in a 'world come of age'. In the first letter he wrote to him from prison, dated 18 November 1943, Bonhoeffer would tell Bethge: 'I wish I could talk it over with you every day, indeed, I miss that now more than you think. I may often have originated ideas, but the clarification of them was completely on your side.'[22]

Bethge spent Christmas with Bonhoeffer at Ettal, where they worked out a strategy for evading the next military call-up. But Bonhoeffer was already involved in planning his journeys on behalf of the conspiracy. So the days at Ettal included meetings with Justice Minister Gürtner, several representatives from the Vatican (including Pius XII's personal secretary, Robert Leiber), Carl Friedrich Goerdeler, the mayor of Leipzig, who had become a key figure in the resistance, and Josef Müller, a Catholic lawyer with Vatican connections.[23] The focus of the group was the peace feelers being sent from the resistance circles to both Protestant leaders in Geneva and Vatican leaders in Rome; Müller and Bonhoeffer were the couriers of these messages.[24] But soon Bonhoeffer's life became ever more frenetic and fragmentary; he was constantly on the move until his eventual arrest and imprisonment on 5 April 1943.

From 24 February to 24 March 1941 Bonhoeffer made his first visit to Switzerland on behalf of the Abwehr. Shortly after his return to Germany a decree was issued from the Reich Security

---

22. Bonhoeffer, *Letters and Papers from Prison*, p. 130.

23. Bethge, *Dietrich Bonhoeffer*, p. 725; *In Zitz*, pp. 126–7.

24. See Victoria Barnett, 'Communications between the German Resistance, the Vatican and Protestant Ecumenical Leaders', in *Religion im Erbe: Dietrich Bonhoeffer und die Zukunftsfähigkeit des Christentums*, ed. Christain Gremmels and Wolfgang Huber (Gütersloh: Kaiser Gütersloher Verlag, 2002), pp. 54–75.

Office banning him from any further writing and publishing. Clearly the authorities did not appreciate his regular circular letters to former students and pastors, many of whom were serving on the war front and looking to him for guidance. Following his visit to Switzerland he spent the next few months travelling between Berlin, Klein-Krössin and Munich, but then returned to Switzerland again from 28 August to 26 September 1941. He was at home in Berlin for the following two months and then spent Christmas with Bethge at Kieckow.

At this time, Bethge himself was busily engaged in the work of the Gossner Mission in Berlin, which meant that the two friends were able to spend time together whenever Bonhoeffer was there, as he was for much of the first four months of 1941. But then, on behalf of the Abwehr and the resistance, he went to Norway and Sweden from 10 to 18 April. The following month, from 12 to 16 May, he visited Switzerland for the third time. In June he returned to Sweden, and from 26 June to 10 July he was in Italy. The rest of his time was spent travelling between Berlin, Munich and Klein-Krössin, but with visits to Freiburg and Pätzig. Despite the unsettled nature of their lives during this period, Bonhoeffer and Bethge made every effort to keep in touch, meeting when they could, but writing to each other regularly when they were separated. After the intense life together at Finkenwalde, these periods of separation provided a space that was undoubtedly important for Bethge's own development as a theologian.

At the outset of their separation in November 1940, Bonhoeffer had expressed the desire to send a daily greeting to Bethge.[25] This indicates not only how much he sought to keep in regular contact, but also his interest in and support for Bethge's work at the Gossner Mission and especially the Bible weeks he regularly conducted in congregations. Bonhoeffer expressed regret that they were no longer preparing for these together;[26]

---

25. Letter to Bethge, 28 November 1940, in Bonhoeffer, *Konspiration und Haft*, p. 79.

26. See, for example, the letter from Munich dated 4 November 1940, in Bonhoeffer, *Konspiration und Haft*, p. 67.

indeed, to him it seemed quite unnatural that he was unable to help Bethge in this way.[27] They had grown accustomed to working as a team. But separation and letter writing enabled their friendship to flourish in new ways. Bonhoeffer increasingly looked to his confidant not only for support and companionship but also for critical comment on his ideas, respecting him even more as a theological thinker who was able to give order and shape to his own thoughts. This was especially reflected in the remarkable correspondence that now began to flow between them, virtually unbroken until August 1944, after which there was only agonizing silence. The correspondence was far more open than the earlier letters from the Finkenwalde period, and its importance for both men throughout the war cannot be overestimated. Not only did they know each other better, they both needed the support and counsel of the other as never before.

The Gossner Mission and Military Intelligence

Already in 1936, the Gossner Mission headquarters had provided a home for the first preachers' seminary of the Confessing Church. For the 'illegal' pastors, the Mission was now a refuge, a place where the urgent issues of the time, not least military conscription, were discussed in ways with which they could identify.[28] The director of the Mission, Pastor Hans Lokies, was a member of the Council of Brethren of the Confessing Church in Berlin-Brandenburg. Lokies was a friend of Bonhoeffer's, someone whose opinion Bonhoeffer held in high esteem.[29] Lokies in turn understood and supported what Bethge and Bonhoeffer were doing for the pastors they had trained in Finkenwalde and the confessing congregations in East Prussia. So Bethge was able

---

27. Letter to Bethge, 28 November 1940, in Bonhoeffer, *Konspiration und Haft*, p. 80.

28. Bethge, *In Zitz*, p. 114.

29. See Bonhoeffer's letter from prison on 23 January 1944 to Eberhard and Renate Bethge, in Bonhoeffer, *Letters and Papers from Prison*, p. 195.

to continue his work among the young 'illegals', in so far as wartime conditions permitted, just as Lokies himself continued with the examination of candidates for the ministry in the Confessing Church in Berlin-Brandenburg.[30] In the fall of 1941 Lokies and 22 other members of the Confessing Church examination board were arrested and held at Plötzensee prison until their trial in December.[31] Bethge visited him in prison to discuss matters regarding the mission and to keep him informed about people and events. After his release in January 1942, Lokies returned to work at the Gossner Mission.

The Gossner Mission Hall, together with the Dahlem parish church, where Bethge preached on occasion, became a meeting point for people involved in the Confessing Church. Invariably during the intercessions prayers were made on behalf of those who were in prison. In this way information about them became available to members of the congregation. Bethge regularly composed prayers for this purpose. The Gossner Mission Hall also became the focal point for the Friedenauer Confessing Church congregation, and a meeting place for 'non-Aryan' Christians – Christians of Jewish descent now threatened with deportation. In December 1940, the Gestapo had closed the Grüber office established by the Confessing Church and led by Pastor Heinrich Grüber, which helped between 1,700 and 2,000 Jews and 'non-Aryan' Christians emigrate.[32] On a far more modest level, the Gossner Mission continued to help 'non-Aryan' Christians. But Bethge later recalled with shame a man, whose name he never learnt, who came to the Mission for employment at the time of the Berlin deportations in October 1941, but whom they could not help and who was sent to the Theresienstadt concentration camp.[33]

Bethge's responsibilities at the Gossner Mission were three-fold: he was involved in strengthening its evangelization activities (*Volksmission*); he continued to work with Confessing

---

30. Bethge, *In Zitz*, p.122.
31. Bethge, *Dietrich Bonhoeffer*, p. 689.
32. See Barnett, *For the Soul of the People*, pp. 144–6.
33. Bethge, *In Zitz*, p. 120.

Church groups in Berlin and the surrounding regions; and he was given special responsibility for the Mission's work in India. Most of his time and energy, however, went into the second of these tasks, supporting those congregations affected by the war, for at this point both lay and clerical leaders of the Confessing Church were working under immense strain and pressure.[34] Bethge spent a great deal of his time in congregations, using the insights and lessons learnt from his experience at Finkenwalde. Much of this centred on group study of the Bible and the conducting of Bible weeks. Judging from two mission conference papers which Bethge gave in Berlin, one at the beginning of his time at the Gossner Mission (22 April 1941), and the other at the end (3 May 1943), the two major themes of his teaching and preaching were the need to confess Christ concretely within the life of the church, and costly discipleship as the presupposition of mission whether at home or abroad.[35] Both themes he had learnt, of course, from Bonhoeffer.

One of the joys of Bethge's work was the opportunity to visit former Finkenwalde colleagues, one of whom was Albrecht Schönherr, who was a pastor in Brüssow.[36] During this time Bethge's friendship with Schönherr deepened; this later became especially important in the post-war years when, as the Lutheran bishop of East Berlin, Schönherr became a key interpreter of Bonhoeffer's legacy in East Germany. At that time, however, many of the former Finkenwaldians were already serving in the German army. Approximately 3,000 pastors or those being trained as pastors would die as German soldiers on the front. Over half the 'illegal' pastors and vicars in the Confessing

---

34. Bethge gives us an insight into some of his activities in his letters to Bonhoeffer during this period. See, for example, his letters of 14 and 20 January 1941, in Bonhoeffer, *Konspiration und Haft*, pp. 104–5, 111–12.

35. Bethge, *In Zitz*, pp. 120–1.

36. See, for example, the references to Schönherr in Bonhoeffer's letter to Bethge of 8 February 1941, in Bonhoeffer, *Konspiration und Haft*, p. 135. See also Bethge's letter of 11 February 1941 written in Brüssow, in Bonhoeffer, *Konspiration und Haft*, pp. 139–40.

Church, including 36 of those who had studied under Bonhoeffer in Finkenwalde, fell in action.[37]

In these early stages of the war, Bethge and Bonhoeffer attempted to obtain exemptions for their students,[38] and Bonhoeffer's regular circular letters to his former students expressed deep concern for their well-being, both physical and spiritual.[39] Both he and Bethge were acutely aware of their own privileged position in remaining free from military service. 'I don't know yet how much longer you will now be free,' Bonhoeffer wrote to his friend in November 1940. 'But it is undoubtedly a great gift . . . a genuine reprieve. So it's important that we use it well . . . we must help one another.'[40] As Bethge later recalled, 'the entire three years from 1940 to 1943 were really constantly accompanied by the struggle to renew the UK classifications[41] again and again'.[42] Great emphasis was placed on solidarity – and the continuation of the community begun in Finkenwalde – between those who remained at home and those who were now on the front.[43]

Bonhoeffer had developed good relations with the Roman Catholic Steyler Mission (the Catholic *Volksmission*) in Munich, and encouraged Bethge to join him so that he too might get to

---

37. Barnett, *For the Soul of the People*, p. 159; Bonhoeffer, *Finkenwalde*, pp. 1050–3.

38. See, for example, Bonhoeffer's letter to von Dohnanyi, probably March 1942, a letter later used by the prosecution in Bonhoeffer's trial: Bonhoeffer, *Konspiration und Haft*, pp. 251–2.

39. Bethge, *Dietrich Bonhoeffer*, p. 691.

40. Letter to Bethge, 29 November 1940, in Bonhoeffer, *Konspiration und Haft*, p. 83.

41. UK, an abbreviation for 'unabkömmlich', that is, someone whose services were essential to the military and who was therefore not conscripted as a soldier.

42. Eberhard Bethge, 'Drei Kriegsjahre bei Gossners: Erinnerungen an die Zeit bei der Gossner Mission', in *Wegmarken, Einschnitte und Wendepunkte in der 150-Jährigen Geschichte der Gossner Mission (1836–1986)*, ed. Bärbel Barteczko-Schwedler and Hanns-Uve Schwedler (Berlin: Gossner Mission, 1986), p. 81.

43. See also the *Rundbrief* sent either in April or October 1942, in Bonhoeffer, *Konspiration und Haft*, p. 252.

know what the Catholics were doing. 'I find that the people there are open and cooperative,' wrote Bonhoeffer, 'so that I could imagine a fruitful conversation between you . . . I think it will indeed be interesting for you and perhaps objectively apropos for one to take advantage of this kind of thing . . . Tell Lokies that I think it is important now to make these contacts again!'[44] The letter may have been a ploy on Bonhoeffer's part to provide Bethge with a reason to visit him, something that he was continually trying to arrange.[45] Bonhoeffer was also keen that Bethge experience the Benedictine hospitality and spiritual life at Ettal, something akin to what was expressed in *Life Together*.[46] Yet by fall 1940, every meeting and contact served multiple agendas. In any case, Bethge's theological conversations with his Catholic counterparts resulted only in 'a suitcase full of Steyler material et al. . . . it didn't go deeper or further'.[47]

Bethge became privy to the conversations and plans of the German resistance when, during Christmas 1940 in Ettal, he and Bonhoeffer met with Robert Leiber, as well as Ivo Zeiger and another Vatican representative. The meeting also included Josef Müller, Wilhelm Schmidhuber, and Hans von Dohnanyi, as well as Franz Gürtner, Dohnanyi's former chief and a man in whom the conspirators placed great hope, but who, in one of history's ironies, died suddenly weeks later. Bethge was characteristically reticent about his own role in the conspiracy. Nonetheless, in the Bonhoeffer biography, many of his descriptions of events within the resistance (including the December 1940 meetings at Ettal) are eyewitness accounts. Certainly at the beginning, Bethge was present in his capacity as Bonhoeffer's friend. Yet – as in Finkenwalde and the subsequent period of the underground pastorates – Bethge quickly became an independent agent.

---

44. Letter to Bethge, 18 November 1940, in Bonhoeffer, *Konspiration und Haft*, p. 73.

45. See his letter to Bethge, 18 November 1940, in Bonhoeffer, *Konspiration und Haft*, p. 73.

46. See his letter to Bethge, 23 November 1940, in Bonhoeffer, *Konspiration und Haft*, pp. 75–7.

47. Bethge, 'Drei Kriegsjahre', p. 81.

Bethge's UK status was increasingly under pressure as the war progressed. In September 1942, a church application for its continuation not only stressed the fact that he was by that point the only ordained minister available, but emphasized the strategic wartime importance of the mission's work: 'In terms of the wartime economy, the Gossner Mission field lies in and around the most important and productive industrial regions of India'.[48] However, when, at the end of 1942, the church application was rejected, von Dohnanyi stepped in and Bethge received an Abwehr assignment to continue working for the Gossner Mission. Dohnanyi cited as reasons 'the course of the war with the Japanese advance' and the 'anti-British factions in India' that might be of use to German military intelligence. Accordingly, Bethge wrote several fictitious reports for the Abwehr about Japanese troops on the India–Burma border, various independence movements against the British, the armaments factories in Jamshedput, and the visit by Stafford Cripps.[49] Bethge had no personal experience of the Gossner Mission's work in India, although he tried to become sufficiently informed about its history and the current state of the work so that he could write reports which would satisfy those who were suspicious of his activities.[50] As Ruth von Kleist-Retzow ironically observed, while he was not involved in saving India, India in a sense saved him from possible death on the eastern front.[51]

Although Dohnanyi had arranged for Bethge to become a member of the Abwehr in order to avoid military conscription, he had come to trust Bonhoeffer's friend, and considered how he could help the resistance. So in April 1943 Bethge received a visa to visit Switzerland, ostensibly to meet with representatives of partner mission organizations. But the Abwehr had its own

48. Bethge, 'Drei Kriegsjahre', p. 83.

49. Bethge, 'Drei Kriegsjahre', p. 83.

50. See the document among Bethge's private papers entitled 'Eberhard Bethges Abwehrangelegenheit'. There are two reports entitled 'Bericht über Indien', the first dated 20 October 1942, the second 5 July 1942.

51. See the letter of Ruth von Kleist-Retzow to Bonhoeffer and Bethge, 13 June 1940, in Bonhoeffer, *Konspiration und Haft*, pp. 44–5.

agenda for his visit – an agenda that had already changed by the time Bethge travelled to Switzerland in July, for Dohnanyi and Bonhoeffer had been arrested in April and were in prison. By his own account, Bethge spent far more time in Switzerland bringing Bonhoeffer's friends and contacts up to date than he did with mission partners. He took information to Willem Visser 't Hooft at the World Council of Churches, and he visited Karl Barth, who gave him a cigar to take to Bonhoeffer in prison.[52] For his Abwehr report, he collected news from the Swiss missionary societies about what the Japanese were doing in China and the Far East. Upon his return to Germany he spent many evenings with Klaus Bonhoeffer, working on a report that would cover his tracks sufficiently and provide 'useful' information for military intelligence.[53] But with Dohnanyi now in prison and the Gestapo on the trail of the Abwehr office's foreign contacts, Bethge's UK days were numbered. He was drafted into the military in August 1943.

At the same time, his ongoing ministry to the scattered Finkenwalde community and his work in the Gossner Mission, particularly during the period of the imprisonment and trial of Lokies and the other Confessing leaders, saw Bethge taking initiatives independently of Bonhoeffer and thus making his own characteristic mark on developments. In doing so he remained deeply influenced by Bonhoeffer's theological insights; in many ways what he did anticipated his later work as the interpreter of Bonhoeffer's theology.

---

52. Bethge was able to deliver it personally during a prison visit in November 1943; Bonhoeffer wrote afterward: 'Karl's cigar is on the table in front of me, and that is something really indescribable': *Letters and Papers from Prison*, p. 145.

53. Bethge, 'Drei Kriegsjahre', p. 84.

5

A 'Singular Friendship'

Although theological, political and church matters were of
paramount importance to Bethge and Bonhoeffer, much of their
correspondence during this period focused on more mundane
and also more intimate matters so important for their friendship.
They discussed plans to meet or to share holidays,[1] and Bonhoeffer expressed how upset he was when they were unable to see
each other, notably when they were separated during February
and March in 1941.[2] They also discussed Bonhoeffer's relationship to Maria von Wedemeyer,[3] and Bethge's role in the process
that led to the engagement.[4] There was ongoing consultation
about the purchase of joint Christmas presents for family and
friends, and the state of their finances.[5] They discussed books
they were reading or music they enjoyed.

Bonhoeffer welcomed Bethge's interest in the writings of
George Santayana,[6] and Bethge wrote to him explaining what
he liked about his work.[7] Bonhoeffer told of concerts he had

---

1. See, for example, Bonhoeffer's letter of 19 February 1941, where he
expresses the hope that they could meet at the family holiday home in
Friedrichsbrunn: Bonhoeffer, *Konspiration und Haft*, p. 152.

2. Letter to Bethge, 19 February 1941, in Bonhoeffer, *Konspiration und
Haft*, p. 153.

3. Bonhoeffer, *Konspiration und Haft*, pp. 325, 370, 372.

4. See the letters during Advent 1940, in Bonhoeffer, *Konspiration und
Haft*, pp. 85–7, 88–9, 91–93.

5. See the letters during Advent 1940, in Bonhoeffer, *Konspiration und
Haft*, pp. 67–102.

6. Bonhoeffer, *Konspiration und Haft*, p. 117.

7. Bonhoeffer, *Konspiration und Haft*, p. 133.

attended in Munich, and expressed his indebtedness to Bethge
for introducing him to the music of Heinrich Schütz, a composer
who predated and had a remarkable influence on J. S. Bach.[8]
Bonhoeffer also told Bethge how much he appreciated his talent
as a singer, and how greatly he missed the opportunity to accompany him on the piano or listen to music together.[9] Bethge, he
would later acknowledge, was the first one who had really opened
up for him 'the world of music-making'.[10] And in a letter of
January 1941 Bonhoeffer expressed his delight that Bethge could
'write such wise and helpful letters in the midst of human
difficulties', adding that it hardly surprised him given the fact
that Bethge had such special talents. 'What you have to say on
such human questions', he wrote, 'is usually simple and clear;
and for that one who is in the midst of complications is especially
grateful.'[11]

Friendship, Romance and Marriage

Perhaps the most revealing letter around this time came in
response to Bethge's birthday letter in which he wished
Bonhoeffer 'good friends'. Bonhoeffer replied that the heart
longs even more for a singular friendship: 'There are individual
relationships without loyalty and loyalty without individual
relationships. Both are to be found in the plural. But together
(which is seldom enough!) they seek the singular, and happy is he
who has "this great success".'[12] Here Bonhoeffer is quoting
Friedrich Schiller's famous poem 'Ode to Joy' which Beethoven

---

8. Letter to Bethge, 4 February 1941, in Bonhoeffer, *Konspiration und Haft*, p. 129. Bonhoeffer's later recollection in prison that Renate Bethge had introduced him to Schütz was presumably wrong; see Bonhoeffer, *Letters and Papers from Prison*, p. 40, n. 34.

9. Letter to Bethge, 14 February 1941, in Bonhoeffer, *Konspiration und Haft*, p. 144.

10. Bonhoeffer, *Letters and Papers from Prison*, p. 135.

11. Bonhoeffer, *Konspiration und Haft*, p. 120.

12. Letter to Bethge, 4 February 1941, in Bonhoeffer, *Konspiration und Haft*, p. 128; translation from Bethge, *Friendship and Resistance*, p. 88.

used in his Ninth Symphony. In his later reflections on 'Bonhoeffer's Theology of Friendship', Bethge went on to comment that Bonhoeffer's letter was 'a declaration of love from a friend, who rejoices in noting the shape of the relationship and takes pleasure in communicating it in the nocturnal letter to his partner as a wonderful reassurance'.[13] Such friendship did not need theological justification; it was simply understood as a gift to be received, shared and expressed. As he later wrote, such friendship 'breaks open the divine mandates in fruitful illogic'.[14]

The correspondence clearly shows how close these friends had become. In February 1941 Bethge wrote to Bonhoeffer on the occasion of Bonhoeffer's birthday, wishing him strength for the following year in all he was doing, including his work on his *Ethics*, but also expressing the hope that there would be good times of relaxation with his friends. And then he thanked Bonhoeffer for their friendship:

in summary I will say thanks to you – perhaps this works in writing – for your concern and loyalty, your patient, friendly work on me, being available in all personal and official duties, intellectual and spiritual generosity and allowing me to be part of things, use of your tie and shoes, creativity and inspiration. How should I summarize it? The secure feeling of knowing there is someone with whom there is advice and solutions in all circumstances. You will naturally find this goes too far.[15]

As it happened, Bethge's letter crossed with one from Bonhoeffer, written on the same day, which revealed the extent to which Bonhoeffer had come to depend upon his friend:

Since 1936 I can hardly imagine a birthday without you. . . . the fact that the two of us could be connected for 5 years through work and friendship is, I believe, a rather unique

---

13. Bethge, *Friendship and Resistance*, p. 88.

14. Bethge, *Friendship and Resistance*, p. 96.

15. Letter to Bonhoeffer, 1 February 1941, in Bonhoeffer, *Konspiration und Haft*, p. 123.

piece of fortune in a human life. To have a person who understands one objectively as well as personally, and in whom one in both respects has a true helper and adviser, that is indeed already a great deal. And you have always been both for me.

Bonhoeffer continued:

You have also patiently withstood the endurance tests of such a friendship, particularly through my undoubted volatility (which I myself loathe in myself and of which you fortunately have repeatedly and once openly reminded me) and you have not become embittered by it . . . in countless questions you have decisively helped me through your great clarity and simplicity of thinking and judgement, and I know from experience that your prayer is a genuine source of power for me. So I wish for myself that this will remain so in the new year and become even better, so that both of us will be helped through it even more, also spiritually. I wanted to write you this today.[16]

Some years later, when he was in prison, Bonhoeffer would again acknowledge that he had sometimes made life hard for Bethge,[17] referring specifically to his 'tyrannical' nature which, he says, Bethge knew so well![18] Perhaps it was this that led him to write on another occasion: 'I don't know anyone who does not like you, whereas I know a great many people who do not like me . . . the reason is probably that you are by nature open and modest, whereas I am reticent and rather demanding.'[19]

Fashioned as it was during their life together at Finkenwalde, the relationship was clearly more than a friendship based on

---

16. Letter to Bethge, 1 February 1941, in Bonhoeffer, *Konspiration und Haft*, p. 125.

17. Bonhoeffer, *Letters and Papers from Prison*, p. 129.

18. Letter to Bethge 28 November 1943, in Bonhoeffer, *Letters and Papers from Prison*, p. 148.

19. Letter to Bethge, from Tegel, 18 January 1944, in Bonhoeffer, *Letters and Papers from Prison*, p. 189.

mutual interest and liking for each other; it was also based on a shared spiritual commitment. Neither Bethge nor Bonhoeffer wore their piety on their sleeves, and they seldom if ever expressed their deep feelings publicly. But they did in their letters. Bonhoeffer especially shared his own inner feelings and failings, as he did in a letter from Ettal in which he reminded his friend to maintain the discipline of daily prayer, something particularly important given the unsettled nature of his life and work, and something necessary to gain clarity for what he was doing.[20] Bethge, we recall, had become Bonhoeffer's confessor at Finkenwalde, and he continued to fulfil this role though in a much less formal way.

In virtually everything he later wrote about these years Bethge focused on his friend. Yet there were other matters on Bethge's mind that were beginning to shape the nature of their 'singular friendship'. As noted earlier, Bethge's frequent stays at the Bonhoeffer family home at Marienburger Allee 43 had given him an opportunity to become better acquainted with the extended Bonhoeffer family and, in particular, Dietrich's niece, Renate Schleicher, who lived next door. Thinking back to those days, he later related:

> You should also realize that the window of that room looked out over the garden of the neighbouring house at number 42, where the presence of the Schleicher children became for me more and more exciting and attractive . . .[21]

The Schleicher parents soon became aware of Bethge's interest, and of that shown by their daughter in Dietrich's likeable friend and companion from Saxony. In a sense, Bethge had already become a member of the family, but now the relationship would be sealed by marriage. By early 1943 preparations were being made for the wedding. Indeed, on his way home from

---

20. Letter to Bethge, 14 February 1941, in Bonhoeffer, *Konspiration und Haft*, p. 144.

21. Bethge, *Friendship and Resistance*, p. 73.

Switzerland, Bethge bought a gold wedding ring for his fiancée, something it was now impossible for him to buy in Germany.[22]

No one was happier about the pending wedding than Bonhoeffer, who had become engaged to Maria von Wedemeyer earlier in the year on 17 January. But how would the two friends work out their relationship? Could they remain as intimate in the future as in the past? Despite Bonhoeffer's pleasure at the thought of Bethge's marriage, the relationship between marriage and friendship was obviously one that was difficult for him to come to terms with. However, the joys of romance and the anticipated marriages were marred by a momentous turn of events. In Bethge's words:

> On April 4 – that was a Sunday – Renate and I had travelled to my mother's place about 100 kilometres away from Berlin and had come back either the evening of that Sunday or on Monday morning. We went to 42 Marienburger Allee. Dietrich came over from his parents' house, telling us that he had rung Christel von Dohnanyi and strange voices had answered the call, so he knew what was happening.[23]

The Gestapo had arrived to search the Dohnanyi household; they arrested Hans von Dohnanyi and, briefly, his wife. The next day, 5 April 1943, Bonhoeffer was arrested by the Gestapo and imprisoned in Tegel Prison.

It is remarkable that in his first letter to Bethge from prison Bonhoeffer returned to the subject of how their respective marriages might affect their friendship. This was something that clearly gave him considerable anxiety. He wrote: 'Sometimes I've thought that it is really very good for the two of you [Eberhard and Renate] that I am not there. At the beginning it's not at all easy to resolve the conflict between marriage and friendship; you're spared this problem, and later it won't exist.'[24] Reflecting on the difficulties ahead, Bonhoeffer wrote a few days

22. Clements, *What Freedom?*, p. 40.
23. Quoted in Clements, *What Freedom?*, p. 39.
24. Bonhoeffer, *Letters and Papers from Prison*, p. 131.

later: 'Thank God that you have Renate; and you yourself know well enough that behind her there is a family all of whose members count you one of themselves and will always stand by you'.[25] With respect to himself, he told Renate, she should stop calling him 'uncle' and think about him as 'your husband's friend'.[26]

While it was through Bonhoeffer that Bethge had come to know Renate Schleicher, Bethge himself had been involved in making Bonhoeffer's engagement to Maria possible through his conversations with her grandmother in which he expressed support for it. So it was now Bonhoeffer's wish that his friend should do all he could to assist Maria during these difficult days, not least because she had to relate to the wider family under such trying circumstances without having had much opportunity to get to know them previously. 'Please think of her, too, when you think of me,' Bonhoeffer wrote.[27] Maria's relationship with Bethge was undoubtedly strengthened by the fact that both of them were outsiders to the Bonhoeffer family, though, of course, Bethge had long been welcomed into its life. 'I keep feeling very sorry', Bonhoeffer writes to Bethge, 'that Maria has really come to know the family only under the pressure of last year.'[28] Was it with regard to Maria that Bonhoeffer penned his thoughts about 'what mothers-in-law should do' and not do, when he wrote to Bethge on 7 May 1944?[29] Many years later when Bethge commented on the publication of the correspondence between Bonhoeffer and Maria, he would write: 'I can now read a correspondence that originated when I was not only close to Dietrich but his ally in the face of family misgivings about prospective partnerships for life between people of widely differing ages, first

---

25. Bonhoeffer, *Letters and Papers from Prison*, p. 133.

26. Bonhoeffer, *Letters and Papers from Prison*, p. 176.

27. Bonhoeffer, *Letters and Papers from Prison*, p. 132.

28. Letter to Bethge, 2 April 1944, in Bonhoeffer, *Letters and Papers from Prison*, p. 245.

29. See also the comments in Bonhoeffer's letters to Maria, for example, in his letter of 11 March 1944 – in Bonhoeffer and von Wedemeyer, *Love Letters from Cell 92*, p. 168.

in my case and then in his.'[30] In saying this, he might well have
been recalling that the Schleichers were also initially very upset
by the age difference between him and Renate, which was just as
great.

Ever planning their future together, Bonhoeffer suggested in
one letter to Bethge that after the war he and Maria, together
with the Bethges, should visit Italy as the two of them had done
in 1936. But he added that the two of them could then go to
Palestine, leaving their wives behind to wait for them![31] Bethge
had some reservations about this, and certainly at first the
two friends did not see eye to eye on how their relationship
should now develop. In one of his letters Bethge responded to
Bonhoeffer by saying that marriage was 'what remains stable in
all fleeting relationships'; Bonhoeffer agreed, but lest marriage
should detract from their friendship, he hastily added, 'we
should also include good friendship among these stable things'.[32]
This prompted Bethge to write back:

> You write that, after marriage, our friendship is to be counted
> among the stable things of life. But that is not the case, at least
> as far as the recognition and consideration of others is con-
> cerned. Marriage is recognised outwardly – regardless of
> whether the relationship between the couple is stable or not –;
> each person, in this case the whole family, must take it into
> account and finds it the right thing that much should and must
> be undertaken for it. Friendship – no matter how exclusive
> and all-embracing it may be – has no *necessitas*, as father put it
> over the question of visiting . . . Friendship is completely
> determined by its content and only in this way does it have its
> existence.[33]

In one of the few letters written to both Renate and Eberhard,
Bonhoeffer, who had patently been brooding on the subject,

---

30. Bonhoeffer and von Wedemeyer, *Love Letters from Cell 92*, p. 313.
31. Bonhoeffer, *Letters and Papers from Prison*, p. 171.
32. Bonhoeffer, *Letters and Papers from Prison*, p. 164.
33. Letter to Bonhoeffer, from Lissa, 2 January 1943, in Bonhoeffer,
Letters and Papers from Prison, p. 181.

returned to the theme of marriage and friendship on 23 January 1944. Now his thoughts were decidedly more theological in character. He agreed with Bethge that friendship, unlike marriage, 'depended entirely on its own inherent quality'.[34] And then, in an attempt to give it a theological basis, he distinguished between marriage as one of the divine mandates, and friendship as something that belonged to the 'sphere of freedom':

> Just because friendship belongs to this sphere of freedom . . . it must be confidently defended against all the disapproving frowns of 'ethical' existences, though without claiming for it the *necessitas* of a divine decree, but only the *necessitas* of *freedom*. I believe that within the sphere of this freedom friendship is by far the rarest and most priceless treasure . . .[35]

Eberhard and Renate Bethge were married in May 1943. Bonhoeffer, who had attended the civil ceremony in March, obviously could not be present on this occasion, but he wrote the wedding sermon from prison. The sermon did not arrive in time, perhaps fortunately, because in later years the Bethges were embarrassed by its conservative tone. Reflecting on it later, Renate Bethge, in a revealing comment, wondered whether 'the reason why Bonhoeffer brought out so strongly the serving role of the woman and the responsibility-role of the man was to help Eberhard to make his voice also heard in the big Bonhoeffer family, and because he knew how strong his family was, being used to planning and deciding everything (and this of course mainly on the part of the women)'.[36] Maybe that was so, but Bonhoeffer, a man of his time, was undoubtedly patriarchal in his views.

The newlyweds had little time to celebrate. With both von Dohnanyi and Bonhoeffer in prison, Bethge was informed that

---

34. Bonhoeffer, *Letters and Papers from Prison*, p. 192.
35. Bonhoeffer, *Letters and Papers from Prison*, p. 193.
36. Renate Bethge, 'Bonhoeffer's Picture of Women', in *Bonhoeffer's Ethics: Old Europe and New Frontiers*, ed. Rene van Eyden, Guy Carter and Hans-Dirk van Hoogstraten (Kampen: Kok Pharos, 1991), p. 198.

his service in the Abwehr was no longer necessary. In July he was conscripted into the military and sent to Lissa in Poland to do his basic training. He remained there until January 1944, when he was sent to an Abwehr unit on the Italian front. Meanwhile, on 30 July 1943 Bonhoeffer was informed by the military authorities that the enquiries about his case were concluded and that an indictment was being prepared. He was also now given additional letter-writing privileges that included permission to write to Maria, though all correspondence continued to be censored. This, then, was the background for the prison correspondence that would reveal so much more about the friendship and Bethge's role as theological sounding board for Bonhoeffer's new thinking.

Letters from Prison

The correspondence between Bonhoeffer and Bethge that was published in the early editions of *Letters and Papers from Prison*[37] was but a small selection, largely material that had some theological significance.[38] In making that selection, Bethge was seeking to honour both Bonhoeffer's wishes that his correspondence was for Bethge's eyes only,[39] and the growing post-war interest in his theology. Certainly, the letters that he sent to other members of the family, and especially to Maria, were very personal. Indeed, the letters to Maria, most of which were only published in 1992, revealed a romantic intimacy not previously recognized. Reflecting on them late in his life, Bethge wrote: 'It [also] delighted me to hear my friend say, again and again: I want you,

---

37. The German title *Widerstand und Ergebung* (Resistance and Submission) comes from Bonhoeffer's letter to Bethge of 21 February 1944 (in Bonhoeffer, *Letters and Papers from Prison*, p. 217) where he is reflecting on his experiences, especially within the resistance movement.

38. On the history of the publication of this correspondence see the introduction to Dietrich Bonhoeffer, *Discipleship*, Dietrich Bonhoeffer Works, vol. 6 (Minneapolis: Fortress Press, 2001).

39. See for example Bonhoeffer's letter to Bethge, 20 May 1944, in Bonhoeffer, *Letters and Papers from Prison*, p. 302.

only you, and just as you are!'[40] But Bonhoeffer probably anticipated that some of his letters to Bethge would not remain private
for ever. As he told Bethge, one reason, if not the chief reason,
why he wrote at such length and so frequently was 'no one knows
how much longer things are likely to last. And since one day you
will be called to write my biography, I want to put the most complete material possible at your disposal!'[41] He also observed that
one 'writes some things more freely and vividly in a letter than in
a book', and that he often had 'better thoughts in a conversation
by correspondence' than by himself.[42]

Many years later, Bethge told the remarkable story about how
he received the letters from Tegel Prison, and how many of them
were preserved during the war years in gas mask containers in
the Schleichers' garden at Marienburger Allee 42, so that they
could be retrieved afterwards. This correspondence, unlike the
censored letters sent to the members of his family and Maria, was
smuggled out of Tegel through the good services of one of
Bonhoeffer's guards, Corporal Knobloch, who mailed them from
home. Several letters, both from Bonhoeffer and from others,
were lost, some having never reached their destination in the first
place,[43] and others having been misplaced in the chaos of the
times. There were others, notably Bonhoeffer's letters to Bethge
in September 1944, which were destroyed for security reasons.

The first edition of the prison writings was published in 1950
and was intended 'to make available to a group of people who
were interested in Bonhoeffer some short, specifically theological, meditations from Tegel'.[44] At the same time, Bethge had to
make it clear that this slender volume of fragments was not a
theological monograph but part of an ongoing correspondence
with him and with other family members about many things. As

---

40. 'Postscript' to Bonhoeffer and von Wedemeyer, *Love Letters From
Cell 92*, p. 314.

41. Letter to Bethge, 1 February 1944, in Bonhoeffer, *Letters and Papers
from Prison*, p. 202.

42. Bonhoeffer, *Letters and Papers from Prison*, p. 347.

43. See Bonhoeffer, *Letters and Papers from Prison*, p. 363, n. 5.

44. Bonhoeffer, *Letters and Papers from Prison*, p. vii.

is apparent on reading the letters, Bonhoeffer's theological reflections in prison were often triggered by events such as Bethge's marriage, family visits, air-raid bombings, and his own experiences of loneliness. As Bonhoeffer told Maria, he was not interested simply in 'profound, intellectual discussions' but as much in 'the ordinary things of life'.[45] Nonetheless, Bethge was not only cautious about including passages that related to personal and family affairs, but assumed that readers would only be interested in theological matters.

This anticipation was, in his own words, 'completely put in the shade by the reception that has actually been given to [the prison letters] throughout the world'.[46] Not only did the book rapidly become a Christian classic, as the English publishers asserted, but the debate about Bonhoeffer's theological explorations in prison required that they be put in the broader framework of his life and his ongoing discussions with Bethge. This eventually led to a much-expanded version. As Bethge observed, after 25 years personal and family considerations had 'retreated into the background' and Bonhoeffer's life and thought had 'long since left the private sphere'.[47] An even larger version has now appeared as volume 6 in the *Dietrich Bonhoeffer Werke*,[48] and, in addition, the correspondence with Maria has been published[49] as well as a volume on Bonhoeffer's *Fiction from Tegel Prison*.[50]

During the first few months of Bonhoeffer's imprisonment, Bethge was in the military training camp in Lissa, although he had occasional opportunities to spend time in Berlin with his wife. This also gave him the chance to visit Bonhoeffer in prison on 26 November 1943, together with Bonhoeffer's parents and Maria, the 'four people', Bonhoeffer wrote, 'who are nearest and

---

45. Bonhoeffer and von Wedemeyer, *Love Letters From Cell 92*, p. 169.

46. Bonhoeffer, *Letters and Papers from Prison*, p. vii.

47. Bonhoeffer, *Letters and Papers from Prison*, p. viii.

48. Dietrich Bonhoeffer, *Widerstand und Ergebung*, Dietrich Bonhoeffer Werke, vol. 6 (Gütersloh: Chr. Kaiser/Gütersloh Verlagshaus, 1998).

49. Bonhoeffer and von Wedemeyer, *Love Letters From Cell 92*.

50. Dietrich Bonhoeffer, *Fiction from Tegel Prison*, tr. Nancy Lukens, ed. Clifford J. Green, Dietrich Bonhoeffer Works, vol. 7 (Minneapolis: Fortress Press, 2000).

dearest to me.'[51] Bonhoeffer was delighted that their separation had not in any way affected their relationship: 'That's the advantage', he wrote after the visit, 'of having spent almost every day and having experienced almost every event and discussed every thought together for eight years.'[52] A few weeks later, on Christmas Day 1943, he wrote: 'I had become so used to talking everything over with you that the sudden and prolonged interruption meant a profound change and a great deprivation.'[53] He wrote in a later letter that

> The mind's hunger for discussion is much more tormenting than the body's hunger for food, and there is no one but you with whom I can talk about some things and in one way. A few pregnant remarks are enough to touch on a wide range of questions and clear them up. This ability to keep on the same wavelength, to play to each other, took years to cultivate, not always without friction, and we must never lose it.[54]

But Bonhoeffer was now thankful that through their correspondence, 'we're at least in touch again'.[55]

Bonhoeffer returned to this theme often in his letters, trusting that once he was released and the war had ended, he and Bethge would continue as before in both their friendship and ministry. But in the meantime they could write to each other, and though Bonhoeffer would not always tell others all about the harsh side of prison life, he would 'not deceive' Bethge 'in any way', 'nor', he told his friend, 'must you deceive me'.[56] Meanwhile Bethge, who much preferred to read Bonhoeffer's letters than to write his own,[57] found those letters most encouraging, giving him a sense

---

51. Bonhoeffer, *Letters and Papers from Prison*, p. 144.
52. Bonhoeffer, *Letters and Papers from Prison*, p. 145.
53. Bonhoeffer, *Letters and Papers from Prison*, p. 160.
54. Letter to Bethge, 16 December 1943, in Bonhoeffer, *Letters and Papers from Prison*, pp. 177–8.
55. Bonhoeffer, *Letters and Papers from Prison*, p. 160.
56. Bonhoeffer, *Letters and Papers from Prison*, p. 173.
57. Bonhoeffer, *Letters and Papers from Prison*, p. 184.

'of tranquillity and assurance' that he otherwise would not have had, and helping to clarify points of disagreement between them.[58] During his train journey to Munich and then on to the Italian front on 9 January 1944, he wrote: 'It seems to me that you have made things about yourself clearer and more comprehensible, the difference in our backgrounds – yours and mine; what it meant for you to become a theologian and to be one in *this* family.'[59]

In his first letter to Bonhoeffer in prison, sent from Charlottenburg, Berlin, on 30 November 1943, Bethge expressed the thought that he 'felt military life' had brought him 'very close' to his friend 'because of the loss of the ability to determine our own actions, which is so utterly unfamiliar to the two of us'.[60] This theme, of somehow being in the hands of fate or providence, runs through the letters and, of course, is reflected in the German title of the published volume, *Widerstand und Ergebung* (Resistance and Submission). How to resist fate, yet submit to the God of history is indeed a central theme in the prison writings. But where does one draw the line between the two in practice and not just in theory?[61] How difficult it was to accept that one could not do much to help oneself in these circumstances. More and more Bonhoeffer became aware of the fragmented nature of life and the need for a *cantus firmus* that can hold things together.[62] Bonhoeffer's thinking about this was triggered not only by the fateful events of the time and his own imprisonment, but also by the frightful and incessant bombing of Berlin and its environs, much of it very close to the prison – in fact, the bombing killed several inmates and at least one good friend among his prison guards. His letters to Bethge are full of experiences associated with the

---

58. Letter to Bonhoeffer, from Bethge in Charlottenburg, 8 January 1943, in Bonhoeffer, *Letters and Papers from Prison*, p. 182.

59. Bonhoeffer, *Letters and Papers from Prison*, p. 183.

60. Bonhoeffer, *Letters and Papers from Prison*, p. 154.

61. Letter from Bonhoeffer to Bethge, 21 February 1944, in Bonhoeffer, *Letters and Papers from Prison*, p. 217.

62. 23 February 1944, in Bonhoeffer, *Letters and Papers from Prison*, p. 219.

bombings, his own reaction and that of his fellow prisoners, but also the spiritual problems relating to these events, notably the difficulty of praying in times of trouble.[63]

After the initial expectations that he would be tried and released relatively soon, Bonhoeffer began to accept that perhaps things would not work out as he and his family and friends had hoped. He would have to submit to whatever would happen. Thus, as the months passed, Bonhoeffer's letters to Bethge began to reflect doubt about their future together, wondering whether they would 'have to be content with what has been. They were', he added, 'really quite wonderful years.'[64] But it was clear that the delay in his trial, quite apart from his separation from family, fiancée and Bethge, often made Bonhoeffer despondent, something he tried to hide from his family and Maria, but not from Bethge, now posted to serve in the German army in Italy.

---

63. See the letters to Bethge in Bonhoeffer, *Letters and Papers from Prison*, pp. 199, 231.

64. Letter to Bethge, 19 March 1944, in Bonhoeffer, *Letters and Papers from Prison*, p. 235.

6

A Soldier in Italy

The correspondence between Bonhoeffer and Bethge is usually read and considered in terms of Bonhoeffer's situation and experience, his role in the resistance and his imprisonment. But Bethge's context was equally significant, and his letters to Bonhoeffer during his ten months on the Italian front are equally revealing. Ironically, the fact that Bethge had been sent to Italy for military duty was initially a relief for Bonhoeffer and the other members of the family; after all, he could have ended up on the Russian front. Moreover, the fact that he worked as a clerk for the commanding officer of his unit also meant that he would be saved from the dangers of front-line combat. Much of this good fortune came as a result of family intervention through contacts in the Abwehr.[1] For Bonhoeffer there was an added reason for his delight in Bethge's posting to Italy, for it brought back to mind their brief holiday there together in 1936. But no one realized that Bethge was being sent to Italy at the very moment when the German army was getting caught between the Allied troops and Italian partisans.

A Growing Disgust

In January 1944 additional Allied troops had just landed at Anzio, south of Rome, to supplement the forces that had arrived six months earlier. In radio broadcasts the Allies called for support from Italian partisans throughout the country, and

---

1. Bethge, *Friendship and Resistance*, p. 39.

encouraged the partisans to shoot at the Germans. Bethge's ten months in Italy would coincide with the German army's move toward the north, away from the Allies and involved in constant battle along the way with partisan forces.

Bethge was assigned to a small Abwehr unit of sixteen men in the 10th Army, which was under the command of General Heinrich von Vietinghoff. Together, the 10th and the 14th Army constituted Army Group C, under the command of Field Marshal Albert Kesselring. Bethge's unit was charged with bringing intelligence to Kesselring, but most of the time he served as chauffeur, secretary and night watchman.[2] Vietinghoff, who had served in Poland and the Balkans before his assignment to Italy, was 'a solid, if not ostentatious, former Prussian guardsman . . . a by-the-book officer who was ruthlessly efficient'.[3] Little is known about the smaller, non-combat Abwehr units, but in Italy at the beginning of 1944 they, like the rest of the German army, were part of 'the intensified fight against the Italian partisan movement'.[4]

Hitler had ordered that fifty Italians be killed for every German soldier who fell. At his 1947 trial for war crimes Kesselring defended himself by noting that he had reduced the figure to only ten Italians for every German. And this was precisely what occurred in March 1944, when, in reprisal for a bomb attack that killed 32 German soldiers, 320 Italian partisans, diplomats and civilians were murdered in the Ardeatine caves south of Rome. While this was the most infamous such incident, there were numerous smaller ones; one writer estimates that at least a thousand Italians, including women and children, were killed.[5] German soldiers also engaged in widespread plunder and

---

2. Bethge, *Friendship and Resistance*, p. 39.

3. Tim Ripley, *The Wehrmacht: The German Army in World War II 1939–1945* (New York: Fitzroy Dearborn, 2003), p. 242.

4. Julius Mader, *Hitlers Spionagegenerale sagen aus: Ein Dokumentarbericht ueber Aufbau, Struktur und Operationen des OKW Geheimdiestamtes Ausland/Abwehr mit einer Chronologie seiner Einsaetze von 1933 bis 1944* (Berlin: Verlag der Nation, 1971), p. 390.

5. Richard Lamb, *War in Italy: A Brutal Story 1943–1945* (New York: St Martin's Press, 1994), pp. 66–8.

destruction of property. In June 1944 Vietinghoff noted that the problem had 'increased in its ugliest forms' in the 10th Army and feared that the soldiers would damage the army's reputation.[6] This was the situation in which Bethge found himself. Both his correspondence at the time, and his later account of this period, offers a strange juxtaposition of the beauty of his surroundings and the horror of what was happening.

Bethge was first stationed at Rignano, which gave him an opportunity to journey south to Velletri, from where he saw the Allied fleet in the distance near Nettuno and Anzio, and heard their guns. This was shortly after the Allied invasion occurred on 22 January. He was also able to revisit Rome and attend an audience with the Pope, though to his disappointment, the Pope gave no sign of responding to his hurried comment, when introduced, that he was 'an illegal pastor of the Confessing Church'.[7] What time he had, he spent in St Peter's Basilica, where Michelangelo's Pietà made 'a great impression' on him.[8] Bethge did not see many towns or cities other than Rome, but he did experience much of the countryside and the beautiful lakes of Alba and Nemi near the papal summer residence.[9]

Bethge had long shared Bonhoeffer's interest in culture, and there is a great deal in their letters about art and music appreciation, and what Bonhoeffer in one place refers to as the importance of 'aesthetic existence'.[10] But while Bethge enjoyed and wrote to Bonhoeffer about the beauty and culture of Italy, expressing pleasure without reserve, he also wrote about the horrors of war – and what it meant to be confronted by them. On one occasion Bethge drove his immediate superior, Major Tilp, to Rome on a trip that he later realized was connected to the

---

6. Friedrich Andrae, *Auch gegen Frauen und Kinder: Der Krieg der deutschen Wehrmacht gegen die Zivilbevölkerung in Italien 1943–1945* (Munich: Piper Verlag, 1995), p. 67.

7. Bethge, *Friendship and Resistance*, p. 41.

8. Letter to Bonhoeffer, 15 February 1944, in Bonhoeffer, *Letters and Papers from Prison*, p. 214.

9. Bonhoeffer, *Letters and Papers from Prison*, p. 224.

10. See Bonhoeffer, *Letters and Papers from Prison*, p. 193.

Ardeatine cave massacre.[11] A letter he wrote immediately after that incident requested that Bonhoeffer destroy the first page; in the passage that opens the remainder of the letter, Bethge wrote of his isolation:

> When you are drafted, first of course comes a period of being a recruit and only then come the demands. Sometimes I become afraid about being here, but then all kinds of reasons for comfort occur to me. The chief [Tilp] here and his immediate subordinates, both very nice to me personally, are nonetheless so modern [a coded reference to their being Nazis] and so soldier-like in their attitude that up to now I have not been able to talk about my problems and I fear will never be able to speak in the way I would sometimes like to . . . an underling who was drunk recently said to me that in peacetime after the war such people as me . . . would be taken care of by the Party.[12]

Month by month, Bethge's letters revealed his growing disgust at the events around him. In February 1944, he observed:

> Now I am mainly a secretary and have a great deal to do, some of it interesting, but on the whole it is not pleasant. i.e. outwardly I am lucky and am also treated well. Yet how should I respond to everything that I must go along with? When does something go beyond mere secretarial work and when not? The major is interested in allowing me to work somewhat more independently, very occasionally, and naturally knows nothing else about me. On the other hand I don't wish to make my situation worse . . .[13]

Early in March he wrote:

> The delight of some people in this business is disgusting and it coexists with otherwise nice, human, sympathetic traits of the same people with whom one can converse, laugh, and do mischief. This is naturally a burden.[14]

---

11. Bethge, *Friendship and Resistance*, p. 40.
12. Bonhoeffer, *Widerstand und Ergebung*, pp. 372–3.
13. Bonhoeffer, *Widerstand und Ergebung*, pp. 328–9.
14. Bonhoeffer, *Widerstand und Ergebung*, p. 347.

And, again, in July, he wrote after watching his fellow soldiers looting:

> The confiscation of the very well-tended and cultured house-holds . . . the throwing out of people and snooping through all their boxes, provisions and drawers by our people was the most repulsive thing that I have recently experienced. I had not yet been part of this, the invasion of entirely new areas . . . by our forces. The greed in anticipated pleasures creates a nervousness that waits only for the slightest grounds that these poor people offer, in order to find the proper fury and self-justification for proceeding, and then all the barriers fall. The officers distainfully appeal to 'reasons of defence'; the under-officers, in order to give the troops all the 'necessities', the troops – they're the best of all. Together they spread them-selves around the carved tables, on the upholstery, and drink the cellars dry. And there you stand.[15]

Bethge's only post-war essay about this period is entitled 'How the Prison Letters Survived'. In it, his comments on his experiences in Italy are circumspect. Of his comrades hunting the partisans, he writes: 'There must have been ghastly atrocities there too. I did not ask much about them, or I repressed them quickly.'[16] Once he took food to a captured civilian imprisoned by his unit; upon hearing that Bethge was a pastor, the prisoner asked him to hear confession and give him absolution. Bethge's comment – that Finkenwalde had prepared him somewhat for the encounter – was followed by his acknowledgement that he 'never heard anything more about that man's whereabouts or fate'.[17]

While his focus was naturally on the issues and questions raised in his correspondence, and on his wife and new son at home, Bethge's letters included agonized reflections upon his own situation and how he should behave. It is difficult to imagine that this did not shape Bethge's own thinking later when he

---

15. Bonhoeffer, *Widerstand und Ergebung*, pp. 524–5.
16. Bethge, *Friendship and Resistance*, p. 43.
17. Bethge, *Friendship and Resistance*, p. 43.

1 Eberhard Bethge at 21, 'On the road to Lichtenstein', Ascension
Day, 1931

2 Pastor Bethge and his first confirmation class, Lagendorf, March
1935

3 Eberhard Bethge and Dietrich Bonhoeffer, in the collective
pastorates in Gross-Schlönwitz, 1938

4 Eberhard Bethge and Dietrich Bonhoeffer making music together with the von Dohnanyi children, Ettal, Christmas 1940

5 The wedding of Eberhard Bethge and Renate Schleichen, Berlin, May 1943

6 Eberhard Bethge, preacher and pastor, shortly after World
  War II

7 Eberhard and Renate Bethge on a visit in 1972 to Schwäbisch
  Hall, where Bonhoeffer's ancestors are buried

8 Eberhard Bethge, teacher and interpreter, in South Africa,
   February 1973

9 Eberhard Bethge, Renate Bethge and Albert Schönherr, at the
   International Bonhoeffer Congress, Hirshluh, East Germany,
   July 1984

10 Eberhard Bethge, senior colleague and elder statesman, in his
    late sixties

11 Eberhard Bethge
at his ninetieth
birthday
celebration in Bad
Godesberg, 18
August 1999

12 The 'empty
chair': Eberhard
Bethge's study
after his death

wrote of the 'double life' of the conspirators, yet there is no direct reference to these very central experiences. Bethge's later writings would focus exclusively on his friend; where he brought in his own experience, it is always in reference to the friendship – and, indeed, this is the case with his essay on the Tegel letters. The early editions of the prison letters simply omitted Bethge's messages from the front. But as the excerpts above suggest, the double life that confronted him at the time was not just a division between public behaviour and secret conviction, or the necessary duplicity of the conspiracy – but the situation, as Bethge noted, of otherwise decent people who become participants in terrible deeds. He was referring, of course, to his own situation. Indeed, Bethge experienced this in Italy in a way that was spared his friend. Like so many other Germans, Bethge would later reflect on the great post-war issues of guilt and responsibility – yet this deeply disturbing experience was left out of his letters.

The 'Theological Letters'

Bethge's initial selection of the prison letters for publication was, as we have previously noted, determined by theological interest. And however important it is to read these within the broader framework provided by the rest of the correspondence as we now have it, these letters undoubtedly remain the core of the correspondence. But we need to recognize that Bethge was more than a recipient of these letters. He was also a contributor to the theological reflections that emerged, reflections that, for Bonhoeffer, were deepened by his prison experience, and for Bethge, darkened by his wartime experience and worries about events at home. In June 1944 Bethge wrote his friend:

> You speak in your letter of the continuity with one's own past and that we haven't experienced any break . . . For me personally however there are many matters of taste, of judgements, of ways of living, that have changed a great deal, of which e.g. Renate cannot have the slightest inkling . . .[18]

18. Bonhoeffer, *Widerstand und Ergebung*, p. 497.

Although anticipated in some earlier passages in Bonhoeffer's letters to Bethge, there is no doubt that the theological reflections on Christianity in 'a world come of age' that began with the letter of 30 April 1944 came as something of a surprise. Anticipating this, Bonhoeffer wrote to Bethge:

> You would be surprised, and perhaps even worried, by my theological thoughts and the conclusions that they lead to; and this is where I miss you most of all, because I don't know anyone else with whom I could so well discuss them to have my thinking clarified.[19]

Bethge's later interpretation of Bonhoeffer's 'new theology' from prison will be considered more fully in Chapter 10. At this stage, when Bethge was still receiving the letters and not sure of what was yet to come, he was trying to digest each letter in turn, and responding to Bonhoeffer's thought in an ad hoc manner. But what is not often recognized is that Bethge's thought was itself moving along a parallel track, changing in ways that would prepare him to respond enthusiastically to Bonhoeffer's ideas. Indicative of this is that prior to receiving Bonhoeffer's programmatic letter of 30 April, he wrote:

> Can you tell me anything about the fact that all my feeling and thinking is now really concentrated on personal experience, and that excitement over church affairs, love for its cause, has been caught up in a degree of stagnation? My conscious missionary impulse, which in earlier years was there perhaps more or less naïvely, has given way to the attempt to understand things, people and circumstances and to grasp them in a 'human' way.[20]

And, indeed, after receiving Bonhoeffer's ground-breaking letter, he immediately responded: 'I got your letter of 30 April today. It came very quickly. I am delighted about the things which, I must say, excite me very much. Some of it is echoed in

19. Bonhoeffer, *Letters and Papers from Prison*, p. 279.
20. Bonhoeffer, *Letters and Papers from Prison*, p. 283.

the questions I have written above, though put more naïvely and primitively.'[21] Much to his frustration, Bethge had no one with whom he could immediately discuss Bonhoeffer's ideas or his own responses, though one of his fellow soldiers, J. Rainaltar, a lawyer from Munich, became something of a confidant who showed interest in the issues.[22]

The anticipated birth and the naming of the Bethge baby was a subject of much discussion in the letters. Bonhoeffer was delighted that it would be 'Dietrich' if a boy, but suggested the name of his twin sister, Sabine, if it were a girl.[23] As it happened, 'little Dietrich' was born on 3 February 1944, the day before Bonhoeffer's thirty-eighth birthday. The next day Bonhoeffer was in the midst of writing to Bethge, 'remembering that for eight years in succession we have celebrated together', when he was called downstairs, 'where the first thing with which Maria greeted me was the happy news: "Renate has a little boy, and his name is Dietrich!"'[24] Bonhoeffer was a godfather, along with the good family friend and Confessing Church lawyer Friedrich Justus Perels, to whose son Bethge himself had earlier been the godfather. Bethge received the news on the front:

> When on Friday the major showed and handed me the telegram with completely garbled names, out of joyful shock my knees actually went weak and I trembled throughout my body. It had been completely impossible for me to picture beforehand how it would be when the child arrived. And it is still difficult. The impossibility of seeing Renate and the little one oppresses me again and again.[25]

Bethge was given leave of absence to return to Germany in May to attend the baptism – a fortunate coincidence, because he was

---

21. Letter to Bonhoeffer, 8 May 1944, in Bonhoeffer, *Letters and Papers from Prison*, p. 284.
22. Bethge, *Friendship and Resistance*, p. 39.
23. Bonhoeffer, *Letters and Papers from Prison*, p. 194.
24. Bonhoeffer, *Letters and Papers from Prison*, pp. 207–8.
25. Bonhoeffer, *Widerstand und Ergebung*, p. 326.

away when the Allies captured Monte Cassino on 18 May. He arrived in Berlin and saw his infant son for the first time on the 16th of that month. Although Bonhoeffer could not attend the baptism and preach the sermon (Bethge did) he did prepare a reflection for the occasion in which we get a vivid account of where his new theological thinking was leading him. By 'the time you have grown up', he told the infant Dietrich,

> the church's form will have changed greatly . . . It is not for us to prophesy the day (though the day will come) when men will once more be called so to utter the word of God that the world will be changed and renewed by it. It will be a new language, perhaps quite non-religious, but liberating and redeeming . . .[26]

While in Berlin for the baptism, Bethge had an opportunity, together with Renate, to visit Bonhoeffer in prison on 19 May. This led to a flurry of letters from Bonhoeffer to Bethge in which he reflected on the visit and what they had discussed. In one of them, the day after the visit, a letter 'intended for you only', Bonhoeffer, clearly feeling desperately lonely, gently yet firmly rebuked his friend for some comment he had made in which he expressed his pain at his long periods of separation from his wife and young son. Bethge had complained that Bonhoeffer's letters to his parents, which were shared with his siblings and Maria, were not passed along to him.[27] He also hinted that perhaps Bonhoeffer was better off in prison than he himself was in the Italian theatre of war. Why did Bethge say this? Surely not because of the danger and hardships of army life during wartime; more likely, Bethge was alluding to his knowledge of the massacres to which we referred earlier and about which he could not openly write. Undoubtedly when they met, Bethge shared this information with Bonhoeffer. But in the meantime Bethge's comment made Bonhoeffer a little uneasy. In responding he told Bethge that he had every right to live happily with, and for the

---

26. Dietrich Bonhoeffer, *Christology* (London: Fontana, 1971), p. 300.

27. Bethge, *Friendship and Resistance*, p. 91.

sake of, his wife and young son. He also suggested that he 'was more tired of life' than Bethge. Not that he wanted to be pitied, or wished Bethge to feel any guilt or grief.[28] Rather he wanted him to experience the 'polyphony of life', that is, its full range of experiences including earthly love. But he insisted that this could only be done when the God-given *cantus firmus* is clear and plain.[29] In his later interpretation of Bonhoeffer's life and theology, Bethge would often return to this notion of the 'polyphony of life' and the *cantus firmus*.

Bethge later confessed that the first few days back in Berlin had been difficult, as he experienced an 'unrest and sense of oppression which wouldn't go away'.[30] But the baptism, being with Renate and his young son, and his visit to Bonhoeffer in prison, followed later by a telephone conversation, had made all the difference. 'These three weeks have been incomparably splendid,' he told Bonhoeffer, 'and I'm glad to have found you so well despite all my fears to the contrary.'[31] In response, Bonhoeffer wrote that he, too, found 'it was very splendid for both of us to be together and I can't imagine that anything will change in the years that are to come. That is a real possession, perhaps acquired slowly and laboriously, but how worthwhile have been all the sacrifices that we have made for it!'[32]

Bethge set off from Berlin to return to Italy on 8 June. His journey was interrupted in Munich due to the chaos in northern Italy, which enabled Renate to visit him there for a few days. But eventually, after some difficulty, he rejoined his unit now stationed at Pistoia. There he was promoted to lance corporal, a reward, as he told Bonhoeffer, for the skilful way in which he had found his way back,[33] and there, too, he found several of

---

28. Bonhoeffer, *Letters and Papers from Prison*, p. 305.

29. Bonhoeffer, *Letters and Papers from Prison*, p. 303.

30. Bonhoeffer, *Letters and Papers from Prison*, p. 338.

31. Letter to Bonhoeffer, 3 June 1944, in Bonhoeffer, *Letters and Papers from Prison*, p. 317.

32. Letter to Bethge, 9 June 1944, in Bonhoeffer, *Letters and Papers from Prison*, p. 329.

33. Letter to Bonhoeffer, 27 June 1944, in Bonhoeffer, *Letters and Papers from Prison*, p. 338.

Bonhoeffer's letters awaiting him, one of them (8 June) containing thoughts about and definitions of religionlessness.[34]

Remarkably, during his visit to Bonhoeffer in Tegel Prison,
the two friends had found time to discuss some of Bonhoeffer's
new theological ideas. These questions and observations, Bethge
wrote to tell him on his return to Italy, struck him 'afterwards in
an electrifying way'.[35] Their discussion also led Bonhoeffer to
write: 'I've again seen from our conversation recently that no one
can interpret my thoughts better than you can. That is always a
great satisfaction to me.'[36] But now Bethge began to feel that he
could not keep Bonhoeffer's new ideas to himself. So he asked for
permission to share them with some of their former Finkenwaldian colleagues.[37] To this request, Bonhoeffer promptly
replied that he had no objection, though he himself would not do
it 'because you're the only person with whom I venture to think
aloud, as it were, in the hope of clarifying my thoughts'.[38] But he
did ask Bethge to keep his specifically 'theological' letters just in
case he might want to read them again later. With this in mind,
Bethge made excerpts when he received them. In the last letter
from prison that survived the war, Bonhoeffer refers to these
selections from his 'very provisional thoughts', commenting:

> You can imagine how pleased I am that you're bothering about
> them. How indispensable I would now find a matter-of-fact
> talk to clarify this whole problem. When that comes about, it
> will be one of the great days of my life.[39]

---

34. The 8 June letter is in Bonhoeffer, *Letters and Papers from Prison*,
pp. 324–9.

35. Letter to Bonhoeffer from Sakrow, 3 June 1944, in Bonhoeffer,
Letters and Papers from Prison, p. 316.

36. Letter to Bethge, 5 June 1944, in Bonhoeffer, *Letters and Papers from
Prison*, p. 320.

37. Bonhoeffer, *Letters and Papers from Prison*, p. 339.

38. Letter to Bethge, 8 July 1944, in Bonhoeffer, *Letters and Papers from
Prison*, p. 346.

39. Letter to Bethge, 23 August 1944, in Bonhoeffer, *Letters and Papers
from Prison*, p. 392.

Indeed, Bonhoeffer feels that it all 'sounds too clumsy. It can't be printed yet, and it will have to go through "the purifier" later on.'[40]

Bethge was stationed in a confiscated villa in San Polo d'Enza, near Parma, on the fateful day of 20 July, when the assassination attempt on Hitler in East Prussia failed.[41] 'That evening is crystal clear in my memory', Bethge later recalled. Arrangements had been made with Renate to send him a coded message so that he would know what had happened. But, of course, as the person responsible for dealing with army reports and dispatches, Bethge was the first in his unit to hear about the failed assassination attempt and, moreover, to report it to his superiors. That night he hardly slept. 'If the despatches were even close to accurate, was everything lost by the next day for the family, for their prisoners, for a different Germany? How did things really look back home?'[42] Then, finally, a letter from Bonhoeffer dated 21 July arrived, followed a little later by his poem 'Stations on the Road to Freedom'.[43] From then on, that letter was Bethge's favourite. He even kept it in his possession years later when he gave all the original Bonhoeffer documents to the Berlin library. It was still in his study after his death. The agonizing days of living a double life were coming to an end. The 'long period of conspiracy really was the true path of liberation from the way "decent people" were sucked into complicity with evil'.[44] In his letter, Bonhoeffer also expressed the hope that one day he might be able to talk to Maria in the same way as he talked to Bethge. At this stage correspondence with Maria had, in fact, begun to dry up due to her deep depression, whereas the correspondence between the two friends was flourishing.

Bonhoeffer's letters of September, all of which Bethge destroyed for security reasons, 'showed signs of the darkening

40. Bonhoeffer, *Letters and Papers from Prison*, p. 393.

41. Bethge tells the story in his essay 'How the Prison Letters Survived', in Bethge, *Friendship and Resistance*, p. 38.

42. Bethge, *Friendship and Resistance*, p. 44.

43. Bonhoeffer, *Letters and Papers from Prison*, pp. 370–1.

44. Bethge, *Friendship and Resistance*, p. 45.

skies over the whole family and close friends like Perels', but Bonhoeffer continued to share his theological thoughts with his friend. The last thing Bethge received from Bonhoeffer was an 'Outline for a Book', which provided the framework Bethge used when he later interpreted Bonhoeffer's prison theology.[45] Bethge, in turn, wrote his last letter to his friend on 30 September 1944. It was already far too dangerous to continue the correspondence.[46] 'Once again we're living in a great pause', Bethge wrote. Nonetheless, he added, 'I find your thoughts about the future bold and perhaps even comforting.'[47]

---

45. Bethge, *Dietrich Bonhoeffer*, pp. 853–92.

46. See Bonhoeffer, *Letters and Papers from Prison*, p. 406, n. 27.

47. Letter to Bonhoeffer, 30 September 1944, in Bonhoeffer, *Letters and Papers from Prison*, p. 398.

7

Amidst the Ruins

On 6 June 1944 the Allied invasion began in Normandy, and a few weeks later their forces penetrated into Germany itself. Several weeks later, on the evening of 20 July, several conspirators in the plot to assassinate Hitler were shot, and others were hanged in August at Plötzenzee in Berlin. In mid-August, in one of the last surviving letters from Tegel, Bonhoeffer wrote to Bethge:

> For your new year I wish you – after you've returned to your family and into the ministry – a really great task and responsibility and at the same time the necessary calm to be able to write something very good from time to time. For myself, my wish is that our spiritual exchanges will continue to make it possible for our thoughts to arise, be expressed and clarified, and still more important, that in each other we shall always have someone in whom we can place unlimited trust.[1]

Largely unmindful of the dreadful events unfolding back home, Bethge wrote in reply that things were 'still going remarkably well'.[2] This was despite the fact that the partisans were increasingly active and the German army was retreating northwards. Of course, it is difficult to know what was said for the benefit of the military censors, and what was genuinely the case. And it could be that there was an understanding between the two friends that

---

1. Letter to Bethge, 14 August 1944, in Bonhoeffer, *Letters and Papers from Prison*, p. 387.
2. Bonhoeffer, *Letters and Papers from Prison*, p. 397.

when Bethge said all was going well he actually meant the very opposite.

Imprisonment and Escape

On 22 September, the Gestapo discovered highly incriminating files in the Abwehr offices in Zossen. That changed everything, for now it was possible for the Gestapo to trace the wider connections among the conspirators. The friends' trust in one another was about to be tested to the utmost. On 1 October, the Gestapo arrested Klaus Bonhoeffer, three days later Rüdiger Schleicher, Bethge's father-in-law, and then Friedrich Perels the following day. On 8 October Dietrich Bonhoeffer himself was moved from Tegel Prison to the infamous Gestapo prison in Prinz-Albrecht-Strasse, which Admiral Canaris described as a 'living hell'. At the same time, the Gestapo intensified the interrogations of the Bonhoeffer family members, torturing several of them.[3] The results can be seen in the intelligence report sent on 12 October, 1944 to Martin Bormann from SS General Ernst Kaltenbrunner, who conducted the interrogations.[4] The report revealed the numerous links between Klaus and Dietrich Bonhoeffer, Schleicher, Perels, and other circles of conspirators, and went into detail on Bonhoeffer's church contacts and trips abroad for the Abwehr. Then, ominously, it mentioned Bethge's name under the heading: 'Oppositional stance of the entire family':

> The entire circle of those grouped around the name Bonhoeffer is characterized by the following examples:

---

3. According to Josef Mueller's memoirs, Dietrich Bonhoeffer divulged key information about Oster's involvement after the Gestapo threatened to harm Maria von Wedemeyer: Mueller, *Bis zur letzten Konsequenz: ein Leben fuer Frieden und Freiheit* (Munich: Sueddeutscher Verlag, 1975), p. 243.

4. *Spiegelbild einer Verschwörung: die Kaltenbrunner-Berichte an Bormann und Hitler uber das Attentat vom 20. Juli 1944* (Stuttgart: Seewald Verlag, 1961), pp. 440–4.

1. The daughter of Bonhoeffer is married to a pastor named Eberhard Bethge. According to Schleicher's statement, Bethge, a follower of the confessional front, is a lance corporal in Italy. From his very connection to the confessional front he rejects the National Socialist state. During his last leave they discussed plans for the coup again.[5]

Thus, although Bethge believed at the time that he had not been tied to the Bonhoeffers and to the plot against Hitler, he was wrong. On 28 October, a confidential telegram arrived at the office where Bethge was on duty. Bethge was under instructions to deal with all incoming mail and bring it to the attention of the commanding officer. This telegram, however, was different. It was an instruction from the Reich Security Head Office in Berlin that Lance Corporal Eberhard Bethge be brought forthwith under heavy guard to Berlin. Bethge pondered what to do. In the end he thought it wise to inform the commanding officer, Major Sarstedt, who, to Bethge's amazement, did not take the matter very seriously. But, as ordered, Bethge was sent back to Berlin, though not under heavy guard, but in the company of two amiable NCOs. His guards, who were in no hurry, readily accepted a proposal from Bethge that they should visit Marien-burger Allee to see Renate, his wife, and also eat a special meal cooked by his mother-in-law![6] But a day later they dutifully delivered Bethge to the Gestapo prison at Lehrterstrasse 3, and Bethge was placed in cell 235.

The visit to the Schleicher home provided an opportunity for Bethge to work out a secret code whereby information could be passed between him and Renate once he was in prison. They also worked out a plan to outwit the Gestapo, who had no knowledge that Bethge had been able to visit his wife and mother-in-law. The purpose of the secret code was so that they could know whether or not Eberhard was being interrogated, and whether the questions were about Renate's father, Rüdiger Schleicher, or about Bonhoeffer. As it happened, there was no interrogation to

---

5. *Spiegelbild*, p. 444.
6. Bethge, *Friendship and Resistance*, p. 51.

begin with. That was to follow. But Bethge was able to make
visual contact in the cells with other prisoners associated with the
resistance, and on occasion to share brief moments with them in
the prison exercise yard. Then, towards the end of November, he
was taken for interrogation. Bethge tells us what happened:

> Commissar Baumer interrogated me. A secretary wrote the
> transcript, but only from his dictation. I was not allowed to
> formulate my answers for it. I then had to sign seven copies of
> the transcript. From time to time, Commissar Günther would
> look in and ask pointedly, 'Is he talking?'. . . 'Is he talking yet?'
> . . . 'He'll talk!'[7]

As far as Bethge knew at the time, the Gestapo were not aware of
his close links with Bonhoeffer, nor were they aware of their
correspondence over the past months.[8] At one point in the
interrogation they tried to get Bethge to acknowledge that he
knew Bonhoeffer's signature, but they soon abandoned the
subject. Bethge later came to the conclusion that the reason why
they did not question him about Bonhoeffer was because the
team that interrogated him (Günther and Baumer) was responsible for the group around Schleicher and Klaus Bonhoeffer, while
Huppenkothen and Franz Sonderegger were responsible for the
group around von Dohnanyi and Dietrich Bonhoeffer. In all likelihood this is correct, even though the Gestapo knew more than
Bethge realized. Bethge himself believed that their lack of interest in that regard was largely because he was a peripheral figure.
'What they were interested in', he wrote, 'was the Confessing
Church, my feelings of duty toward Jews, contacts with con-
spiratorial visitors at No. 42, and my failure to report such
friends and relatives.'[9]

Bethge's own description of his imprisonment and interrogation is minimal and almost casual. He always refused to be placed

---

7. Bethge, *In Zitz*, p. 158. Translation by Barbara Green, from a translation of this chapter of *In Zitz* and published separately as a brochure (with
no details of publication).

8. Bethge, *Friendship and Resistance*, p. 55.

9. Bethge, *In Zitz*, p. 161; translation from Barbara Green, *op. cit.* n.7.

among the ranks of those who had suffered most in prison.[10] While it is true that he was never tortured, documents and the recollections of other conspirators who survived the regime indicate how harrowing it must have been, and Bethge's own memories give a glimpse of this. Ever the pastor, Bethge became a chaplain to the other prisoners, a role that was apparently tolerated by his guards and enabled him to visit even those in solitary confinement and awaiting execution, and he became a prison trusty, delivering meals to his fellow prisoners. This enabled him to exchange information with the other prisoners, as well as to minister to them. It also fell to Bethge to clear out the cell of Ernst von Harnack, the son of the distinguished church historian Adolf von Harnack, after his execution. With another prisoner, Catholic priest Father Odilo Braun, Bethge administered Holy Communion to fellow prisoners using some wine left behind by Harnack. As the last one to speak to Harnack, Guttenberg and several other conspirators, Bethge would have the immediate post-war task of passing on their final words to their surviving family members. Already his later post-war role as the mediator of memories from this period was taking shape.

In the spring of 1945 Bethge was formally discharged from the army and was indicted to stand trial before the Nazi People's Court on 15 May. But by then Germany had surrendered. On 25 April, as the Russian troops began to pour into Berlin, the German prison guards fled their posts, apparently opening the cells and thus allowing Bethge and others to walk free. But he walked out into the chaotic dawn of the liberation of Nazi Germany: a country occupied by the Russians, the Americans, the French and the British, who were still fighting final skirmishes with die-hard Nazi troops. Berlin had been heavily bombed and many parts of the city had been reduced to rubble. Bethge's first thought, of course, was to find Renate and young Dietrich. With so many of their family members in prison, the Bonhoeffer parents had remained in Berlin. While in prison, Bethge had befriended a Russian Jew, who fortunately escaped with him. For as they ran through the rubble of the city, dodging bullets

---

10. Bethge, *Friendship and Resistance*, p. 54.

and hiding behind walls, they were accosted by a Russian patrol that was ready to shoot Bethge. But his friend spoke to them in Russian and they let them pass.[11] Eventually they arrived safely at the Schleicher home.

From his prison cell Bethge had passed information on to Renate, who, we may note, was only nineteen years old. She, in turn, kept a list of important dates. These were later discovered in his book of daily devotions for the year 1945, which survives among his private papers. It detailed Renate's visits to her husband in prison (her last visit was 21 April, only four days before Bethge walked free), as well as the dates that her father Rüdiger Schleicher and other conspirators were taken from their cells to be executed. The list also offers a brief record of what the final chaotic days of the war were like for the Bonhoeffer family members in the homes on Marienburger Allee, amidst Allied bombing raids and the entry of the Russians into Berlin:

Sun. 22.4	everyone moved into the cellar [of the Schleicher house]
Thurs. 26.4	futile attempt to drive out [to Sacrow, the site of the Dohnanyi's country cottage]
Fri. 27.4	grenade into house nr. 42. Buried alive.[12]
Sat. 28.4	the first 2 Russians in the cellar
Sun. 29.4	Soviet staff officers in the grandparents' home at nr 43
	6 a.m. ordered to evacuate
Wed. 2.5	Berlin surrenders
Fri. 4.5	second futile attempt to drive to Sacrow. Encounter en route with prisoners from Brandenburg[13]

---

11. These events were recounted by Bethge to Mary Glazener: see her 'A Tribute to Eberhard Bethge', *Newsletter of the English Language Section of the International Bonhoeffer Society*, 73 (June 2000), p. 12.

12. As noted earlier, this was the Schleicher home next to the Bonhoeffer house. 'Buried alive' must have indicated the initial destruction; no one was seriously injured.

13. This may be a reference to concentration camp inmates from one of the camps in the region.

Sat. 5.5	reunion with Renate in Sacrow
Sun. 27.5	move into Marienburger Allee 50
Thurs. 31.5	certainty of father's [Rudiger Schleicher's] and Klaus' death
Sat. 2.6	grave discovered[14]
Wed. 11.6	funeral service for father, Klaus and the others

Yet Dietrich's fate remained uncertain. No one in the family knew what had happened to him, whether he was dead or alive.

Pastor to the Desolate

Bonhoeffer's ecumenical friends were the first to learn of his death. Willem Visser 't Hooft learned of it in May from Josef Müller, Bonhoeffer's Catholic counterpart, who was now in US custody. Visser 't Hooft wired the news to George Bell and Bonhoeffer's sister Sabine Leibholz and her husband in Cambridge. Franz Hildebrandt, who happened to be in Cambridge at the time, heard the sad news from the Leibholzes and wrote on 5 June to tell Herbert Jehle, one of Bonhoeffer's students in Germany. Meanwhile the ecumenical office in Geneva issued a press release citing Bonhoeffer's ecumenical contributions and concluding: 'The Church of Jesus Christ has become the poorer by the loss of a highly gifted worker and the richer by a martyr.'[15] But as there was virtually no communication between the citizens of occupied Germany and the outside world, the family in Berlin still did not know what had happened to Dietrich, and continued to hope that he had survived. After Bethge discovered the fate of Klaus and his father-in-law Rüdiger Schleicher at Berlin-Moabit, he continued to contact various officials to ascertain Dietrich's fate. Maria von Wedemeyer was travelling on her

---

14. This was the crude grave where the bodies of Klaus Bonhoeffer, Rüdiger Schleicher, Friedrich Perels and the other conspirators had been dumped by the Gestapo.

15. Press release, I.C.P.I.S. Geneva, no. 22, June 1945; copy in Eberhard Bethge's private papers (hereafter 'Bethge papers').

own trying to trace Dietrich's whereabouts; she learned of his death in June but could not get word to the Bonhoeffers in Berlin.

Then, on 27 July a memorial service was held for Dietrich Bonhoeffer at Holy Trinity Church in Kingsway, London. The service was conducted by Julius Rieger, who had been Bonhoeffer's colleague in London in 1934; George Bell and Franz Hildebrandt both spoke; the choir was from the German congregation in London that Bonhoeffer had served. On 29 July, the BBC in London broadcast a fifteen-minute excerpt of the service on its European station. It was in this way that Bonhoeffer's parents, and Eberhard Bethge, received definitive word that Dietrich Bonhoeffer had been hanged on 9 April 1945, in Flossenbürg.

The Bonhoeffers had now lost four members of the immediate family in the resistance against Nazism. After Russian troops had entered Berlin, Dietrich's brother Klaus and Rüdiger Schleicher were shot, along with several other conspirators, during the night of 22 April at the Lehrter-Strasse Prison by SS guards. Hans von Dohnanyi had been killed on 8 or 9 April in Sachsenhausen.

These tragic losses were magnified by the executions of other close friends and distant relatives from the various resistance circles. Paul von Hase, a cousin of Bonhoeffer's mother, had been hanged on 8 August 1944, shortly after the failed coup. Russian troops had arrested Justus Delbrück (brother of Klaus Bonhoeffer's wife Emmi) to interrogate him about the conspiracy; he died of diphtheria in October 1945. Other close friends were executed in the final months of the Third Reich: Hans Otto, Ernst von Harnack, Ewald von Kleist-Schmenzin, Hans Oster, Friedrich Justus Perels, Hans-Bernd von Haeften, and Karl von Guttenberg.

Publicly, at least, the Bonhoeffers bore these losses stoically, yet their private emotional devastation was evident in a letter from Karl Bonhoeffer to a colleague who had emigrated to the United States:

I hear you know that we have suffered greatly and have lost two sons and two sons-in-law through the Gestapo. As you can imagine, this has taken its toll on us old folk. For years, we endured the tension, the anxiety . . . But since we all agreed about the necessity of action, and my sons were also fully aware of what they could expect if the plot miscarried, and had resolved if necessary to lay down their lives, we are sad, but also proud of their straight and narrow attitude. We have fine memories of both sons from prison . . . that move both of us and their friends greatly.[16]

These personal losses were felt even more deeply in light of the physical and spiritual destruction of Germany that was quite visible in the weeks and months following the defeat of the Third Reich. Berlin had been largely destroyed by Allied air raids. Nazi Germany had murdered millions of human beings and devastated Europe. Yet in the weeks that followed the collapse of the Nazi regime, Germans focused on their own personal losses and the devastation of their own country. There was a pervasive sense of political uncertainty, particularly in the eastern part of the country, now under Soviet control. This was where the only surviving Bonhoeffer son, Karl-Friedrich, found himself in June 1945. As the US forces prepared to hand Leipzig over to the Soviet troops, Karl-Friedrich feared that he might not survive, and so he wrote his own letter to his children, giving an account of what he knew of the final days of his brothers and in-laws 'there in the ruins from which no news comes to us'. This poignant letter ended with Karl-Friedrich's own uncertainty about the fate of the entire family. He had last spoken to his parents two months before:

What may have happened since the capture of Berlin by the Russians? A man came from there who said that they had executed 4000 political prisoners beforehand . . . Is everyone still alive? Have the grandparents been able to survive these bitter days? Both were already at the end of their tether . . . Uncle Dietrich spoke to someone at length on 5 April, in the neighborhood of Passau . . . From there he is said to have gone to the concentration camp at Flossenbürg. Why isn't he here yet?[17]

---

16. Bethge, *Dietrich Bonhoeffer*, p. 933.
17. Bonhoeffer, *Letters and Papers from Prison*, pp. 409–10.

The losses of the Bonhoeffer family were symbolic of a far more widespread loss that was most evident to the immediate survivors of the resistance. In the months that followed the failed coup of July 1944, the Nazis executed 11,448 people suspected of being involved in various resistance groups.[18] These were people from all walks of life – the churches, the Communist and social-ist parties, the civil service, the military – who had been engaged in some kind of activity to overthrow the Nazi regime and to create a foundation for what would follow. The Nazi regime, even in its death throes, had managed to eradicate its most articulate and thoughtful opponents.

At Christmas 1942, along with an excerpt from a manuscript of his *Ethics*, Bonhoeffer had sent a pensive essay to Bethge, Oster and von Dohnanyi entitled 'After Ten Years'.[19] In it Bonhoeffer had identified precisely the ethical spectres that would haunt Germans in the decades to follow. He spoke of the costs of complicity and compromise, the ethical seduction and corruption of his fellow Germans, the 'dearth of moral courage' and the first-hand experience of betrayal, the demands of 'free responsibility' and the importance of making one's 'whole life an answer to the question and call of God'. He prefaced this haunting essay by expressing his 'constant sense of gratitude for the fellowship of spirit and community of life that have been proved and preserved through the years'.[20]

Eberhard Bethge's life after 1945 would bear testimony to the themes that Bonhoeffer had addressed, as well as to the 'fellow-ship of spirit' that he had shared with his murdered friend. Yet, like most Germans, Bethge's immediate post-war concerns were far more pragmatic. At the top of the list were his responsibilities to the Bonhoeffer family. Not only did he have Renate and their children to think of, but both he and Karl-Friedrich had begun to shoulder responsibilities for the entire family, particularly Bonhoeffer's now-fragile parents (Karl Bonhoeffer would die in

---

18. Marie Vassiltchikov, *The Berlin Diaries 1940–1945 of Marie 'Missie' Vassiltchikov* (London: Methuen Ltd, 1987), p. 234.

19. Reprinted in Bonhoeffer, *Letters and Papers from Prison*, pp. 1–21.

20. Bonhoeffer, *Letters and Papers from Prison*, p. 3.

1948, his wife Paula three years later) and their daughters Christine and Ursula, now widows.

In material terms, the Bonhoeffers were better off than many in Germany; as news of Dietrich Bonhoeffer's death spread to his many friends abroad, a number of CARE packages were sent directly to the Bonhoeffer family.[21] Nonetheless, it was a time of deep anguish for all. Dietrich's sister Christine von Dohnanyi was particularly devastated, not only by her husband's torture and execution, but by the post-war accusations by Hans-Bernd Gisevius, who had been active in another resistance group, that Hans von Dohnanyi's preservation of certain documents had enabled the Gestapo to arrest a number of conspirators. Gisevius claimed that the Gestapo would never have discovered many of the conspirators had it not been for von Dohnanyi, claims later refuted by Christine.[22]

During this period Bethge himself also had to fill out the Allied denazification and other forms that led to his classification in 1946 as a 'victim of fascism',[23] a status that enabled him to travel abroad. The denazification form offered a complete résumé of his activities during the Nazi era, including his travels abroad with Bonhoeffer and his brief trip to Switzerland in 1943 for the resistance.

At the same time, Bethge was aiding the family in its search for justice. The circumstances under which Klaus and Dietrich Bonhoeffer, Hans von Dohnanyi, and Rüdiger Schleicher had

---

21. Emmi Bonhoeffer spoke of this in a 16 May 1986 interview with Victoria Barnett: see *For the Soul of the People*, pp. 242–3. Bethge also wrote a one-page report (dated 19 December 1945; Bethge papers) on the circumstances of the Bonhoeffer, Schleicher and Dohnanyi families that clearly described their needs.

22. See below, p. 153.

23. The forms found in Bethge's private papers include the six-page 'Military Government of Germany Fragebogen', which Bethge signed on 22 December 1945; a letter from Bishop George Bell, dated 30 October 1945; and an official certificate from the Berlin government, dated 13 April 1946, declaring him a 'victim of fascism' and permitting him to have an 'interzone passport'. There is also a typewritten statement listing his activities in the Confessing Church and the resistance, dated 2 May 1947.

died were now clearer. Bethge began to write up his own recollections of the resistance communications, particularly the role
and activities of Dohnanyi, and he contacted others in Berlin who
could help him reconstruct the history of their arrests and
deaths.[24] With this evidence in hand, Christine von Dohnanyi,
Bethge and Karl Bonhoeffer now sought the arrest and trial
of five Nazi officials directly implicated in their deaths. These
included Franz Sonderegger, the Gestapo official under
Manfred Roeder who had interrogated their family members,
and Walter Huppenkothen, an SS official who had summarily
'tried' Dietrich Bonhoeffer before his execution in Flossenbürg.[25] In 1946 Bethge wrote a report on the circumstances of
their deaths and began to correspond with judicial authorities in
the Soviet-occupied zone as well as with Allied officials. The
family's efforts led to the arrest of Sonderegger in 1946, and
family testimony was instrumental during the trials of Huppenkothen in the early 1950s.

The controversy surrounding Hans von Dohnanyi would be
the first of several larger debates about conflicting versions of
historical truth. In the early post-war period, however, these
debates were often waged on a personal level, propelled by raw
emotions and grief. German society was racked by distrust and
accusations. In this atmosphere Bethge now emerged as an
important and trusted pastoral figure. In one such case, he tried
to mediate between the parties, and wrote to the accuser:

> I came across our comrade L. again and, indeed, in a condition
> of utter desolation. I had the impression that he could barely
> keep control of himself. He looked terribly pitiful. I then
> invited him over and on Saturday had a long conversation with
> him. In particular I gained more precise information about the

---

24. Bethge's papers include a number of such documents from 1945 and
1946.

25. In a letter of 19 November 1946 to Karl Bonhoeffer, A. L. Petersen,
a US attorney for war crimes with the Allied military government in Berlin,
told Bonhoeffer that he had compiled files, including photographs, 'of the
five people whose names you gave to me' (Bethge papers).

charge you passed on from Mrs M., that L. was to blame for
Mr M.'s disappearance. After a complete explanation I now
have the impression that one shouldn't say that . . . It is understandable that for a woman like Mrs M. who has been
wounded so badly, the matter is very one-sided . . . should we
not try together to do something for L.?[26]

Bethge also spent a great deal of time helping the widows of
executed resistance leaders negotiate the legal and bureaucratic
system as they sought pensions, reparations, and in many
cases legal recognition of the innocence of their deceased family
member. In some instances, the families of those with whom
Bethge had been imprisoned needed his testimony about the final
hours of their loved ones so that they could have them declared
dead, and thus settle their financial affairs.[27] Because this entailed
dealing with Allied authorities, German courts, and often very
recalcitrant German bureaucrats, the process was a protracted
one for many families. As late as 1960 Bethge was asked to attest
to someone's involvement in the resistance, and he became a
regular witness at trials and other legal proceedings, not only on
behalf of the Bonhoeffer family, but for others as well.[28] Even
years later, in 1986, Bethge was involved in arranging a pardon
for Otto John, who, after his disappearance in 1945, had re-
appeared in 1954 and been accused of spying for the KGB.
    Some of the widows of resistance figures also turned to Bethge
for any information he could give them about the last days of

---

26. Letter to unknown recipent, 23 August 1948, Bethge papers.

27. In Bethge's papers there is correspondence concerning this from
May and July 1949 between Bethge and Therese Guttenberg, the widow of
Karl Ludwig von Guttenberg.

28. Bethge's private papers include a statement of January 1960 on
behalf of resistance figure Hans John, a summons of June 1957 to testify in
the criminal case against Gestapo official Josef Baumer, an August 1955
summons to testify in the trial of several Gestapo officials involved in the
prosecution of the July 1944 conspirators, and a great deal of correspondence surrounding the trial of Walter Huppenkothen, who had been
responsible for the interrogations of Bonhoeffer and others in Flossenbürg.

their husbands. In October 1945 the widow of Ewald von Kleist wrote him a poignant letter:

> As I have learned in a roundabout way, you were with my husband during his final night and were able to give him the eucharist. Would it be possible for you to report everything, everything to me? I would be so terribly grateful to you for this . . .[29]

Bethge replied to her letters, as to all other such letters, at great length and with obvious pastoral concern:

> My dear lady! What should I tell you about your husband's sense for the real situation of those weeks, of how he spoke with such chivalrous love and faithful confidence about the dreadful final weeks for you in Schmenzin . . . it is my own opinion that he had as much confidence in the strength of his nearest relations as he did in his own, and that the most important thing for him was to stand in human dignity and Christian faith whatever happened, whatever must be borne . . .[30]

Thus, Eberhard Bethge became an early leader of the '20 July group', which consisted of the families of those executed, survivors of the conspiracy itself, and their supporters. Although he probably perceived his own role at this early stage as largely pastoral, he had his own strong opinions about how the conspirators should be honoured – opinions that give us some insight into how he viewed this history in the early post-war period.

In 1947, a group of surviving families planned a memorial service and published a lengthy obituary notice in several German newspapers. The obituary listed the names of over one hundred executed conspirators, and announced that they had 'died a heroes' death in the free, honourable battle for truth and justice, for the freedom of the German people, for the purity and

---

29. Letter to Bethge, October 1945, Bethge papers.
30. Letter to Margarethe von Kleist, 31 January 1946, Bethge papers.

honour of German arms, as deliberate atonement before God for the injustice our people carried out'.[31] In the name of the Bonhoeffer family Bethge wrote to Count Carl-Hans Hardenberg, who had published the notice, that

> I personally would not yet have wished to use the term 'heroes' death', since it is still too tainted . . . I always believe that the simplest words are the most appropriate and the greatest honour for our dead. Of those on the list, the men who were close to me were primarily representatives of the German bourgeoisie and attempted to atone for their guilt and turn it around. Humanity and a sense of being citizens of the world were probably more important to them than the purity and honour of German arms.'[32]

In addressing this history, Bethge was not only doing so against the backdrop of evolving German history but within the specific realm of the post-war German Protestant church. While he would eventually play a prominent role in shaping the retrospective view of the German resistance, his real impact would be less among historians than within the church and among theologians – and ironically, he would have greater impact in theological circles abroad than in Germany.[33]

---

31. Translation by Victoria Barnett, from a copy of the obituary notice in the Bethge papers.

32. Letter to Count Hardenberg, from the Bonhoeffer home in Marienburger Allee, 3 June 1947, Bethge papers.

33. For an interesting analysis of this, see Andrew Chandler, 'The Quest for the Historical Dietrich Bonhoeffer', *The Journal of Ecclesiastical History* 54:1 (January 2003), pp. 89–97.

8

Post-war Reconstruction

In the summer of 1945, Bethge accepted an assignment to serve as assistant to Bishop Otto Dibelius. Dibelius, a former church superintendent and member of the Confessing Church, was 65 years old at the time and would remain bishop of Berlin-Brandenburg until 1966. Dibelius was a powerful and complex figure, both during the *Kirchenkampf* and in the post-war church scene. Although in the early post-war period he portrayed himself as one of the heroes of the church struggle, Dibelius had in fact been a strong nationalist and conservative in church circles who, among other things, preached openly anti-Semitic sermons during the 1920s and defended the Nazi anti-Jewish boycott in 1933. During the church struggle he had viewed Bonhoeffer as far too radical. Yet Dibelius had also come under pressure from the Nazi regime and in August 1945 was one of the German church leaders who signed the Stuttgart Declaration of Guilt.

In December 1946 Bethge's classification as a 'victim of fascism' permitted him to travel on behalf of Dibelius to England, where he was able to visit the Leibholzes and Julius Rieger.[1] One of the most moving aspects of his visit, he later wrote to his host, Oliver Tomkins, was the 'kindness I could observe just towards Germans. Reports on the only too comprehensible attitude of Dutch, French and Norwegian people did not allow me to expect this without further ado.'[2] In the same letter he also referred to his visit to German pastors who were serving in POW camps in

---

1. Bethge refers to this visit in his letter to Oliver Tomkins, 28 December 1946, Bethge papers.
2. Letter to Tomkins, 28 December 1946.

England, recommending that they should be given special training to minister to those in their care. He also expressed his own willingness to participate in organizing such courses, which would involve German theologians who were able to help the chaplains deal with the spiritual and social issues facing the imprisoned soldiers.

The Future of the Church?

Bethge described his duties under Dibelius in a November 1948 letter to Baron Schroeder, one of the church council members at the Sydenham parish that Bonhoeffer had served in London in 1933–4:

> Bishop Dibelius assigned me to look after the relations between him and the church government on the one hand and the western military governments in Berlin on the other, and in the weekly meetings with Allied religious officers to discuss the problems that came up between the church in the western sectors of Berlin and the occupation forces.[3]

Bethge's job had both ecclesiastical and political implications, for with the Soviets in the east and the western Allies governing the western sector of the city, Berlin was already at the heart of the dawning Cold War. Thus, his role was affected by the growing tensions between the western Allies and the Soviets, and it was complicated by the conflicts within the church itself. Already a debate was raging within the German Protestant church about what kind of institution it should be in the wake of Nazism.

In the increasingly polarized atmosphere of the early Cold War, many of the former members of the Confessing Church (and the resistance) were beginning to move in different political directions. Martin Niemöller, Helmut Gollwitzer and others associated with the 'Dahlemite' faction of the Confessing Church

---

3. Letter to Baron Schroeder, dated either 6 October or 6 November 1948, Bethge papers.

became advocates of rapprochement with the Soviet Union and opposed the western tilt of the Adenauer government. Dibelius, on the other hand, was a fervent anti-Communist and was one of the leading voices for reconstruction – that is, for preserving the traditional structures and form of the church. But the former young radicals in the Confessing Church, including Bethge and many of Bonhoeffer's students, sought a new kind of church – in effect, a continuation of the 'Confessing' church that would repudiate German Protestantism's long history of loyalty to state authority, an alliance that had proved so seductive, and fatal, under Nazism. As it was, in Berlin and the surrounding regions, some parishes continued to identify themselves as Confessing parishes, and the Confessing 'Council of Brethren' even continued to meet until the mid-1950s, despite the re-establishment of the official church hierarchy in Berlin and elsewhere.

Led by former Bonhoeffer student Wolf-Dieter Zimmermann, several of the younger pastors of the Confessing Church, in pursuit of their vision for the future of the church, founded the 'Unterwegs' ('on the road') circle in Berlin and for several years published a journal by the same name. This group called for a new model of the church and cited Bonhoeffer's vision in Finkenwalde as one possible option. In the Unterwegs circle Bethge found an early and congenial group of colleagues whose friendship went back to the beginning of the *Kirchenkampf*: Zimmermann, Claus Westermann, Rudolf Weckerling and his wife Helga, Winfried Maechler, Martin Fischer, the French military chaplain Georges Casalis and Gertrud Staewen.[4] Together they sought to reawaken the spirit of the Barmen and Dahlem synods in the post-war German Protestant church, strongly influenced by Barth's *Church Dogmatics*, by Bonhoeffer's writings, particularly *Life Together*, and by the example set by Bonhoeffer's involvement in the resistance. Through Bethge they were also becoming aware of Bonhoeffer's own

---

4. See Friedrich-Wilhelm Marquardt's account of the history of their friendships in his article on Horst Dzubba, 'Ein Berliner Nachbar von Frans Breukelman', *Text und Kontexte* 90 (February 2001), pp. 4–31.

thoughts about the future of the church as expressed in his prison letters. As Friedrich-Wilhelm Marquardt would later write:

> It was no wonder, then, that the Unterwegs circle, through its members and others who had been involved with Bonhoeffer, received something of the spirit and intent of Bonhoeffer . . . This circle was the first recipient of Bonhoeffer's legacy from Tegel, and participated in Bethge's own exploration of this.[5]

Thus the Unterwegs group provided Bethge with an early chance to reflect with others on Bonhoeffer's striking (and controversial) concepts, such as 'religionless Christianity' and what it meant to be 'the church for the world'.

Although he never spoke publicly about it, Bethge's special assignment under Dibelius must have been problematic in the Unterwegs group, and it undoubtedly ran counter to his own personal convictions, both with respect to the church and the political scene. In his brief memoir on the Gossner Mission, Bethge noted that 'before 1945 the Gossner Mission, welcoming the risks, had opened itself to the impulses to build and alter a confessing church'. But after 1945 'its environment, German Protestantism, returned completely to the old *volkskirchlich* regional churchdom':

> Now it was no longer heretical Nazi Christians and their aides to power who made the lives of the illegals difficult – but also worthwhile; now it was attrition and the temptations of the status quo that made the disruptions of renewal so difficult.[6]

Recovering the Truth

Just as his friend Bonhoeffer, frustrated by the inertia of his church and by the political situation, had looked abroad in late 1933, Bethge now began to explore possibilities outside Germany.

---

5. Marquardt, 'Ein Berliner Nachbar', p. 10.
6. Bethge, 'Drei Kriegsjahre', p. 85.

His 1948 letter to Baron Schroeder was actually a tentative job enquiry; he had heard of a possible opening in one of the German-speaking congregations in London. As this letter showed, Bethge was concerned about the continued dangers of the post-war German situation, particularly those that had come up in his work for Dibelius in the eastern zone. Berlin in the late 1940s was beginning to feel more dangerous:

> with the gradual heightening of political tensions more and more people approached me, whom I had to help flee, via the Allied officials, to the western zones of Germany on behalf of the bishop or on my own initiative. Several indications lead me to assume that these matters, which I could not avoid, have become known by the Russians. Russian offices have repeatedly demanded of one pastor in Potsdam, who by the way hardly knew me, to give them a report about my person and my activities . . . they always referred to me only as an 'American agent' and finally told the pastor to invite me sometime to his parsonage in Potsdam (I live in the British sector of Berlin) and then let them know. This naturally didn't come to pass.

Bethge continued:

> Another factor is that as the closest relative and friend of the pastor Dietrich Bonhoeffer who was murdered by the Gestapo . . . I have very close ties to his resistance group . . . . The Russians are well informed about the 20 July circle and possess many documents. Recently in the Russian zone they attempted to get hold of all the people who had anything to do with the former Abwehr. I am threatened even more by this. Since of the five male members of our family who were arrested back then by the Gestapo, four were murdered, and I am the only male who escaped this fate, for me it is a question of the responsibility for the surviving relatives of these men, not to place myself in new life-threatening circumstances if this is not absolutely necessary. Since this new threat has emerged from an activity that is not immediately related to my religious faith and my ministry as pastor of a parish, I think that leaving

is a possibility for me and, in the event of a decisive threat under the circumstances in Berlin is justified.[7]

It would be 1953 before Bethge actually took a position in England, as pastor of the German congregation in Sydenham, London, where Bonhoeffer had served. Yet in early 1949 he was able to leave Germany for a three-month visit to the US as part of a Marshall Plan programme, organized by the US military authorities in Berlin, 'to be re-educated democratically'.

Bethge made the journey to the United States with mixed feelings. On the one hand, he had to leave behind his wife and three young children – Dietrich, who was then five; Gabriele, who had been born in January 1946; and Sabine, born in June the following year.[8] On the other hand, the visit provided an opportunity for him to meet friends with a Bonhoeffer connection, notably Paul Lehmann, then at Princeton Theological Seminary, and Reinhold Niebuhr at Union Seminary in New York. Bethge brought along Bonhoeffer's diary from the fateful days of summer 1939 in New York, and he took it with him when he went to visit Paul Lehmann in Princeton:

> I now found it self-evident to tell Paul about Dietrich's final years. And in the process I discovered that he was now transferring his friendship with Dietrich, cemented in 1930 at Union Theological Seminary, renewed in 1933 in Berlin, preserved in 1930 in New York, immediately and without reservation over to me. I gave him the diary that was so relevant to him. He compiled for me the correspondence with him, with Reinhold Niebuhr, with Henry Leiper, that Dietrich had had in that summer of 1939 and that I was unfamiliar with.[9]

Lehmann was to become a major supporter of Bethge's work.

---

7. Letter to Baron Schroeder, 6 October or 6 November 1948.
8. Letter to Käthe (not Bethge's sister, but identity otherwise unknown) 14 January 1949, Bethge papers.
9. From a draft in Bethge's private papers of the article cited in Chap. 9, n. 31.

Not only had he known Bonhoeffer well, but he was also one of the very few major theologians in the United States who had a thorough grasp of his theology. His seminar on Bonhoeffer at Union Seminary, coupled with a more widespread interest in Bonhoeffer, awakened a new generation of North American scholars to the importance of Bonhoeffer's legacy. Some of these scholars were to play an important role in supporting Bethge's work and in establishing an international network of Bonhoeffer scholars.[10] Lehmann, as we shall see, also made it possible for Bethge to revisit the United States a decade later in order to devote more concerted attention to his task of retrieving Bonhoeffer's legacy.

Thus, the brief sojourn in the United States opened several avenues for Bethge. Personally, he was able to make his own budding friendships with Bonhoeffer's friends there. He had also gained his own first-hand impressions of the world Bonhoeffer had encountered in the United States. Bethge spent his three months visiting colleges and universities in order to learn about the role of the church and the influence of Christianity among students. Making these contacts was important for the tasks that awaited him and, as it turned out, significant in opening up opportunities that would have otherwise not materialized.

Bethge returned to Berlin in April 1949 and continued his work as a student chaplain at both Humboldt University and the technical college. At the same time he remained active in the Unterwegs circle. He had already published several articles and portions of Bonhoeffer's writings in *Unterwegs*. The first post-war volumes would soon follow: the original German edition of *Ethics* appeared in 1949; the collection of the prison letters would be published in 1951.

At the time of the publication of these early volumes, Bonhoeffer was still a controversial figure in the German church, and there was considerable ill-will toward the 20 July conspirators within the general population, who considered the resistance

---

10. Among this new generation of Bonhoeffer scholars were Jim Burtness, Clifford Green, Geffrey Kelly, Burton Nelson and Larry Rasmussen.

figures to have been traitors.[11] The reasons for this probably included the widespread desire in Germany to lay the past to rest and the troubling questions raised by the fact of the resistance. After all, the resistance figures (and their survivors) were reminders that resistance against Nazism had indeed been possible.

Although Bonhoeffer had been a powerful influence on his students and was well known abroad, and although he had been a significant radical leader within the *Kirchenkampf*, formally speaking he had actually been a minor figure. He was young and held no leading church position, he had spent key periods during the Nazi era abroad (he was not at the Barmen Synod, for example), and his longest period of activity on behalf of the Confessing Church had occurred in the remote Pomeranian countryside. When he had attracted the attention of church leaders in Berlin, it was usually because of his controversial actions, such as his outspokenness at ecumenical conferences. Now, in a post-war landscape in which many Germans preferred to forget the recent, problematic past, Bonhoeffer was particularly controversial in the church because of his role in the 20 July conspiracy. Bavaria's Bishop Meiser said bluntly that Bonhoeffer had been a political martyr, not a religious one.[12]

Thus, *Ethics* and *Letters and Papers from Prison* – the two works by Bonhoeffer that had been written during his work for the resistance – were published when attention was centred on his resistance rather than his church activities. This was particularly due to the trials during the early 1950s of Walter Huppenkothen, the SS colonel who participated in the investigations of the 20 July conspirators. He had 'tried' Bonhoeffer and several others at Flossenbürg, and was charged with having ordered their executions.

The Allies imprisoned Huppenkothen from 1945 to 1949;

---

11. See Barnett, *For the Soul of the People*, 198–204. See also Friedrich Wilhelm Marquardt's recollection that the German people believed 'that one should hang the entire Canaris gang': 'Ein Berliner Nachbar', p. 15.

12. Eberhard Bethge, *Bonhoeffer: Exile and Martyr* (London: Collins, 1976), pp. 159–60; Barnett, *For the Soul of the People*, p. 200.

after that the German courts ordered him to be held as he
awaited trial. It was during this period that the Bonhoeffer family
pushed for his trial and Bethge gathered as much evidence as
he could about the circumstances of Dietrich Bonhoeffer's
death. Although Huppenkothen would actually stand trial three
times, he was never convicted. The German courts during the
1950s agreed with his defence attorneys that the executions of
Bonhoeffer and others had been 'legal' within the context of Nazi
law. The Huppenkothen verdict and others were appealed all the
way to the German Supreme Court, which in 1956 upheld the
lower court decisions. Only in 1995 did the German Supreme
Court finally declare Bonhoeffer, Dohnanyi and other conspirators 'innocent' of the Nazi charges of treason against them. After
his acquittal, Huppenkothen found a position in industry, yet his
past continued to haunt him; he was interrogated as one of the
witnesses, for example, in the 1961 trial of Adolf Eichmann.

For Eberhard Bethge, the Huppenkothen trial, like all war
crimes trials, served the purpose not only of trying the defen-
dant, but also of establishing the historical truth.[13] In the wake of
Huppenkothen's acquittal, the latter task gained even greater
importance. Bethge and the Unterwegs group were outraged by
the final acquittal of Huppenkothen, and sent a protest letter to
West German federal president Theodor Heuss. Certainly,
Bethge and the rest of the Bonhoeffer family could not feel that
justice had been served. But Bethge had learned a great deal
about the conspirators' final days. His own testimony in the trial
illustrated both his growing certainty about the historical facts
and his own drive to discover as much as possible about the
circumstances under which Bonhoeffer had died. In the process,
he argued with the court, refuted Huppenkothen's testimony,
and on one occasion in the proceedings posed the question that
clearly haunted him and the entire family:

---

13. A copy of the entire transcript of the three Huppenkothen trials is in
the Harold Deutsch papers, Army War College archive, Carlisle,
Pennsylvania.

I can only ask why people searched for four men from one family from all over the place, just in order to murder them: Klaus and Dietrich Bonhoeffer, Hans von Dohnanyi and Rüdiger Schleicher. There must be something more behind this. Hans von Dohnanyi was very much part of everything, but the others only a very little. There must have been a clear, unambiguous decision behind this, that all four were picked up in order to kill them. I am the only one who got out of this; but then I only married into the family.[14]

The Bonhoeffers suspected that only a direct order from Hitler could have led to the execution of all four men. This suspicion was never confirmed, but the Huppenkothen trial did provide Bethge with a clearer understanding of the fate of all four family members, as well as a look behind the scenes of his own imprisonment. Bethge also provided the court with the evidence he had compiled, based upon his conversations with other survivors such as Josef Müller. Over the course of several days, as Bethge continued to testify and on occasion correct Huppen-kothen's version of things with conflicting evidence, the court acknowledged the importance of Bethge's knowledge. By the final day of Bethge's testimony, the court was turning to him for additional information and overruling motions by Huppen-kothen's lawyer to disregard the evidence.

In and through all these developments, Eberhard Bethge was beginning to reconstruct the history of Bonhoeffer in all its complexity: as friend, as pastor and mentor, and as 'man of his times' – a life that his friend was now reflecting upon not in isolation, but within the overall, highly charged, difficult process of coming to terms with the past, *Vergangenheitsbewältigung*. This process would itself be altered in the decades to follow, and Bethge, too, would confront different aspects of that history as he began to encounter different questions from different areas of the world.

---

14. Huppenkothen 1952 trial transcript, vol. i, p. 173.

9

Retrieving a Legacy

Bethge was a pastor, not an academic theologian or scholar in the formal sense. Although he received wide acclaim and recognition for his work and was appointed an honorary professor at the University of Bonn in 1969, unlike Bonhoeffer he never sought to fulfil the requirements for teaching in a German university. Even though he was regularly invited to give university lectures and seminars, he stood outside the academic guild. His major sphere of influence was the church – the regional church of the Rhineland, the wider ecumenical church, as well as the German lay academies and the Kirchentag, that large biennial gathering of laypeople, young and old, that had its origins in the church struggle and continues to play an influential role in German church circles. But Bethge was also a skilled researcher, writer and editor, all gifts that were now essential for retrieving the legacy of his friend Bonhoeffer.

First Steps in Publishing

A glance at the bibliography of Bethge's writings of this early period shows how soon after the war he was engaged in giving talks and publishing essays on Bonhoeffer's life and thought, starting with his first contribution in *Unterwegs*, and a memoir published in 1946 in *Neue Zeit* in East Berlin.[1] At this stage many other former friends and colleagues of Bonhoeffer were still

---

1. Eberhard Bethge, 'Leben ohne Ausflucht: Zur Erinnerung an Dietrich Bonhoeffer', *Neue Zeit*, 29 (3 February 1946).

alive,[2] some of whom were also interested in telling his story and sharing his theology and writings.[3] One or two of them were a little envious of Bethge's emerging role and growing reputation, and some disagreed with his interpretations. Bethge in turn defended his views energetically, but always acknowledged the contribution of others, especially those who, like Albrecht Schönherr, had been so faithful to the Bonhoeffer legacy.[4] On one occasion he commended Otto Dudzus, a former Finkenwaldian, 'who so painstakingly and unselfishly worked on Bonhoeffer's legacy'.[5]

Bethge was especially sensitive to the feelings of Franz Hildebrandt, Bonhoeffer's friend and confidant since their student years in Berlin and through the early years of the *Kirchenkampf.* Hildebrandt's friendship prior to the Finkenwalde period paralleled that of Bethge's from then on, with a brief overlap in which Bethge began to take his place. He was a scholar of considerable ability, passionate in his devotion to Luther's theology yet, like Bonhoeffer, highly critical of the way in which it had been distorted and betrayed. Given this, and the fact that he had shared so much with Bonhoeffer so intimately before being forced into exile in 1937, he, if anyone, could have played a major role in interpreting Bonhoeffer's theology after the war,

---

2. The following were present at the Second International Bonhoeffer Congress in Geneva in 1976 in addition to Renate Bethge: Emmi Bonhoeffer, widow of Klaus Bonhoeffer; from the ecumenical movement, P. C. Toureille; from the time Bonhoeffer spent at Union Seminary in New York, Erwin Sutz; from his time as lecturer in Berlin, Franz Lehel; from Finkenwald, Winfried Maechler, Albrecht Schönherr, Hans Pompe and Heinz Fleishack; from the church struggle, Kurt Scharf; from his second visit to New York, Theodor Gill; from Tegel Prison, Gaetano Latmiral; and his former fiancée, Maria von Wedemeyer.

3. A collection of some of these memories is in *I Knew Dietrich Bonhoeffer.*

4. See the dialogue between Bethge and Schönherr on the occasion of Bethge's ninetieth birthday celebration, 11 September 1999, in Eisenach, published in *Bonhoeffer Rundbrief,* 61 (March 2000), pp. 3–4.

5. From Bethge's typed notes of a talk at the celebration of Bonhoeffer's seventieth birthday in Geneva during the Second International Bonhoeffer Congress, 4 February 1976, Bethge papers.

especially in the Anglo–Saxon world that became his home. And, indeed, Hildebrandt did on occasion seek to do this. But he had strong reservations about the direction in which Bonhoeffer's theology was moving from the *Ethics* onwards, not helped at all by the way in which the discussion developed in Britain and the United States.[6] He also felt out of touch with post-war German theology, and the debate about interpreting Bonhoeffer's theology. But it was largely for personal reasons that he refrained from becoming involved. As he once remarked in an interview: 'The friendship [with Bonhoeffer] was of an intimacy which makes it impossible for me to enter the debate about him. I have quite deliberately kept out of that.'[7]

Whatever others might have thought about Bethge's role in retrieving Bonhoeffer's legacy, no one could doubt that he had been Bonhoeffer's closest companion during the final decade of his life;[8] that he had been his assistant, colleague and confessor at Finkenwalde and in the collective pastorates; and that it was to Bethge that Bonhoeffer had himself entrusted the task of writing his biography.[9] In addition, there was the anticipation of Bethge's role by Bonhoeffer, confirmed by the family. Already in May 1939 Bonhoeffer had written a will in which Bethge was made responsible for disposing of his goods as well as the recipient of any royalties from his works. Again, in November 1943, shortly before his arrest, Bonhoeffer listed everything that he wanted Bethge to inherit; among these was the whole of his library. He also asked Bethge to give a book to each of several former students and friends, the names of which were recorded.[10] Furthermore,

---

6. Holger Roggelin, *Franz Hildebrandt: Ein lutherischer Dissenter im Kirchenkampf und Exil* (Göttingen: Vandenhoeck & Rupprecht, 1999), pp. 262–9.

7. Quoted in Roggelin, *Franz Hildebrandt*, p. 262.

8. Bethge's own account of these various friendships with Bonhoeffer, including his own, is described in *Friendship and Resistance*, pp. 82–8.

9. See Eberhard Bethge, 'The Editing and Publishing of the Bonhoeffer Papers', *Andover Newton Bulletin* 52: 2 (December 1959), p. 1.

10. There were three *Abschriften* (attested copies of his testament), dated 22 May 1939, 27 May 1939, and 23 November 1943, all of which survive in Bethge's private papers.

Bonhoeffer's mother Paula drafted a statement in July 1949 confirming that Bethge was the executor of her son's literary estate.[11]

The only remaining member of the family who might have fulfilled this role was Bonhoeffer's eldest brother, Karl-Friedrich, to whom he had been particularly close. In one of his last major essays, Bethge wrote about this relationship, saying that 'the steady presence of his family, and especially his brother Karl-Friedrich, was probably more motivating and important than that of many theological colleagues', among whom Bethge even included Karl Barth.[12] But Karl-Friedrich did not have the same intimate connection with his younger brother's legacy as Bethge did, and his health suffered after the war, leading to his death in 1957 at the relatively young age of 58. Thus, not only did Bethge take on the task of retrieving Bonhoeffer's legacy, but other family responsibilities also fell onto his shoulders.

Bethge knew that the task awaiting him would be considerable, but he never anticipated the extent of his role as the person responsible for Bonhoeffer's legacy; that only gradually dawned on him as the process unfolded. As he lacked any previous experience in editing and publishing, he also felt inadequately prepared for such a massive and demanding task. But his commitment to the task made up for any lack of professional qualifications. Next to his 'chosen profession as pastor' Bethge was moved, as he said, 'only by the mandate to assure the estate of my friend and make it available'.[13]

Despite his protest to the contrary and his position outside the academy, Bethge was a scholar and theologian in his own right. He was also a born historian. Not only did he keep copious notes

---

11. The statement is dated 29 July 1949, and is found in the Bethge papers among correspondence between Bethge and Maria von Wedemeyer.

12. Eberhard Bethge, 'The Nonreligious Scientist and the Confessing Theologian: The Influence of Karl-Friedrich Bonhoeffer on his Younger Brother', in *Bonhoeffer for a New Day*, ed. John W. de Gruchy (Grand Rapids: Eerdmans, 1998), p. 42.

13. Quoted by Bishop Wolfgang Huber in his sermon at Bethge's funeral service, 25 March 2000, Marienforst Church, Bad Godesberg; translation by Victoria Barnett in *International Bonhoeffer Society English Language Section Newsletter* 73 (June 2000), p. 8.

of people he met, places he visited, and events in which he participated, but he hoarded papers and documents that he sensed were of historical importance, as well as those that he anticipated might be of value at some stage either to himself or to others. As Bonhoeffer teased him in a letter from prison, 'You've always liked lists – reminiscences of the sixth form'.[14] This orderly trait, so important for a historian and custodian of memories, was confirmed later with the discovery of diaries stretching back many years in which Bethge kept details of letters written and phone calls made.[15] Of chief interest among the documents he preserved and kept close at hand in his study were those many papers, sermons, lectures, and manuscripts of Bonhoeffer's that survived the war. All of this material was, for him, of great importance and interest. But only gradually did he become aware of how significant it might be for many others as well.

Bethge had at least one other gift that was significant for his task. He was able to see and appreciate things with a disarming directness – a gift that enabled him to communicate easily with others whether in conversation or teaching, writing or preaching. In a letter to Bethge from prison in August 1944, Bonhoeffer, commenting on this ability, described it as a great intellectual achievement. He went on to say:

> I believe that with a sure touch you've found the appropriate form for yourself – narrative, first person – and the right subject-matter – what you yourself have experienced, seen, observed, been through, felt, thought. Your gift of *seeing* seems to me to be the most important thing. And precisely *how* and *what* you see. This is no urgent, analytical, curious seeing, that wants to pry into everything, but clear, open and reverent seeing.[16]

---

14. Bonhoeffer, *Letters and Papers from Prison*, p. 220.

15. The diaries were found in his study, arranged in chronological order.

16. Letter to Bethge from Tegel, 11 August 1944, in Bonhoeffer, *Letters and Papers from Prison*, p. 385.

This kind of seeing, Bonhoeffer continued, was precisely what he himself sought to achieve in doing theology. And perhaps, he added, it was this that accounted for their 'strong spiritual affinity'; indeed, he suggested, it was 'the most important result of our long spiritual friendship'. Yet he noted a difference: 'with me it's a matter of seeing with the intellect, whereas you use your eyes and all your senses'.[17] No wonder that Bonhoeffer was delighted that Bethge was interested in passing on his ideas to others.[18]

Bonhoeffer's early academic works, *Sanctorum Communio* and *Act and Being*, had been published during his lifetime, as were *Discipleship* and *Life Together*. But Bonhoeffer always regarded his proposed *Ethics* as the book he most wanted to complete and publish. That was not to be, though he had worked a lot on it during the final hectic years of his life when he was involved in the conspiracy. Bethge, however, inherited the various manuscripts and working notes and, knowing Bonhoeffer's desire, decided as his first priority to edit and publish them. At the suggestion of Bishop George Bell, Bonhoeffer's elder confidant in England, Bethge's own bishop in Berlin, Otto Dibelius, gave him sufficient time to work on this project, as well as secretarial help,[19] with the result that the book appeared in 1949. Given the nature of the manuscript, the task of ordering the text was not easy – indeed, it was a task that would be undertaken afresh several times in the years ahead. But sadly, for Bethge, its publication was a non-event. 'The echo, when it came,' Bethge later recalled, 'was scarcely audible.'[20] Scholars, even those who knew of Bonhoeffer and his role during the Third Reich, had little interest in a treatise on ethics that was incomplete, apparently devoid of systematic cohesion, and so critical of traditional

---

17. Bonhoeffer, *Letters and Papers from Prison*, p. 385.

18. See Bonhoeffer's letter to Bethge from Tegel, 23 August 1944, in Bonhoeffer, *Letters and Papers from Prison*, p. 392.

19. Bethge's photocopied notes for a lecture on Dibelius, 'Otto Dibelius: Autobiographisches', delivered at the University of Heidelberg, 23 May 1989, p. 3; Bethge papers.

20. Bethge, 'The Editing and Publishing of the Bonhoeffer Papers', p. 2.

approaches. In an ironic twist of history the *Ethics* would eventually become what many regard as Bonhoeffer's most significant work, exactly as Bonhoeffer had hoped. But that was yet to be. Nonetheless, Bethge had begun what was to become his life's work, and a relationship was being forged with Chr. Kaiser Verlag in Munich that was to continue until his death fifty years later. This personal relationship with a distinguished publishing house was of inestimable value and importance for Bethge, for Bonhoeffer scholarship as a whole, and for making Bonhoeffer's legacy known within Germany at both an academic and a more popular level.

Given the apparent failure of the *Ethics* to attract attention, it would have been understandable if Bethge had thrown in the towel and if Chr. Kaiser Verlag had lost interest. But instead Bethge continued editing and arranging for the publication or republication of Bonhoeffer's books. Many of these now appeared for the first time in English. The first of the English translations was an abridged version of *Nachfolge* (Discipleship) published under the title *The Cost of Discipleship* by Macmillan in 1948 with a foreword by Bishop Bell.[21] The fact that this volume came out before any of the others meant that the initial Anglo-Saxon image of Bonhoeffer was that of a man of great faith, courage and sanctity who had lived faithfully according to the Sermon on the Mount and died a martyr's death. This image was reinforced with the subsequent publication of *Life Together* in 1954,[22] but it was soon to be challenged by another, that of Bonhoeffer the radical theologian of the prison letters. And it was Bethge, without fully realizing the consequences of what he was doing, who brought this about.

The remarkable story of how Bonhoeffer's letters and other writings from prison survived the war years has already been

---

21. On the history of the publication and translation of *Nachfolge* see Dietrich Bonhoeffer, *Discipleship*, Dietrich Bonhoeffer Works, vol. 4 (Minneapolis: Fortress Press, 2001), pp. 29–30.

22. For publication details see Dietrich Bonhoeffer, *Life Together; Prayerbook of the Bible*, Dietrich Bonhoeffer Works, vol. 5 (Minneapolis: Fortress Press, 1996), pp. 20–1.

told. Equally remarkable is the story of their editing and publication, and the impact that successive, and increasingly more
substantial, editions of *Widerstand und Ergebung*, published in
English as *Letters and Papers from Prison*, have had around the
world. The German edition was first published in 1951, the
English in 1953, and those in other languages subsequently,
Dutch and Danish among the earliest. Although, as we have
seen, Bethge was excited by the theological insights contained in
the letters he received from Bonhoeffer in Italy, and had wanted
at the time to share them with his former Finkenwaldian
colleagues, he did not recognize their full significance. In fact he
later wrote that for a long time he was not aware of what lay
hidden in his desk 'in the form of those letters smuggled out of
the Tegel prison cell in 1943 and 1944'. In fact, Bethge tells us it
was six years before he 'dared to hand a selection of them to the
publisher, without the slightest idea that they would produce
such a wide and lasting effect'.[23]

But the result was, in Bethge's own words, 'a theological
sensation' caused 'by a book which Bonhoeffer had not intended
to write'.[24] As later described in a Festschrift on the occasion of
his seventieth birthday, the publication of these 'theological
letters' was 'wie eine Flaschenpost' – like a message in a bottle.
Bethge now expectantly awaited the response.

The critical theological letters were those dated between 30
April and 21 July 1944. Bethge later recalled that subsequent
letters came in September, but these had been destroyed for
security reasons. 'Today', he wrote in 1959, 'I am afflicted with
the tormenting afterthought that I was responsible for the
destruction of what may have contained decisive developments
of Bonhoeffer's ideas, but developments which I can no longer
recall.'[25] Maybe these would have clarified some of the issues that
were hotly debated at the time the letters were published.
Certainly it is tantalizing to think about what these letters, and
the other material that did not survive, might have contained.

---

23. Bethge, *Bonhoeffer: Exile and Martyr*, p. 19.
24. Bethge, *Bonhoeffer: Exile and Martyr*, p. 20.
25. Bethge, 'The Editing and Publishing of the Bonhoeffer Papers', p. 4.

For as Bethge tells us, Bonhoeffer continued working on his new
theological thoughts even after his transfer to Prinz-Albrecht-
Strasse prison and took what he had written with him to
Flossenbürg. It was there, where Bonhoeffer was hanged, that
Walter Huppenkothen, the Gestapo officer responsible for the
case against both Bonhoeffer and von Dohnanyi, burned the
remaining documents on 9 April 1945.[26] Whether or not he
destroyed letters and papers that would have altered anything is
impossible to say. But we might hazard the opinion that while
Bonhoeffer might well have clarified his concepts more adequately, he would hardly have backtracked on the line he had
been taking, given the trajectory of his thinking at that time. In
any case, we can only speculate on such matters. As Bethge put it:
'He may possibly have chosen some other subject than that of the
nonreligious interpretation, but if he did we know nothing about
it.'[27]

Abroad and at Home

In 1953, on the recommendation of Martin Niemöller, Bethge
became the pastor of the German-speaking congregation in
Sydenham, London. So he was in Britain during the years
that witnessed a growing international interest in Bonhoeffer's
theology following the publication of the first English edition of
Letters and Papers from Prison. Bethge knew the British theological and church scene remarkably well, and was therefore able to
interpret Bonhoeffer's ideas to an audience that was somewhat
stunned by the new image of the saintly martyr that was emerging. In a paper he gave to the Brompton Ecumenical Fellowship
in London in February 1956 he spoke about the 'contradictory
formulations' to be found in Bonhoeffer's writings. He examined

---

26. Bethge, 'The Nonreligious Scientist and Confessing Theologian',
p. 56. This detail is not mentioned in the biography, though Bethge does
say there that Bonhoeffer was working on his theological writings right up
to the end, even in Buchenwald: Bethge, *Dietrich Bonhoeffer*, p. 910.

27. Bethge, *Dietrich Bonhoeffer*, p. 910.

four portraits, which he labelled 'the monk-like Bonhoeffer, the orthodox, the liberal and the political Bonhoeffer'. In speaking of the 'liberal Bonhoeffer' of the prison letters, he remarked:

> Bonhoeffer's suggestions do not spring from any capitulation in the face of modern godlessness, they spring from the deepest concentration upon the Founder of our faith as He was and as He lived. He does not try to make palatable by subtraction whatever the customs-barrier of modern thought may consent to pass; he wants to pursue the track of Christ's presence today, to understand it better and to bear witness of it. Here the twin notions of 'modernist' and 'Orthodox' break down, but there remains a man walking with Christ, free and equipped with seeing eyes.[28]

Bethge received an increasing number of invitations to speak about Bonhoeffer in various parts of Britain, including opportunities to give talks on the BBC, the first being on 14 November 1955. On 13 March 1960, he was the adviser to a radio programme on Bonhoeffer that included interviews with Reinhold Niebuhr, Willem Visser 't Hooft (General Secretary of the World Council of Churches), Franz Hildebrandt, Henry Louis Henriod (who had been Secretary of the World Alliance) and Hetty Bell, the recently widowed wife of the bishop of Chichester. The name and significance of Bonhoeffer was obviously beginning to attract fresh British interest as a result of Bethge's labours.

Bethge's life and work abroad was by no means confined to talking about Bonhoeffer. He was the pastor of a suburban congregation and, as always, he and Renate were deeply interested in the history and culture of their surroundings, as well as current social and political events. An interesting vignette of life in the Bethge household comes from the pen of one of Bethge's younger German colleagues in England, Ferdinand Schlingensiepen, pastor of the Lutheran congregation in Bradford.

---

28. Bethge, 'Dietrich Bonhoeffer: the Man and his Witness', mimeographed copy of a paper read to the Brompton Ecumenical Fellowship, 21 February 1956, p. 7; Bethge papers.

Schlingensiepen's friendship with Bethge was not initially connected with any interest in Bonhoeffer. What brought them into
contact was a plan, instigated by the Lutheran World Federation,
to establish a united Lutheran Church in England that would
bring all the German congregations into one denomination. This
led to many visits to the Bethge home, Manor Mount, in
Sydenham, the 'grotesque old pastor's house' where Bonhoeffer
had lived thirty years previously.[29] Schlingensiepen recalls the
three Bethge children, Dietrich, Gabriele and Sabine, who
'humorously made allowances for their father's English', the
chamber music they played together, the four-part songs they
sang, and the visits they made to the various historical sites of
London. 'All of this', Schlingensiepen comments, 'had scarcely
anything to do with Bonhoeffer.'[30]

By the late 1950s, Bethge's reputation as the close confidant of
Bonhoeffer, as the editor of his writings, and increasingly as the
major interpreter of his life and theology, was well established.
But as the minister of a London parish, there was little time for
him to pursue the task that he had set himself. Fortunately
another visitor to Manor Mount was Paul Lehmann who, seeing
all Bonhoeffer's papers in Bethge's study, expressed concern that
he did not have the freedom to edit and publish them. As Bethge
later recalled:

> It must have been the summer of 1955. Paul Lehmann sat in
> my dark study of the dilapidated German parsonage in
> London-Forest Hill . . . we sat in the same room in which
> Dietrich had once worked . . . he posed to me the question that
> until then I had neither posed to myself nor would have been
> able to reply to in that moment. He asked: who in the German
> church or in one of the theological faculties back home is
> giving you the means and time to order, secure, and make
> available Dietrich's papers down there on your bookshelves? I

---

29. Ferdinand Schlingensiepen, 'Für Was biste gekommen?', in *Wie
eine Flaschenpost: Ökumenische Briefe und Beiträge Für Eberhard Bethge*, ed.
Heinz Eduard Tödt (Munich: Chr. Kaiser Verlag, 1979), p. 18.
30. Schlingensiepen, 'Für Was biste gekommen?', p. 18.

replied: no one. The thought had really never occurred to me
. . . Paul appeared to understand this only with great difficulty.
He was well able – more than I – to assess what remained
hidden and had not been worked through and what was in
danger of being totally lost. . . . Paul didn't say much more
about it. Certainly he said his characteristic 'This is unheard
of.' I don't quite know how he then arranged things. In any
case, two years later I sat at Harvard Divinity School.[31]

Lehmann, who was then teaching at Harvard University, had
arranged for Bethge to be a visiting professor at Harvard in
1957/8.[32] As Bethge wrote in his later account, Lehmann, more
than anyone else, gave the impetus to bringing Bonhoeffer's story
to the world. The Bethges were delighted with the opportunity
to spend an extended period of time at Harvard. Quite apart from
the opportunity this provided for Eberhard to work on the
Bonhoeffer legacy, it also provided an opportunity to become
better acquainted with the United States. Moreover, it meant
that Bethge could renew contact with Maria von Wedemeyer,
who was already living in Boston.

Bethge had stayed in touch with Maria over the years since the
end of the war and since she had emigrated to the United States.
Initially he felt a particular responsibility towards her since
Bonhoeffer had asked him to give her support when he was in
prison. Then later, after the war, he felt the need to maintain
contact between her and the family, and to keep her informed
about the growing interest in Bonhoeffer's legacy and writings.
There was an additional reason, namely the question of what
should be done about the letters between her and Bonhoeffer
written during his imprisonment. Even though these 'love
letters' from Tegel Prison were not of direct theological interest,
Bonhoeffer 'the man' was now of interest to a much wider circle
of people, theologians included, who were naturally intrigued by
the possible content of these letters. Although executor of

31. Bethge, 'Paul Lehmann's Initiative', *Union Seminary Quarterly
Review* 29: 3–4 (1974), pp. 151–2.
32. Information provided by John Godsey, personal communication.

Bonhoeffer's literary estate, Bethge readily agreed that the letters
were Maria's property and later, in November 1967, formally
signed a declaration to that effect. He was very sensitive to her
feelings and wanted to honour them, not least in writing
Bonhoeffer's biography. The press detected this at the time when
the biography was published, leading some media reviewers to
write about 'passionate letters on the way to execution' – Maria
regarded these remarks as the 'height of kitsch'.[33] Although most
of the letters were subsequently published after her death, her
fear of the sensational exploitation of her relationship to
Bonhoeffer was justified, as some later movies about his life
demonstrated.

From this period onwards, after living in London and Boston,
the Bethges learnt to straddle the divide between Germany and
the Anglo-Saxon world with considerable ease. This living in
two worlds would characterize much of the rest of their lives, and
profoundly influence the way in which both Eberhard and
Renate would engage in Bonhoeffer interpretation. There were
opportunities to settle in Britain or the United States that were
very tempting, for they found both cultures congenial, refreshing
and open. But they could not deny, nor did they wish to escape,
their roots in Germany, its culture and history, its theology and
church life, its towns and countryside. Moreover, for Eberhard,
the choice to remain in both worlds was a statement about how he
chose to approach his country's history:

> I believe that the lesson for us . . . is that we are Germans and
> remain so . . . In 1957–1958 we were at Harvard for one year.
> The question came whether we didn't want to stay longer. But
> the separation from our kind of German culture, German
> liberalism, German theology as well – I never wanted that, or
> could do it, and never seriously considered it.[34]

Living in Germany yet in regular contact with the wider world
was necessary in order for Bethge to fulfil his life's commitment

---

33. Letter to Bethge, 30 December 1967, Bethge papers.
34. Quoted in Barnett, *For the Soul of the People*, p. 303.

to retrieving Bonhoeffer's legacy. On the one hand, Bethge had to be close to the sources and the resources that made his work possible. Moreover, his understanding of his responsibility as a survivor of the *Kirchenkampf* and the resistance was to interpret Bonhoeffer's legacy within the post-war and contemporary German context. Bethge could not have been true to this task had he not engaged in the post-war discussions about the reconstruction of the church in Germany, or later, about the Holocaust and Jewish–Christian relations. By staying in Germany he was true to Bonhoeffer's own sense of responsibility for the reconstruction of Germany that brought him back from New York to Germany on the eve of the Second World War.[35]

On the other hand, much of the stimulation and support Bethge received for his task came from circles beyond Germany. Moreover, the legacy for which he was responsible was of ecumenical significance; it had to do with the role of the church in the global struggle for justice and peace. And, in any case, like Bonhoeffer, there was a cosmopolitan side to Bethge's character that thrived through engagement with other cultures and the opportunities that modern-day travel made possible. Fortunately, living in these two worlds did not detract from his task, but made it possible in ways that would not have otherwise been so. Bethge was able to work on Bonhoeffer's legacy with all the resources that were available at home, including regular discussion with friends and colleagues, and at the same time engage in conversation with many others around the world whose interest in Bonhoeffer, and whose questions about his life and work, opened up fresh avenues of exploration and interpretation. Living in these two worlds also meant that Bethge was in a better position both to help the German church understand its ecumenical and global responsibility, and to interpret the German experience to a world-wide audience.

---

35. See Bonhoeffer's letter to Reinhold Niebuhr, June 1939, in Bonhoeffer, *Sammelvikariate*, p. 210.

10

Interpreting Bonhoeffer

During his stay at Harvard in 1957/8, Bethge gave a lecture to the theological faculty on the editing and publishing of Bonhoeffer's papers.[1] In it he set out what had been accomplished thus far, and what he was now planning to do. Bethge was convinced, as he told his audience, that Bonhoeffer's theology could not be properly understood if only some of his writings were available, or if he was studied in a piecemeal way. Hence his commitment not only to edit and publish or republish all of Bonhoeffer's books, especially those previously neglected, but also to gather together, edit and publish everything that could be recovered – sermons, lectures, exegetical studies, seminar presentations, notes, and conference papers, as well as letters both from and to Bonhoeffer.

With all this in mind, Bethge told the Harvard faculty at some length and in detail about the publication of Bonhoeffer's completed collected writings (the *Gesammelte Schriften*), two volumes of which had already been completed,[2] and two more planned.[3] In

---

1. Eberhard Bethge, 'The Editing and Publishing of the Bonhoeffer Papers', *Andover Newton Quarterly* 52:2 (December 1959), pp. 1–24; Bethge's handwritten outline and notes for this lecture are in his private papers.

2. Dietrich Bonhoeffer, *Ökumene: Briefe Aufsätze Dokumente 1928–1942*, Gesammelte Schriften (GS), vol. 1 (Munich: Chr. Kaiser Verlag, 1958); Dietrich Bonhoeffer, *Kirchenkampf und Finkenwalde: Resolutionen Aufsätze Rundbriefe 1933–1943*, GS, vol. 2 (Munich: Chr. Kaiser Verlag, 1959).

3. Eventually published as Dietrich Bonhoeffer, *Theologie Gemeinde: Vorlesungen Briefe Gespräche 1927–1944*, GS, vol. 3 (Munich: Chr. Kaiser

the end, six volumes were published,[4] and a selection was also published in English in three volumes.[5] The *Gesammelte Schriften* anticipated the much larger project, the sixteen-volume *Dietrich Bonhoeffer Werke*, which was to occupy Bethge years later after his retirement. It is noteworthy, as Bethge would observe, that the first reviews of the *Gesammelte Schriften* appeared in Jewish journals.[6] His overall aim, he said, was to make a fivefold contribution:

(1) to recent church history, whose documentation in Germany is difficult and the object today of a widespread search; (2) to the history of the ecumenical movement in the thirties; (3) to the history of National Socialism and its relationships with the Christian church; (4) to the question of responsible opposition to tyranny; and (5) to theology, in that here a way is taken independently of Karl Barth.

With respect to Bonhoeffer's biography, he told his audience

Verlag, 1960); and Dietrich Bonhoeffer, *Auslegungen Predigten: Berlin London Finkenwalde 1931–1944*, GS, vol. 4 (Munich: Chr. Kaiser Verlag, 1961).

4. The final two volumes were: Dietrich Bonhoeffer, *Seminare Vorlesungen Predigten: 1924–1941. Erster Ergänzungsband*, GS, vol. 5 (Munich: Chr. Kaiser Verlag, 1972); Dietrich Bonhoeffer, *Tagerbücher Briefe Dokumente: 1923–1945 Zweiter Ergänzungsband*, GS, vol. 6 (Munich: Chr. Kaiser Verlag, 1974).

5. Dietrich Bonhoeffer, *No Rusty Swords: Letters Lectures and Notes 1928–1936*, Collected Works of Dietrich Bonhoeffer, vol. 1 (London: Collins, 1977); Dietrich Bonhoeffer, *The Way to Freedom: Letters Lectures and Notes 1935–1939*, Collected Works of Dietrich Bonhoeffer, vol. 2 (London: Collins, 1966); Dietrich Bonhoeffer, *True Patriotism: Letters Lectures and Notes 1939–45*, Collected Works of Dietrich Bonhoeffer, vol. 3 (London: Collins, 1973). These volumes were all edited by Edwin H. Robertson, who was also the general editor of the first abridged edition of Bethge's *Dietrich Bonhoeffer* (London: Collins, 1967).

6. Eberhard Bethge, 'The Challenge of Dietrich Bonhoeffer's Life and Theology', *Chicago Theological Seminary Register* 51:2 (February 1961), p. 2. Bethge mentions the paper of the Judische Lehrhaus published in Zurich, and the *Allgemeine Wochenzeitung der Juden in Deutschland*.

7. Bethge, 'The Editing and Publishing of the Bonhoeffer Papers', pp. 7–8.

that that story must wait for a later day.[7] But Bethge was already gathering material for the biography he was planning, and which he now regarded as essential for placing Bonhoeffer's theological development in its proper historical context. How important this would be for the interpretation of Bonhoeffer's theology would soon become apparent – following the publication of Bonhoeffer's letters from prison.

Giving Structure to the Task

The impact of *Letters and Papers from Prison* on a post-war generation of theologians was as dramatic as the publication of Barth's commentary on the letter to the Romans had been in 1918. By this time many of the new generation had moved beyond Barth and were engaged with Rudolf Bultmann's programme of demythologization, Paul Tillich's reinterpretation of Christian symbols, and the escalating debate about God in a secular age. Bonhoeffer's prison theology spoke directly to these concerns. As a result he was elevated to the company of seminal twentieth-century theologians. This was not without considerable opposition or caution on the part of those for whom Barth, Emil Brunner and Bultmann remained pre-eminent. Bonhoeffer's ideas about Christianity in 'a world come of age' certainly did not find a ready welcome within the German theological academy. But they nonetheless attracted widespread attention in a way that contrasted remarkably with the lack of attention previously given the publication of the *Ethics*.

Barth's own response to the 'new Bonhoeffer' of the prison letters was largely negative. In particular he found Bonhoeffer's comments about his 'positivism of revelation' both 'incomprehensible and unintelligible'.[8] But more generally, Barth found Bonhoeffer's thoughts about 'non-religious interpretation' unsatisfactory and hoped that his reputation as a theologian would not depend on such incomplete and relatively unexplanatory

---

8. Letter to Eberhard Bethge, reprinted in Karl Barth, *Fragments Grave and Gay*, p. 120.

fragments. Many others shared Barth's reservations.[9] As noted previously, Bonhoeffer had been a largely unknown figure during the *Kirchenkampf* itself, and he was a controversial figure in the post-war German churches because of his role in the political resistance. Both these factors led more established German theologians to discount the radical elements in his prison writings, although there was some appreciation for his earlier writings and his theological contribution to the *Kirchenkampf*.

Significantly it was a North American doctoral student of Barth's, John Godsey, who wrote one of the first major studies on Bonhoeffer's theology.[10] This was certainly to Barth's credit, and was unlike some Barthians who felt that Bonhoeffer had little to contribute to contemporary theology. Barth, of course, had previously met Bethge during the war when Bethge had visited Switzerland on behalf of the Abwehr, so he knew of Bethge's relationship to Bonhoeffer and was aware of his role in publishing Bonhoeffer's work. Thus it was both natural and necessary for him to encourage Godsey to turn to Bethge, then in London, for help. Not only did Bethge have all the extant Bonhoeffer papers in his possession, he was also now recognized as a key interpreter of his thought.

Despite the widespread lack of interest among German academics in Bonhoeffer at this time, the growing international interest of some scholars, such as Godsey, and the emerging debate about the interpretation of Bonhoeffer's theology gave Bethge's task of preserving the legacy a new urgency and significance. Whereas previously his task had been primarily conceived as one of historical reconstruction, archival organization, and biographical narration, now theological interpretation became equally important and inescapable. And, most significantly, for Bethge, the inseparable relationship between the two tasks, that of biography and that of theological interpretation, was becoming more evident.

---

9. For a reassessment of these issues, see Andreas Pangritz, *Karl Barth in the Theology of Dietrich Bonhoeffer* (Grand Rapids: Eerdmans, 2000).

10. John Godsey, *The Theology of Dietrich Bonhoeffer* (London: SCM Press, 1960).

Although Bethge was in a unique position to engage in this task, he was not alone. Former Bonhoeffer students and colleagues who had survived the war, and who knew his theology from earlier times, were also keen to find out more about the theology of the Bonhoeffer they did not know, the Bonhoeffer of the *Ethics* and prison letters, and to discuss his legacy more generally. Bethge, as we know, had hoped to share Bonhoeffer's new and more radical ideas with some of them at the time he first received the letters. That proved impossible. But in August 1954, largely through the efforts of Bethge, former Finkenwaldians gathered together at Bethel to discuss Bonhoeffer's 'new' theology and its interpretation when the Evangelical Academy Hemer hosted a study conference on the theme of 'Dietrich Bonhoeffer's Legacy for Theology and Church'. The papers from that occasion were published soon after as *Die mündige Welt: Dem Andenken Dietrich Bonhoeffers*, a volume that initiated a series under the same title.[11] The opening chapter in that collection was a lecture which Bethge himself gave in Bonn a few months after the conference on 'Dietrich Bonhoeffer: Person und Werk'.

The Bethel conference was followed a year later by a second conference at Weisensee in East Berlin, where the topic under discussion was 'The Problem of "Non-Religious" Interpretation'.[12] But by now the issues were of theological interest beyond the Bonhoeffer circle of former students and friends. Remarkably, at a meeting of the prestigious German Society for Evangelical Theology in Wuppertal (1956) the distinguished Professor Ernst Wolf could say that the subjects Bonhoeffer had raised in his letters had even overtaken the issues raised by Bultmann. Moreover, he said this during a session devoted

---

11. *Die mündige Welt: Dem Andenken Dietrich Bonhoeffers*, ed. Eberhard Bethge (Munich: Chr. Kaiser Verlag, 1955). A selection of these essays was included in English translation in *World Come of Age: A Symposium on Dietrich Bonhoeffer*, ed. Ronald Gregor Smith (London: Collins, 1967).

12. *Die mündige Welt II*, ed. Eberhard Bethge (Munich: Chr. Kaiser Verlag, 1955).

to putting questions to Barth![13] Bonhoeffer's theology had suddenly become a serious topic for academic debate and study in Germany.

These study conferences in the nineteen-fifties took on a life of their own and led to several more such events, the outcomes of which were usually published in successive editions of *Die mündige Welt*. They also laid the foundation for the First International Bonhoeffer Congress, which was held in 1971 at Kaiserswerth near Düsseldorf, a subject to which we will later return. But the question remained. How was Bonhoeffer's prison theology to be interpreted? How did it relate to his earlier theological works as reflected in his academic treatises, or his exegetical studies during the *Kirchenkampf*? And, not least, what was the connection between such questions and Bonhoeffer's life and fate?

The first major book-length study of Bonhoeffer's theology by a German theologian was by Hanfried Müller, entitled *Von der Kirche zur Welt* (From the Church to the World), published in 1956.[14] It was Müller's contention that the only interpretation of Bonhoeffer relevant for our time was one that built on his radical prison reflections. Living in what was then Communist East Germany, it is not surprising that Müller's interpretation was distinctly Marxist and stood in marked contrast to that of the American theologian Godsey, whose *The Theology of Dietrich Bonhoeffer* stressed the continuities in his theological development and the influence of Barth. These two pioneering studies, with their differing interpretations, along with discussions on Bultmann, set the boundaries for the debate about Bonhoeffer interpretation at the end of what Bethge described as 'the first wave of interest in Bonhoeffer'.[15] They also contributed to the way in which Bethge constructed his own approach to the subject of Bonhoeffer interpretation.

---

13. Bethge, 'The Editing and Publishing of the Bonhoeffer Papers', p. 5.

14. Hanfried Müller, *Von der Kirche zur Welt* (Hamberg-Bergstedt: Herbert Reich Evang. Verlag, 1956).

15. Bethge, *Dietrich Bonhoeffer: Exile and Martyr*, p. 23.

The critical questions were, as Bethge discerned, the nature of the change that occurred in Bonhoeffer's later thought, and whether that took place before he began to write the *Ethics*, or between his work on that project and his prison theology.[16] With regard to the nature of the change, the issue at stake was whether Bonhoeffer's later theology represented a break with his earlier theology, or whether the discontinuities were to be understood within a broader, underlying continuity. In response to Müller's interpretation, Bethge argued that, despite its brilliance, he had failed to do justice to the continuity between Bonhoeffer's earlier theology and that of the prison letters, and on that basis had exploited 'Bonhoeffer's ideas in the interest of Marxism'.[17] In response to Godsey, with whom he had greater affinity on the issues, Bethge stressed more the extent to which Bonhoeffer, undoubtedly influenced by Barth, became critical of and went beyond Barth.[18] While Godsey's treatment of the discontinuities in Bonhoeffer was 'reliable', Bethge nonetheless found him 'over-cautious'.[19] There was, after all, a significant change of direction. So although Bethge disagreed with Müller's understanding of the significance of the change, he did not wish to minimize the fact.

Another scholar who also stressed discontinuity, and placed the change between the *Ethics* and the prison letters, was Bethge's Scottish friend Ronald Gregor Smith, who saw connections between Bonhoeffer and Bultmann at this point rather than Bonhoeffer and Barth, though he had great admiration for Barth as well.[20] But Smith, unlike Müller, recognized the importance of Bonhoeffer's earlier theology, insisting that the revolution

---

16. Bethge, *Dietrich Bonhoeffer*, p. 859.

17. Bethge, *Dietrich Bonhoeffer: Exile and Martyr*, p. 23.

18. Though it could be argued, with Pangritz, that 'in the way in which Eberhard Bethge presents it in his superb Bonhoeffer biography, the theological closeness between Bonhoeffer and Barth is minimized more than it is overstated': Pangritz, *Karl Barth in the Theology of Dietrich Bonhoeffer*, p. 70.

19. Bethge, *Dietrich Bonhoeffer: Exile and Martyr*, p. 23.

20. See Keith Clements, *The Theology of Ronald Gregor Smith* (Leiden: E. J. Brill, 1986), pp. 60, 45.

in his thought had to be seen in relation to his earlier life and writings.[21] In fact, Smith was so determined to see Bonhoeffer's *Sanctorum Communio* published in English that he translated it himself, and arranged for it to be published in 1963. As it turned out, this was a very significant event in the second phase of Bonhoeffer interpretation. For it was becoming evident, through Bethge's work and that of others,[22] that Bonhoeffer's later theology could only be understood as a development that, for all its radical newness, already had its foundations in *Sanctorum Communio* and *Act and Being*. Smith's friendship with Bethge, we may note, was important for both of them. It was Smith who took the lead in introducing Bonhoeffer studies to the British scholarly community,[23] and who recommended Bethge for an honorary doctorate from the University of Glasgow, which was conferred on him in 1962.

There was a further, critical issue in interpreting Bonhoeffer, namely the relationship between his theology and his historical context. Bethge recognized the danger of linking these in such a way that Bonhoeffer's life and martyrdom were misused in giving uncritical approval to his theology. He had no truck with attempts at creating a 'Bonhoeffer cultus', and he had great respect for theologians, such as the Roman Catholic scholar Ernst Feil, who treated Bonhoeffer's theology strictly on its intrinsic merits.[24] Nonetheless, for Bethge it was impossible to interpret Bonhoeffer's theology without constant reference to his biography. This did not mean that his ideas should not be critically examined and evaluated on their own merit, or that his martyrdom gave them a status that could not be challenged. But

---

21. This is made clear in Smith's essay 'Bonhoeffer and This-Worldly Transcendence': see Clements, *The Theology of Ronald Gregor Smith*, p. 183.

22. Notably Clifford Green: see his *Bonhoeffer: Theology of Sociality* (Grand Rapids: Eerdmans, 1999).

23. See Clements, *The Theology of Ronald Gregor Smith*, pp. 76–7. Smith's German wife, Käthe, translated into English the collection of essays co-edited by the Finkenwaldian Wolf-Dieter Zimmermann, *I Knew Dietrich Bonhoeffer* (cited Chap. 2, n.7).

24. Ernst Feil, *The Theology of Dietrich Bonhoeffer*, translated by Martin Rumscheidt (Philadelphia: Fortress Press, 1985).

it did mean that the development of Bonhoeffer's theology was so related to his historical context and the way in which his life unfolded that any interpretation that did not take both into account would fail to understand him fully. What Bethge now needed to do was to provide a coherent overview of Bonhoeffer's life and theology in which he could develop this thesis fully.

The Bethges visited the United States again in January 1961 when Eberhard was invited to give the Alden-Tuthill Lectures at Chicago Theological Seminary. If his earlier visit to Harvard had provided him with an ideal opportunity to reflect on what had been achieved and what still needed to be done to edit and publish Bonhoeffer's work, the visit to Chicago gave him a chance to develop his interpretation of Bonhoeffer's life and theology in a more structured and coherent way. Without the first, he could not have become the major interpreter of Bonhoeffer's theology; without the second, his work would have remained largely archival and biographical. The key was how to bring these together. In pursuing that task Bethge's real genius as biographer *and* interpreter became ever more evident.

A large number of pastors, seminarians and theologians attended these lectures in Chicago intent on discovering more about the martyr-theologian whose legacy had now begun to attract such widespread attention. But the lectures also demonstrated Bethge's own skill as an interpreter, accomplished teacher and communicator. Howard Schomer, then the president of the seminary, described the setting:

As soon as Eberhard Bethge mounted the platform at Ministers' Week in January, the several hundred participants sensed that they had three wonderful evenings before them. Their lecturer, a big man, moved with natural grace and spoke with engaging directness. His humor, like his smile, was not the contrived artefact so common among intellectuals. From time to time it bubbled to the surface from a deep and generous store of good nature, released by something genuinely amusing in the material related. From the outset of the first address the somewhat stiff atmosphere of a university lecture hall was dispelled. Everyone sensed that Eberhard Bethge had flown over from Europe to talk with friends about a question of immense importance for them as for himself.

Schomer went on to say that 'the delivery of these lectures was itself an *event*. As Eberhard Bethge painted the portrait of Dietrich Bonhoeffer, his comrade and mentor, many of his hearers were as deeply stirred by the lecturer's selfless witness as by the full-blooded, contemporary theologian whom he depicted.'[25]

The lecture series was entitled 'The Challenge of Dietrich Bonhoeffer's Life and Theology' and the three lectures were:

I. Foundation: the Quest for the Concrete Nature of the Message
II. Concentration: the Narrow Pass for Christianity
III. Liberation: Christianity without Religion

As Bethge said in his introductory remarks, these marked the three periods in which Bonhoeffer acted and taught, 1927–33, 1933–40, and 1940–5. 'Theologically', he said, 'these same periods might be called the dogmatic, the exegetical, and the ethical; or, again, the theoretical period in which he learned and taught at Berlin University, the pastoral period in which he served the Confessing Church in a preachers' seminary, and the political period in which his life became ambiguous.'[26]

Anyone familiar with these lectures knows that they provide the framework within which Bethge, and many others who have learnt from him, have sought to understand and interpret Bonhoeffer's life and theology. Although the lectures were systematic in character, Bethge did not try to force Bonhoeffer's thought into a system. Given the diverse and fragmentary nature of so many of his writings, as well as the difference in style and content between Bonhoeffer's early academic treatises, his

---

25. Howard Schomer, 'A Winsome Witness', *The Chicago Theological Seminary Register*, 51:2 (February 1961), inside front cover.
26. Bethge, 'The Challenge of Dietrich Bonhoeffer's Life and Theology', p. 3.

writings during the *Kirchenkampf*, and his prison theology, such
an aim would have inevitably led to distortion. Bonhoeffer's
times and circumstances simply did not give him the opportunity
of standing back and producing a systematic theology or ethics in
the surroundings of the academy. His theology in general, like
his *Ethics* and prison theology in particular, had not been constructed in that way. And, in a profound sense, his challenge lay
precisely in this open-ended, provisional character of his theology, in the fact that he was always one step ahead of most others
in thinking and acting theologically in response to both the
gospel and his context.

Bonhoeffer, as Bethge showed, did not answer all our questions; rather, he helps us ask the right questions, and suggests
how we might find our way forward as much in faithful action as
in critical reflection. For Bonhoeffer as Bethge understood him,
the central question, and the one that gave coherence to his
theology as a whole, was 'Who is Jesus Christ, for us, today?', a
question that brought together the Christological foundations of
faith, the existential demands of obedient discipleship, the
nature and role of Christian community, and the contextual
location within which the question must be asked and answered.
It was this Christological *cantus firmus*, as Bonhoeffer described it
in prison, drawing on musical theory that allowed meaningful
polyphony and prevented the fragments from flying apart.[27]
Christ was at the centre of Bonhoeffer's theology from beginning
to end, hence the importance, as Bethge often stressed, of Bonhoeffer's seminal lectures on 'Christology' that he gave in Berlin
in 1933.[28] But the way in which Bonhoeffer dealt with the
Christological question changed in shape and intensity as his life
unfolded, becoming ever more concrete, ever more related to
the reality of God and the world, ever more costly, and leading
inexorably towards its finale in the prison writings and martyr-

---

27. Bonhoeffer, *Letters and Papers from Prison*, p. 303.

28. These lectures, which Bethge carefully reconstructed from notes
by Bonhoeffer's students, were first published in Bonhoeffer, *Gesammelte
Schriften*, vol. 3, pp. 166–247, and then in English in Dietrich Bonhoeffer,
Christology (London: Collins, 1966).

dom. As Bethge summed up his Alden-Tuthill Lectures: 'This in three words the lectures wanted to point to: the message of Christ is *concrete* in itself; as such it is to be preserved *costly* and to be kept *worldly* from any escapism.'[29]

Bonhoeffer's confidence in Bethge as the one who was most equipped to interpret his thoughts[30] was fully justified by these lectures, which from then on were frequently used and quoted by those intent on understanding Bonhoeffer's theology in relation to his life and historical context. But the lectures also demonstrated something more. They showed Bethge's consummate skill in giving structure and form to Bonhoeffer's theology; in showing its relationship to contemporary debates; in discerning the most appropriate phrase or word in Bonhoeffer's varied writings to highlight key moments in his theological development, showing both continuity and discontinuity; and in weaving together a complex life story and an intellectual journey in a narrative that is both compelling and convincing. After the Alden-Tuthill Lectures, which in many ways prefigure the structure of the biography, it would be difficult to think about Bonhoeffer's life and theology in any other way. Yet developments were on the horizon that would wrench that legacy out of the domain of theologians, pastors and seminarians, and thrust it into a larger public domain. These developments would make Bethge's contribution even more necessary and significant for understanding Bonhoeffer.

Going Beyond Bonhoeffer?

The publication of Bishop John Robinson's *Honest to God* in Britain in 1963 was a major media event. A little book of 140 pages, *Honest to God* sold more than 350,000 copies in the Anglo-Saxon world and soon appeared in German and many other

---

29. Bethge, 'The Challenge of Dietrich Bonhoeffer's Life and Theology', p. 38.

30. See, for example, Bonhoeffer's letter to Bethge, 5 June 1944, in Bonhoeffer, *Letters and Papers from Prison*, p. 320.

languages, including Japanese.[31] Suddenly what Bultmann, Tillich, and now Bonhoeffer had said about God in a secular world had become newsworthy, not least because an Anglican bishop had identified with much of what they were about – and been publicly rebuked by the Archbishop of Canterbury for doing so. The ensuing '*Honest to God* debate' showed that Robinson had not only touched a raw nerve within the church establishment, but had also gained the attention of many on the periphery of the church. Some theological reviewers even regarded his book as a means of evangelism in a new key. Robinson agreed with this view – was this not precisely what Bonhoeffer was hoping to achieve through his prison theology?[32]

Robinson had first encountered extracts of the letters from prison that Bethge had published in *The Ecumenical Review* (January 1952), but 'felt at once that the Church was not yet ready for what Bonhoeffer was giving us as his last will and testament before he was hanged by the SS: indeed, it might be understood properly only a hundred years hence'.[33] At the same time, he recognized that Bonhoeffer had begun to speak to people 'where "religion" does not penetrate'.[34] But whether or not Robinson achieved what he had hoped, the name 'Bonhoeffer' had become a household word. Whereas previously he had been known among some clergy and informed laypeople through the publication of *The Cost of Discipleship*, now, in the popular mind, he was a radical theologian who advocated a 'religionless Christianity'. It was assumed, albeit wrongly, that by this Bonhoeffer was promoting a form of Christianity apart from the church, prayer and worship. This caused a major upset among those for whom the testimony of the saintly martyr had struck such a deep chord.

Tillich, one of those whom Robinson also expounded in

---

31. *The Honest to God Debate*, ed. John A. T. Robinson and David L. Edwards (London: SCM Press, 1963), p. 7.

32. *The Honest to God Debate*, p. 274.

33. John A. T. Robinson, *Honest to God* (London: SCM Press, 1963), p. 23.

34. Robinson, *Honest to God*, p. 25.

Honest to God, would later remark that he was not sure whether the bishop had fully understood what Bonhoeffer was about, but there was no doubt in his mind that Robinson's book had opened up Bonhoeffer's ideas, as well as his own, to a new and curious public.[35] Moreover, Tillich, added, it had certainly led to an escalation in the sale of his books – and, we might surmise, Bonhoeffer's as well. Bethge shared Tillich's view. But for Bethge, Robinson's treatment of Bonhoeffer was too eclectic. Nonetheless, he recognized the significance of what the bishop had achieved, for without the stirring of the *Honest to God* debate Bonhoeffer's writings as a whole might have remained largely unknown in the wider Anglo-Saxon public sphere. In fact, Bethge acknowledged that Robinson's book 'unleashed a new search for the specific nature of Bonhoeffer's contribution beyond the continental borders of Europe, in the English-speaking world, and beyond denominational barriers as well, among Roman Catholics'.[36] He also appreciated the fact that Robinson himself had made it clear that he had not attempted to 'give a balanced picture of Bonhoeffer's theology as a whole', and that he referred readers to the Alden-Tuthill lectures for such an introduction to Bonhoeffer's theology.[37] Yet for Bethge, Robinson's interpretation remained unbalanced. At the same time, the *Honest to God* debate that followed highlighted the great extent to which the German and Anglo-Saxon reception of the prison letters differed. For the former, it was a matter of hermeneutics, the 'non-religious interpretation of Christianity'; for the latter, it was about 'religionless Christianity', that is, the life and worship of the church in a secular age. Bonhoeffer, Bethge was convinced, was concerned about both of these, and therefore separating them led to distortion.[38]

But what bothered Bethge far more than Robinson's eclectic

---

35. A comment Tillich made during a seminar led by John Robinson at the University of Chicago during the fall semester 1963, attended by the author.

36. Bethge, *Dietrich Bonhoeffer*, p. 891.

37. Robinson, *Honest to God*, p. 36, n. 1.

38. Bethge, *Bonhoeffer: Exile and Martyr*, p. 24.

treatment of Bonhoeffer, or the disjunction between German and Anglo-Saxon interpretations of the prison theology and its implications, was the 'creative misuse' that was being made of Bonhoeffer in the wake of the *Honest to God* debate by some North American 'secular' and 'death of God' theologians.[39] Referring to them, Bethge wrote:

> Wherever this movement referred to Bonhoeffer, and some theologians like Paul van Buren and William Hamilton for a certain period relied heavily on him, he was misinterpreted and misunderstood. Some even tampered with Bonhoeffer's thought, and with an insufficient knowledge of his work, did violence to or destroyed his dialectical way of expressing himself.[40]

While he was never one to disparage the interpretations of others, and was always open to learning from them, Bethge now saw that his role in interpreting Bonhoeffer's legacy was even more important than he had previously recognized.

Bethge also saw more clearly than before what the key issues were that needed to be addressed. He tackled them with vigour in the many talks, papers and essays he gave or wrote during this period, building on and developing what he had already presented in his Alden-Tuthill Lectures in Chicago. For example, in June 1963, we find him at the Ecumenical Study Centre in Bossey, Switzerland, giving a talk on 'the Church for the World'. In it he traced the characteristics of Bonhoeffer's understanding of 'religion' in terms of individualism, metaphysics, partiality, the *dues ex machina*, and privilege. This approach was later developed more fully in his essay on Bonhoeffer's 'new theology' in the biography.[41] Among all his writings, this essay is one of the best demonstrations of Bethge's skill in interpreting Bonhoeffer's theology in a way that gives it structure and precision in relation to the debates that were taking place at the time.

---

39. Bethge, *Bonhoeffer: Exile and Martyr*, p. 24.
40. Bethge, *Bonhoeffer: Exile and Martyr*, p. 24.
41. Bethge, *Dietrich Bonhoeffer*, pp. 853ff.

Using Bonhoeffer's 'Outline for a Book' as the framework, Bethge examined each of the key theological phrases in the prison letters, showing their origins in the history of theology and ideas, as well as in Bonhoeffer's thought, and demonstrating both the continuities and changes that occurred in these concepts as Bonhoeffer's life entered its final phase.

In 1965, in the midst of the debate about interpreting Bonhoeffer's prison theology, the North American theologian Harvey Cox raised the question whether the time had come to move 'beyond Bonhoeffer'. Theological fads, he reminded us, are always dangerous, and Bonhoeffer's life and work had fallen prey to misunderstanding and abuse. Would it not be better, then, to let Bonhoeffer rest in peace and not use him to justify our own positions or turn him into a cult figure? On reflection, however, Cox concluded his essay by saying that 'we have in no sense finished with Bonhoeffer', and went on to comment:

> Nor do I believe that we can move 'beyond' him until we begin to be the kind of church which lives on the borders of unbelief, which speaks with pointed specificity to its age, which shapes its message and mission not for its own comfort but for the health and renewal of the world.[42]

Looking back to the nineteen-sixties, those years of theological ferment when the name of Bonhoeffer came to the forefront of debate alongside the giants of twentieth-century Protestant theology, Barth, Bultmann and Tillich, it is striking how Bonhoeffer's legacy has endured and even waxed stronger while that of some others has waned. As Cox insisted, talk about going 'beyond Bonhoeffer' in the nineteen-sixties was premature, and would remain so as long as the issues he addressed were pertinent. Yet Cox's question has to be asked, and asked repeatedly, lest we do turn Bonhoeffer's legacy into a cult that would undermine everything for which he stood. Bethge understood this well.

---

42. Harvey G. Cox, 'Beyond Bonhoeffer: The Future of Religionless Christianity', in *The Secular City Debate*, ed. Daniel Callahan (New York: Macmillan, 1966), p. 205.

Thus far we have only considered the first two decades in Bonhoeffer interpretation, and the key role Bethge played in providing direction and structure. Three decades lay ahead of Bethge, decades in which his retrieval of Bonhoeffer's legacy and its interpretation would reach maturity and grow in influence and stature. In anticipation we may well begin to ask to what extent the Bonhoeffer we know today is the creation of Bethge. We may also begin to reflect on the question whether Bethge himself was simply the custodian and interpreter of Bonhoeffer's legacy, or a theologian in his own right who, in remaining faithful to Bonhoeffer, was inevitably drawn beyond him as he engaged the issues of his own times. These questions prompt a further one, namely, how did Bethge understand what it meant to be faithful to the legacy of his friend? Was it a slavish faithfulness that required a rather literal recovery of the Bonhoeffer texts, or was it a faithfulness that went beyond archival retrieval and historical reconstruction and engaged in interpretation that related to a new day beyond Bonhoeffer's historical context? What kind of faithfulness, in other words, would Bonhoeffer himself have expected of Bethge? There can be no doubt that faithfulness demanded truthful accuracy, not 'creative misuse', but there can also be little doubt that it demanded an ongoing engagement with Bonhoeffer's own question: 'Who is Jesus Christ, for us, today?'

Speaking on the occasion of Bonhoeffer's seventieth birthday celebration at the headquarters of the World Council of Churches in Geneva, an event that coincided with the second International Bonhoeffer Congress in Geneva in 1976, Bethge would remind his audience that while Bonhoeffer's theme throughout his life was wrestling with the question about Jesus Christ, his response to that question went through at least three phases. And, significantly, the 'answers were each time more costly, and each new step was threatening and unpopular – as today'.[43] Going 'beyond' yet 'with' Bonhoeffer was not simply a

---

43. Quotations from Bethge's English text (Bethge papers), which so far as I know has never been published. The German text is in *Genf' 76: Ein Bonhoeffer-Symposion*, ed. Hans Pfeifer (Munich: Chr. Kaiser Verlag, 1976), p. 17.

matter of theological enquiry or exploration, but much more a matter of costly discipleship. Thus 'with each new painful learning experience the preacher and conspirator gained a vision of a future process in which Christianity itself would be transformed'.[44] To be faithful to Bonhoeffer's legacy did not mean parroting what Bonhoeffer had said; rather, it required engagement with current issues facing church and society in ways that reflected Bonhoeffer's witness to Jesus Christ and his concern for the world. The truth of the matter was that Bonhoeffer himself kept on moving beyond where he had been as new challenges occurred, and as he wrestled with the question of Jesus Christ in response to them.

One of the key issues in interpreting Bonhoeffer's legacy was, however, the extent to which it could be appropriated in contexts different from his own. Keeping in mind the fact that his life and theology was fashioned within pre-war Germany and the Nazi era, was it possible for others beyond Bonhoeffer's historical situation to interpret him in ways that were both responsible and relevant? Or, to put it in other terms, could Bonhoeffer's legacy be exported without undue distortion? Bethge was acutely aware of this problem, and of the different ways in which Bonhoeffer's theology was being received in various countries and contexts. In his Geneva speech celebrating Bonhoeffer's seventieth birthday he referred to the 'wholly different contextual interests' in the study of Bonhoeffer that brought the participants from around the world together, interests that were not only varied in terms of context but also in terms of discipline: 'systematic-theological, ethical-political, sociological-psychological, biographical and historical'.[45] 'These different interests', he went on to say, 'will define our questions . . . giving different shape to our critique and our tentative answers.'[46]

Going 'beyond Bonhoeffer' was theologically and contextually necessary, but it was also inevitable given Bethge's own personality, experience and commitment. However much he was a

---

44. *Genf' 76: Ein Bonhoeffer-Symposion*, p. 17.
45. *Genf' 76: Ein Bonhoeffer-Symposion*, p. 17.
46. *Genf' 76: Ein Bonhoeffer-Symposion*, p. 17.

protégé of Bonhoeffer's, Bethge was himself a remarkable person, pastor and theologian. Devoted as he was to Bonhoeffer, he was never slavishly so; deeply influenced by Bonhoeffer's theology, he was never uncritical where criticism was warranted. This had been the case during the years of their friendship; it remained the case during the years in which he fulfilled his commitment to Bonhoeffer's memory. But his personality was also different, more ebullient, more outgoing, more embracing, and therefore inevitably influencing and shaping the way in which the legacy would be heard and received. And, of course, Bethge, though only a few years younger than Bonhoeffer, lived much longer. As such he had the hindsight of life-long experience necessary for mature reflection on Bonhoeffer's friendship and legacy – and on life more generally. At the age of 67, as he told his audience in Geneva in 1976, Bethge had difficulty in imagining

> Bonhoeffer amongst us today as a seventy-year-old man. What if, perhaps, he could not agree with us or we with him – that I could imagine. But he certainly would understand us if we honestly struggled for that for which he also cared.[47]

---

47. *Genf' 76: Ein Bonhoeffer-Symposion*, p. 16.

11

The Rengsdorf Years

From 1961, when they returned to Germany from England, until Eberhard's retirement in 1975, the Bethges lived in Rengsdorf, where Eberhard was the director of a pastoral college for the Evangelical Church in the Rhineland. Rengsdorf, a village and health resort set in the hills above Neuwied on the Rhine, is well known for its healing waters and its walking trails in the nearby woods of towering beech trees. On occasion, Bethge would preach in the local parish church. The college, established for the continuing education of ministers, was located in the large and gracious Haus Hermann von Wied, set amidst a well-maintained garden on the edge of the village. A more modern complex adjacent to the house provided space for seminars and a library. The Bethges themselves lived opposite in a two-storey house.

Small groups of pastors in the Rhenish church gathered regularly at Haus Hermann von Wied for refresher courses modelled on the Bible studies and theological discussion that had been characteristic of life together at Finkenwalde. Underlying the conviviality that was always in evidence was a deep commitment to searching the biblical text and exploring theological and pastoral issues related to ministry in the modern world. Bethge usually led the seminars but sometimes he would invite guest professors to provide input and alternative perspectives. Even then, his own stance on issues was always to the fore and clearly stated, yet in a way that enabled those participating to make up their own minds on the issues. He was in his element and ideally suited for the task. Although the historical context was very different, much of this must have reminded Bethge of the days when he and Bonhoeffer had helped prepare pastors for the

Confessing Church. But both the church and the world were now very different. Pastoral formation required fresh theological thinking, however much it drew on previous experience, rather than nostalgic attempts to recapture the past.

Teacher, Traveller, Host

Bethge was a born teacher, able to present his material in a well-structured and imaginative way, always engaging those present in dialogue and conversation. But he was also a pastor-theologian to the pastors, helping them to probe their deepest thoughts, express their doubts and concerns, and find fresh directions for their lives and ministry. On one occasion, after an intense morning of study, Bethge announced that during the coffee break he wanted everyone to think about the question 'What is the meaning of life?' and to share their thoughts on the subject in the next session. The participants were rather taken aback at such a profound question and task, especially during a time designated for relaxation. They returned to the seminar table ready to share their insights, but also eager to have Bethge answer his own question. He did so at the end, simply and shortly. 'The meaning of life', he said, 'is to be spoken to and to respond.'[1]

Indeed, the essence of life for Bethge was found in relationships, for it was in encountering others and responding to them that Christ became a reality, community became possible, and life found its purpose. This profoundly Christological insight had direct relevance for those engaged in ministry, whether in preaching, pastoral care, building community or seeking social justice. Bonhoeffer had provided the theological foundations for this in *Sanctorum Communio*, and the two friends had discovered its significance for themselves both in their own relationship and beyond. But there was a sense in which Bethge, the great conversationalist, listener to and lover of people, perfected the art during his much longer life. And this had a remarkable impact on

---

1. This episode was related to the author by Ruth Zerner, an American professor and friend of the Bethges, who was present on that occasion.

the way in which the Bonhoeffer legacy was retrieved and shared within a growing network of friends and scholars from around the world.

The Bethge home in Rengsdorf became a meeting place for a stream of visitors from many parts of Europe and the rest of the world, the hub of an increasingly wide circle of old and new friends. Some arrived virtually unknown but were soon made welcome. Many were PhD students from around the world who, in pursuit of Bonhoeffer, were overwhelmed by hospitality as the Bethges gave unstintingly of their time, energy and knowledge. A highlight was viewing original Bonhoeffer manuscripts under Eberhard's watchful eye, as he pointed out particular matters of interest. 'Look', he would say, 'at what I wrote in the margin when I received that letter from Bonhoeffer from prison. That is how I understood what he had written at the time, and he would continue with a slightly mischievous laugh, 'I suspect that I was right then – and now!'

But Rengsdorf was not only a place to which others journeyed in search of Bonhoeffer; it also provided a good base from which the Bethges could travel further afield. Indeed, the programme at the college provided the Bethges with many opportunities to travel, not just in continental Europe, which they frequently did, but on many occasions to the United States and Britain, and also to South Africa, Latin America, Japan and South Korea, and often for extended periods. These lecture tours were important for spreading interest in Bonhoeffer, but they also helped Bethge hone his own thoughts and gather fresh perspectives for what he was doing. An examination of the schedules of his various visits to the United States shows how full and intense they were. He not only lectured on Bonhoeffer at colleges, universities and seminaries, but was invariably invited to preach on Sundays, give radio interviews, and present papers at various conferences, especially, from 1970 onwards, those having to do with the Holocaust and Jewish–Christian relations. At the same time Bethge was deeply involved in the issues facing the church in Europe, often giving talks and lectures at the *Kirchentag*, at conferences, and at universities.

Eberhard Bethge was also a remarkable correspondent, as was

Renate, who shared the responsibility of answering letters and who demonstrated her remarkable gift for remembering personal details and matters of interest. Bethge was adept at using a Dictaphone, and many of his letters were typed by a secretary who came once a week for this purpose. But many others were written by him in his strong handwriting (which would become less decipherable as the years passed), or in typescript (he never acquired a computer), answering the many queries he received about details in Bonhoeffer's legacy. And he did so with great thoughtfulness and care. The same was true of the time he devoted to writing letters of reference in support of younger colleagues, and in the growing correspondence that had to do with conferences, lectures or travel arrangements. Despite this extensive correspondence, right up to the end of his life Bethge seldom if ever failed to respond to letters. In what was apparently the last letter he wrote, just before his death, in a shaky but read-able handwriting, he acknowledged receipt of and expressed gratitude for a book that had been dedicated to both Renate and himself.[2]

Renate Bethge's role was by no means confined to providing the normal support one would expect of a pastor's wife. She made her own contribution to the study of Bonhoeffer, one that was increasingly recognized and honoured. Not only did she read and critically comment on much of what Eberhard wrote, she was also widely informed about literature, music and art, and had a particular interest in the women of the resistance and of the Bonhoeffer family.[3] As the niece of Dietrich Bonhoeffer, she provided an important perspective and fund of information on issues relating to his legacy. Increasingly as the years passed, especially after Eberhard's retirement from the Pastoral College in 1976, Renate took on additional responsibilities both as a lecturer and as an editor. She was, as Eberhard told his friend

---

2. This undated letter, to the author, was found on Bethge's desk by his wife shortly after his death. The book was the *Cambridge Companion to Dietrich Bonhoeffer* (Cambridge: Cambridge University Press, 1999).

3. See especially her essay 'Bonhoeffer's Family and its Significance for his Theology', in *Dietrich Bonhoeffer: His Significance for North Americans*, ed. Larry Rasmussen (Minneapolis: Fortress Press, 1990), pp. 1–30.

Wolfgang Gerlach towards the end of his life, someone 'very special'.[4]

Amidst their heavy schedule of teaching, writing and travelling, it must have been an onerous task to provide hospitality at Rengsdorf, answering similar questions and telling the same story time and again in fresh ways. But neither Eberhard nor Renate seemed to lack patience with or interest in either their guests or the subject. They were as generous with their time as they were with sharing a hearty meal washed down with good Mosel wine. One result was the building of new and lasting friendships that soon extended the network of those interested in and informed about the Bonhoeffer legacy. This stretched well beyond the boundaries of Germany, the academy and the church. The Bethges were particularly delighted when guests arrived whose background, interests and life-experiences added fresh perspectives to the discussion – Jews, Roman Catholics, visitors from behind the Iron Curtain, from Japan, or from Africa, Asia or Latin America. Bethge, Wolfgang Huber would later declare, 'was a virtuoso at friendship', something to which he 'devoted a great part of his life's work'.[5]

Bethge, with the help of Ferdinand Schlingensiepen, organized the First International Bonhoeffer Congress, held in 1971 at Kaiserswerth near Düsseldorf, an event that attracted participants from many European countries, the United States and elsewhere. An International Committee, with Bethge as chair, was elected to take the process further and to establish Bonhoeffer archives in Germany and the United States. It was also agreed to establish different sections, the first two being the English Language Section[6] and the German

4. Wolfgang Gerlach, 'Ein Gespann: zur Rolle von Renate Bethge', *Bonhoeffer Rundbrief* 62 (June 2000), p. 16.

5. Bishop Wolgang Huber, '. . . dass das Herz Fest werde: Predigt im Trauergottesdienst Für Eberhard Bethge', *International Bonhoeffer Society Newsletter: English Language Section* 73 (June 2000), p. 7.

6. Though its board is located in the United States, the English Language Section has always included English-speakers around the world. There have also been sections in other countries, including Britain, the Netherlands, East Germany (prior to 1991), Japan and Poland.

Section.[7] Thus emerged the International Bonhoeffer Society for Archive and Research (IBS), as it was initially called. This 'institutionalization' of Bonhoeffer research not only helped Bethge ensure that Bonhoeffer's legacy would be preserved, it also provided the stimulus for much scholarly research and discussion and for the construction of international and ecumenical networks encouraged and stimulated by Bethge's participation.

Despite all his other responsibilities, and these many intrusions into his time, the fifteen years spent at Rengsdorf provided the opportunity for Bethge to pursue his own work on Bonhoeffer's legacy. They also established a pattern that would continue well into his retirement when the Bethges moved to Wachtberg-Villiprott. But above all else, the Rengsdorf years provided the time and space in which Bethge could finally complete his monumental biography, *Dietrich Bonhoeffer: Theologe, Christ, Zeitgenosse (Theologian, Christian, Contempory)*. First published in 1967, it was soon translated into several other languages, including an abridged English version – now fully revised and complete.[8] Berlin's Humboldt University, Bonhoeffer's alma mater, immediately recognized the significance of Bethge's achievement, awarding him an honorary doctorate that same year.

---

7. The German Section (Sektion Bundesrepublik Deutschland) has published a newsletter called *Bonhoeffer Rundbrief*, starting with no. 1 on 24 July 1975. Both the German and the English newsletters have continued to be published through the years and have developed from a few modest duplicated pages into substantial publications, keeping members of the Society aware of events, publications, and conferences relating to Bonhoeffer study and research.

8. Eberhard Bethge, *Dietrich Bonhoeffer: A Biography* (Minneapolis: Fortress Press, 2000). This new, unabridged version of the biography was revised and translated by Victoria Barnett.

The Biography

The early theological debates about Bonhoeffer's significance and the interpretation of his theology, as described in the previous chapter, had an enormous impact upon the writing of the biography. Over a thousand pages long, the biography traced the trajectory of Bonhoeffer's theological development and at the same time gave a detailed account of his life. For Bethge – who had first encountered Bonhoeffer as a theological teacher and mentor and then become part of the family – the two aspects went hand in hand.

Bethge's notes from a faculty lecture he gave at Harvard in February 1958 reveal the ambitious scope of his thoughts at the moment he was just beginning work on the biography. The lecture focused upon the writings that had already been published – the initial edition of the prison letters, the *Ethics*, and the first volumes of the *Gesammelte Schriften* – as well as the different interpretations already offered by Müller and Godsey. Yet in his lecture notes Bethge stated his desire 'to make available the whole of Bonhoeffer's thinking/action'.[9] He wanted to portray Bonhoeffer's contribution to church history and theology, as well as the relevance of his life and work to the larger history of the Nazi era.

Bethge began his work on the biography with the same affinity for dialogical thinking that he had displayed earlier with his friend Dietrich. As the Harvard lecture showed, he was actually constructing his interpretation of Bonhoeffer's life and work *in response to* the questions and interpretations of others. Indeed, this may be one reason for the project's ambitious scope. Given the controversies about the resistance in Germany and the different factions in the German church, and the diversity of early interpretations of Bonhoeffer's work, Bethge had decided by the late 1950s that it would not be enough simply to relate the life behind the theology. The divergent interpretations of Bonhoeffer's work had already shown him that he had to provide his own, and the biography offered a straightforward, methodical

---

9. Bethge's notes for the lecture are in the Bethge papers.

way for him to do so in showing how the theology itself had developed. A major section of the biography thus focused upon Bonhoeffer's theological training, down to the details of the seminars and lectures he attended and the papers he wrote.

Moreover, as a German who had already spent some of the crucial early post-war period abroad, Bethge already was far more sensitive than most of his colleagues back in Germany – including the other former students of Bonhoeffer – to the critical questions people were raising about the Nazi era and the response of the churches, especially to the Holocaust. In the decades that followed, Bethge would receive hundreds of letters from younger colleagues and students seeking answers to the larger questions about resistance and complicity. Not only did he answer many of them at length, but his papers also show how he wove their concerns into new essays and reviews.

Yet while the biography may have been started as a response to the various early interpretations of Bonhoeffer, it soon took on the shape of a far more comprehensive work. In part, this was because of how Bethge himself went about things – as his questions at the Huppenkothen trial in the early 1950s had shown. Although he was in possession of his friends' papers and certainly knew the family history, Bethge began several years of intensive correspondence with Bishop Bell, Visser 't Hooft and others to close the gaps in his own knowledge and resolve the unanswered questions. Hence, in the 1958 Harvard lecture, Bethge could already list with certainty the four areas he planned to examine: the ecumenical period, the church struggle and Finkenwalde, the issues of theology and ministry, and Bonhoeffer's sermons.

In his careful, methodical fashion, he also checked stories. A number of early memoirs had already appeared by the time he began work on the biography, including books by Otto Dibelius, Bishop Würm of Württemberg, Bonhoeffer's fellow conspirator Josef Müller, and Hans-Bernd Gisevius' account of his role in the resistance. Naturally, the portrayal of recent German history in each of these early memoirs expressed the immediate perspective of the author. Bethge, too, had his own experience to draw from. He was also familiar with the strong opinions of the

Bonhoeffer family. Gisevius was the most dramatic example of a very different perspective on the history that Bethge was now in the process of documenting. His book aroused considerable outrage within the Bonhoeffer family, for, as noted earlier, Gisevius claimed that the Gestapo would never have discovered many of the conspirators had it not been for Hans von Dohnanyi, who had refused to destroy his records of information against the Nazi leaders. Dohnanyi's widow Christine angrily refuted the charges, and Bethge incorporated her own account of Dohnanyi's records as an appendix to the biography.[10]

Bethge's quest for details and accuracy was striking. He pieced together much of the biography by the end of the 1950s before moving to Rengsdorf, but he continued to write to people who had known Bonhoeffer, particularly in the ecumenical movement, with long lists of questions. Bethge's own research filled in some of the blanks for Bonhoeffer's ecumenical friends, and the correspondence between Bethge and Visser 't Hooft and Bethge and Adolf Freudenberg shows how these colleagues were in the process of piecing together a much larger ecumenical history.

The biography itself is striking in several respects. It placed Dietrich Bonhoeffer in the foreground in a way that had not been done during the actual history of the German church struggle or, for that matter, in the resistance. Thus, although Bethge later decried the Bonhoeffer 'mythology' that developed in some circles, the sheer scope of the biography placed Bonhoeffer in the centre of his times. At the same time, in the biography Bethge firmly located his own position as being in the background – at the most, a fly on the wall. From 1935 to 1943, Bethge had been omnipresent in Bonhoeffer's life – most of his descriptions of Finkenwalde and the collective pastorates, the war years, and resistance meetings were first-hand accounts – yet Bethge avoided any mention of his involvement. Similarly, the first edition of the prison correspondence, as we have seen, omitted most of Bethge's letters to his friend, including his accounts of his war experiences in Italy.

---

10. Appendix 1, 'The Zossen Files', in Bethge, *Dietrich Bonhoeffer*, pp. 935–41.

As comprehensive and detailed as it was, by today's standards the biography is remarkably reticent. Not only did Bethge leave his own story out of it, but there are few truly personal glimpses of Bonhoeffer the man. These would emerge only much later with the complete publication of his letters and other writings in the *Dietrich Bonhoeffer Werke* series, and most particularly with the publication of his correspondence with Maria von Wedemeyer. Indeed, the cautious tone of the biography reflected Bethge's own generation and culture, as well as his obvious concerns for the privacy of the Bonhoeffer family. Yet it revealed something about Bethge himself that his friend Dietrich had commented on. The final codicil to Bonhoeffer's will, which he revised on 23 November 1943 in his prison cell, began:

> After yesterday's air raid I think it is only right that I should tell you briefly what arrangements I have made in case of my death. The notes given to the attorney might also be destroyed, so it is better that someone knows about them. I hope that you will read them with your usual absence of sentimentality.[11]

In some ways it can indeed be said that the biography revealed an 'absence of sentimentality', yet the portrait of Bonhoeffer's life that emerged from it, and from Bethge's subsequent writings and talks about his friend, was clearly deeply felt. Speaking to the Harvard faculty in 1958, Bethge concluded that Bonhoeffer faced God's questions in both a scholarly and a passionate way:

> The one makes scholars; we need them; the other one makes martyrs – we honour them. Combined, we understand the scholarly questions at once as being questions on the level of life and death, and we experience the honouring remembrance not only as adorning the graves but as some life creating power.[12]

---

11. Bonhoeffer, *Letters and Papers from Prison*. pp. 137–8.
12. Handwritten notes from a lecture at Harvard titled 'Why I Do It', Bethge papers.

The completion of the biography set Bethge free to engage in many other activities, including a more active participation in the debates about the *Kirchenkampf* and the Holocaust. He was acutely aware, as Bonhoeffer had been, that the Confessing Church had failed to respond adequately, if at all, to the persecution of the Jews, and that this issue now had to be addressed with courage and integrity by the German church. The issue was important for at least two reasons. The first was the urgent need for the German church to deal with its past failure and guilt and, in doing so, to engage with Jews in a dialogue that would hopefully begin to heal the wounds. The second was the need to overcome a theological legacy that had both encouraged anti-Judaism and prevented engagement in political resistance. This was particularly necessary in the late nineteen-sixties and early seventies as the ecumenical church became embroiled in controversy about the World Council of Churches' Programme to Combat Racism.

In a paper presented to the First International Scholars' Conference on 'The German Church Struggle and the Holocaust' in 1970 at Wayne State University in the United States, Bethge reflected on the fact that those within the Confessing Church in Germany regarded their struggle as strictly an ecclesial and not a political one. It was a 'resistance lacking any political concept for an alternative Germany'; it had 'no program for political freedom'.[13] Yet within those totalitarian surroundings, Bethge asserted, Barmen 'became not only a witness for but even an organized stronghold of freedom'.[14] Within its context it was a courageous act of resistance. But mindful of the heated debates that were then raging in the churches in Germany about the WCC Programme to Combat Racism, Bethge went on to criticize those who now wanted to recapture the spirit of the *Kirchen-*

---

13. Eberhard Bethge, 'Self-Interpretation and Uncertain Reception in the Church Struggle', in *The German Church Struggle and the Holocaust*, ed. Franklin H. Littell and Hubert G. Locke (Detroit: Wayne State University Press, 1974), p. 171.

14. Bethge, 'Self-Interpretation and Uncertain Reception in the Church Struggle', p. 174.

kampf through simply repeating the Barmen Declaration in opposition to the political engagement of the church in the struggle against racism. In doing so, he argued, they 'create not freedom but only boredom – or even indignant rebellion'.[15] Bethge was particularly mindful of groups, such as those led by Professor Peter Beyerhaus in Tübingen, a former missionary in South Africa, who criticized the Programme to Combat Racism on the basis of the Barmen Declaration.[16] 'Today', Bethge wrote, 'the inflated imitations of Barmen remain completely in the realm of safe verbal exercises . . . the 'new champions' of Barmen refuse to link their efforts expressly (*expressis verbis*) to any humanitarian actions or partnership.'[17] Beyerhaus, we may note in passing, was one of the guest professors invited by Bethge to lead a seminar at Rengsdorf, indicative of Bethge's concern to allow the presentation of perspectives different from his own. Bethge's skill in ensuring that the heated discussion which followed was fruitful, without compromising his own stance, was remarkable.[18]

While the persecution of the Jews during the Third Reich and the oppression of black people in apartheid South Africa were not the same, for Bethge they were clearly related. And the need to deal with the first could not be separated from the need to address the second, both at the practical level of witness and solidarity with the victims and at the theological level, where the traditional Lutheran doctrine of 'two kingdoms' was continually abused to prevent political critique and engagement. As Bethge

---

15. Bethge, 'Self-Interpretation and Uncertain Reception in the Church Struggle', p. 175.

16. Beyerhaus gave his support to the Gospel Defence League in South Africa which, the nineteen-seventies and -eighties, was virulently opposed to those churches and individuals who supported the WCC. The League was funded from Germany, but also received support from the apartheid regime, which used it to provide information about church leaders who were engaged in anti-apartheid activities.

17. Bethge, 'Self-Interpretation and Uncertain Reception in the Church Struggle', p. 183.

18. The seminar took place in 1972 (the author was one of the participants).

became more involved in the discussions about the Holocaust and Jewish-Christian relations, especially after 1970, he was inevitably drawn into the debate about the church's opposition to racism, and in particular to apartheid in South Africa. Thus an invitation made in 1971 to visit South Africa was readily accepted. Perhaps the situation in South Africa could shed light on how the link between confession and resistance, faith and politics, could be forged. Indeed, in a lecture on 'Glaube und Politik' ('Faith and Politics') which he gave in Amsterdam in May 1972 and in which he provided a critique of the abuse of the Lutheran doctrine of the 'two kingdoms', we find written on the manuscript in red ink 'S. Africa!'[19]

---

19. The text of the lecture is in the Bethge papers.

12

The Church Struggle Revisited

The Bethges visited South Africa from 4 February to 9 March 1973 at the invitation of the South African Council of Churches. As always, they were interested in every aspect of their visit – the people, the culture, the terrain, the wildlife, the weather, but especially the social and political situation, and the way in which the churches and theology were responding. The visit evidently made a remarkable impact upon them. It also introduced Bonhoeffer to an audience across the country that was eager to discern his significance for the church struggle in South Africa at a time of deepening despair. Writing a letter of thanks on the flight back to Germany, Renate commented that they had grown 'very fond of South Africa' and would 'follow the events there with keen interest'.[1] Though tempted on several occasions to return to the country, this was never possible again. By the time of the 1996 International Bonhoeffer Congress in Cape Town, Eberhard's health prevented him from attending.

A Confessing Church in South Africa?[2]

The Bethges' interest in South Africa continued well beyond the Rengsdorf years. Part of the reason for this was that their visit brought back vivid memories of the German *Kirchenkampf*. In particular it reminded Bethge of the many discussions and

---

1. Letter to the author, 10 March 1973.
2. Much of this section is based on correspondence between the author and Eberhard and Renate Bethge, spanning the period 1971–2000.

debates that he had had with Bonhoeffer and others around the themes of confession, resistance, military conscription, and expressing solidarity with the victims of totalitarian power. Indeed, the plight of black South Africans was a powerful reminder of the plight of the Jews in the Third Reich. But the visit did more than bring back memories of struggle, suffering and courage. It also stimulated further reflection on these issues as they took on more contemporary contours, whether in South Africa or the United States and elsewhere. Thus, while the visit was only five weeks long, much shorter by comparison with his more frequent and often longer visits to the United States, its significance was far in excess of the time spent in the country.

Bethge's awareness of the emerging church struggle in apartheid South Africa, and of possible Bonhoeffer connections, predated his visit to South Africa by at least a decade, as is evident from his Alden-Tuthill Lectures in 1961. Commenting in those lectures on 'Bonhoeffer's hot theological discussions with Geneva and with Faith and Order in 1934 and afterward' he remarked that they 'would make a good and penetrating textbook for our judgment of the present crisis between the churches in South Africa and the relation of Geneva to this crisis'.[3] Later, in the same lectures, he returned to this subject with the comment that Bonhoeffer 'presented the *Oekumene* with a most delicate demand to accept the condemnation of the heretics, exactly as the archbishop of Cape Town does today'.[4] The crisis to which Bethge referred followed the Sharpeville Massacre in March 1960, and the subsequent call by Anglican Archbishop Joost de Blank for the Dutch Reformed Church to be excommunicated from the World Council of Churches.[5]

We may wonder how it was that Bethge had such an awareness of what was happening in South Africa. After all, news about

---

3. Bethge, 'The Challenge of Dietrich Bonhoeffer's Life and Theology', p. 3.

4. Bethge, 'The Challenge of Dietrich Bonhoeffer's Life and Theology', p. 25.

5. See John W. de Gruchy with Steve de Gruchy, *The Church Struggle in South Africa*, 3rd edn (London: SCM Press, 2004; Minneapolis: Fortress Press, 2005), pp. 60–2.

South Africa was sparse in the German media at that time, especially regarding church affairs. The answer is to be found in the fact that during this period (1953–61) Bethge was a pastor in London, that he moved in ecumenical circles, where there was growing concern about apartheid, and that the British media, especially since the Sharpeville Massacre, was focusing increasingly on what was happening in South Africa. In 1960 Harold Macmillan, the British Prime Minister, made a visit to South Africa during which he gave his historic 'Winds of Change' speech to the Houses of Parliament in Cape Town that helped precipitate South Africa withdrawing from the British Commonwealth. So it is not surprising that in notes Bethge kept of a church meeting he attended in London, he refers several times to people involved in the emerging struggle against apartheid: Chief Albert Luthuli, Bishop Ambrose Reeves of Johannesburg, Father Trevor Huddleston, Canon John Collins, and Archbishop de Blank.[6] The last four were all expatriate Anglican priests who had gone to serve in South Africa, where they had run foul of the apartheid regime and had to return to England. Bethge obviously had all this in mind as he prepared to give his Alden-Tuthill Lectures, but these facts also illustrate well how Bethge's exposure to other cultures and contexts, and his innate ability to see things differently, enabled him to gain fresh perspectives on Bonhoeffer's legacy. Thus he eagerly anticipated visiting South Africa to see things for himself.

Bethge was not disappointed. From the moment of their arrival in Johannesburg until their departure five weeks later, the Bethges were made aware of both the plight of black people and of the church struggle against apartheid. Staying not far from the headquarters of the anti-apartheid South African Council of Churches and the Christian Institute, they were soon introduced to the heated debates on the Programme to Combat Racism that

---

6. Bethge papers. The notes, which are very difficult to decipher, are dated 29 May, but the year is not clear. It appears that the meeting was addressed by several people, on the question of 'church–state' relations in England, during which reference was made to the South African situation and the role of Anglican clergy.

were then, as in Germany, dividing the churches. They also became aware of the discussion about the need for a confessing church in South Africa that would directly address the political situation. In this regard, the Bethges were especially delighted to renew their acquaintance with the director of the Christian Institute, Beyers Naudé, who was the major advocate of a confessing church in South Africa. Naudé had, in fact, attended the First International Bonhoeffer Congress in Kaiserswerth in 1971, where the Bethges met him for the first time.

Naudé had been defrocked by the white Dutch Reformed Church in 1963 on founding the Christian Institute, but was highly regarded within ecumenical circles, not least in Germany, for his principled theological stand against apartheid and his knowledge of the South African situation.[7] Naudé in turn had learned much from the German *Kirchenkampf* and regarded the Christian Institute as an instrument for establishing a confessing church movement, often speaking about the significance of the Barmen Declaration for the church struggle against apartheid. But it was Bonhoeffer's example of always taking the next step, even going beyond the confines of the Confessing Church, that inspired Naudé to identify at great personal cost with the liberation struggle and thus with direct political action and resistance. In this regard, Bethge recognized in Naudé a kindred spirit, indeed, someone who reminded him of Bonhoeffer.

In his lectures he gave at various places around the country, later to be published as *Bonhoeffer: Exile and Martyr*, Bethge avoided speaking directly to the South African situation, or trying to make Bonhoeffer relevant in any overt way. But his audiences immediately sensed a correspondence between Bonhoeffer's theology and witness within the *Kirchenkampf* and their own experience. Though anticipating that this might be the case, Bethge himself was in turn surprised at the extent to which it was.[8] In many ways, Bethge's lectures in *Bonhoeffer: Exile and*

---

7. See the papers in *Resistance and Hope: South African Essays in honour of Beyers Naudé*, ed. Charles Villa-Vicencio and John W. de Gruchy (Grand Rapids: Eerdmans, 1985).

8. See John W. de Gruchy, 'Bonhoeffer in South Africa: An Exploratory Essay', in Bethge, *Bonhoeffer: Exile and Martyr*, pp. 26–42.

Martyr build on his earlier Alden-Tuthill Lectures, showing how his interpretation of Bonhoeffer had developed during the past decade. But it is in his report appropriately entitled 'A Confessing Church in South Africa?', which was published shortly after their return home, and then included in *Bonhoeffer: Exile and Martyr*,[9] that his interpretation of the Bonhoeffer legacy is applied directly to South Africa.

Noting many parallels, yet also sensitive to differences, Bethge necessarily qualified his conclusions. But he detected an uncanny resemblance between the German *Kirchenkampf* and what was developing in South Africa. In his report he wrote:

> The edginess of those who reject the validity of such parallels (the list of which is far from complete) and the constant pre-occupation of those who mull over the consequences these parallels could have for themselves personally (and who, moreover, look to us in Germany to share in their reflections) clearly show that the drawing of such parallels touches a raw nerve.[10]

Theologically speaking, he was particularly struck by points of comparison between the conflicting theologies of the German church struggle. Notable amongst these was the abuse of Luther's 'two kingdoms' teaching and Bonhoeffer's attempts to counter that, and similar tendencies in the South African church situation. Themes that were so central to Bonhoeffer's and his own thinking in the nineteen-thirties (*solus Christus, status confessionis, unitas*) suddenly took on fresh, urgent significance. But, he asked, 'how helpful in fact is this example of the Confessing Church?' His answer was ambiguous. On the one hand, the German experience certainly resonated with the thinking of those engaged in the church struggle against apartheid, suggest-

---

9. Originally published in *Evangelische Kommentare* 6 (6 June 1973); subsequently translated and published by the World Council of Churches in English in *Study Encounter* 3 (1973). With the agreement of Bethge, who also made some changes, the article was then edited and published in *Bonhoeffer: Exile and Martyr*, pp.167–78.

10. Bethge, *Bonhoeffer: Exile and Martyr*, pp. 172–3.

ing that a confessing church, though of a different kind, was a distinct possibility. But on the other hand, the situation had too many variables, whether in church, society or politics, to equate it with the German context. Even the key theological terms of the Confessing Church in Germany took on different contours.

The German Barmen Declaration had avoided any direct reference to the Jews. The anti-apartheid movement in South Africa's churches sought to avoid that fatal error. Thus the *Message to the People of South Africa*, published by the South African Council of Churches and the Christian Institute in 1968, referred to apartheid, whether in church or nation, as a 'false gospel'.[11] So to speak of the unity of the church (*unitas*) without addressing the social and political divisions was unthinkable. The critical issue, after all, was whether white and black South Africans could find each other in church *and* society at a time when apartheid was tearing them apart. Thus, while some white Christians were engaged in a struggle partly inspired by the *Kirchenkampf*, black theologians were developing their own agenda inspired by the Black Consciousness Movement. But maybe Bethge sensed then, as others did, that Bonhoeffer might well provide a bridge between 'confessing theology' and 'black theology' and their respective political agendas.

Bethge was particularly intrigued by the development of black theology in South Africa. On the return trip to Germany, he read the essays in the second issue of the *Journal of Theology for Southern Africa*, noting in particular an article by Ernest Baartman, 'The Significance of Black Consciousness for the Church'.[12] Shortly after he arrived home he received the next issue of the *Journal*, which contained not only one of his own lectures, but also Dr Manas Buthelezi's 'Six Theses: Theological Problems of Evangelism in South Africa', a lecture that had recently been given at the Durban Congress on Mission and Evangelism.[13] These pithy theses, in which Buthelezi called on

11. See de Gruchy, *The Church Struggle in South Africa*, pp. 115–26.

12. Letter to the author from Madrid, 11 March 1973.

13. Manas Buthelezi, 'Six Theses: Theological Problems of Evangelism in South Africa', *Journal of Theology for Southern Africa* 3 (June 1973) pp. 55–6.

blacks 'to evangelize and humanize' whites in South Africa, made a powerful impact on the Congress delegates. Bethge was deeply moved by them, and used them in his own talks and seminars on South Africa.

Buthelezi, a Lutheran who was the leading black theologian in South Africa at the time, was well known in Germany, especially at the University of Heidelberg, where he had briefly lectured in 1972. His close associates there, Professor Heinz Eduard Tödt and Dr Ilse Tödt, who had previously visited South Africa and were involved on behalf of the Lutheran World Federation in dealing with the South African situation, were also close friends of the Bethges. Over the ensuing years they also became increasingly involved with Bethge in Bonhoeffer research. In the summer of 1975 they convened a conference at Heidelberg on theology within the South African struggle in dialogue with Buthelezi. The importance of Bonhoeffer, and of Bethge's interpretation for this dialogue, can be clearly seen from Ilse Tödt's presentation.[14]

Bethge was not present on this occasion, but the previous October he led a seminar on black theology sponsored by the Evangelical Church in the Rhineland, together with a young Anglican priest, Desmond Tutu, and Markus Braun, a Lutheran pastor recently expelled from South Africa. Bethge gave the main address on the subject 'What is relevant theology here today against the background of African Black Theology'.[15] Favourably comparing black theology, as a counter and challenge to white racism, to Barth's dialectical theology as a critique of liberal bourgeois culture of a previous era, Bethge argued that a relevant theology is one that radically renews our understanding of Christ and the church. Black theology, Bethge declared, is a

---

14. Ilse Tödt, 'Parameter der Friendensforschung und die Theologie Südafrika: Nischer Schwarzer', in *Theologie im Konfliktfeld Südafrika: Dialog mit Manas Buthelezi*, ed. Ilse Tödt (Stuttgart: Ernst Klett Verlag, 1976), pp. 214–53.

15. See Bethge's mimeographed notes entitled, 'Bericht über das Seminar "Schwarze Theologie als Versuch einer relevante Theologie", durchgeführt im Rahmen des Pfarrer-Fortbildungsprogramme der Evangelische Kirche im Rheinland von 7–11 Oktober, 1974', Bethge papers.

critique of the tribal religion of whites, the religion of privilege, but also a theology that enables us to discern again the liberating power of the gospel.

Bethge's exposition of black theology shows the extent to which he was familiar with its major themes, and also aware of the struggle going on within the churches in South Africa. But we may also say that his encounter with black theology and the church struggle in South Africa made him more aware of the ongoing relevance of Bonhoeffer's legacy within his own German context and elsewhere. While many people in Europe and North America were then more interested in how Bonhoeffer helped them deal with secularization and atheism, the more burning issues, as Bethge recognized, were those of justice, peace and liberation from oppression.

During the year following their visit to South Africa, the situation in the country rapidly deteriorated as resistance grew and the armed struggle against South Africa in Namibia intensified. Bethge, mindful of Bonhoeffer's as well as his own position during the Second World War, was therefore particularly interested in the debate about conscientious objection that erupted during 1974 within the South African Council of Churches (SACC) and its member churches.[16] Though some conscientious objectors were pacifist, the majority of the young white South Africans who refused to do military service regarded their refusal as a way of identifying with the liberation struggle and the WCC Programme to Combat Racism. In doing so, they often referred to the witness of Bonhoeffer, whose name was also mentioned in debates in Parliament at this time. Bethge found the decision of the SACC 'very exciting', because it reminded him so much of the heated discussions around such issues during the *Kirchenkampf*, giving substance to the debate about the Programme and making it more relevant.[17]

The Bethges were constantly disappointed by the lack of information in the German media on South Africa, especially as they were so often asked to speak on the situation within church

---

16. See de Gruchy, *Church Struggle*, pp. 138–48.
17. Letter to the author, 19 August 1974.

circles and to help formulate responses to the growing crisis. They increasingly felt out of touch. However, Beyers Naudé's trial in 1974 for refusing to give evidence before a government commission investigating the Christian Institute[18] did get church media coverage in Germany, and led to renewed invitations to the Bethges to speak on the situation. A year after their visit to South Africa, Bethge wrote:

> We are constantly reminded of this great journey you had arranged because – funny enough – suddenly we are believed to be experts in South Africa matters and have to speak again and again. Sometimes we seem to be aware of how much things have changed already in this past year, but we try to keep in contact with the news and by means of *Ecunews*.[19] Otherwise our civil papers and broadcast systems are very abstinent in reporting from your part of the world; with our ecclesiastical media things have changed and they are much more in the picture than a few years ago.[20]

When the South African government expropriated the Federal Theological Seminary in Alice in 1975, in a cynical attempt to destroy its influence as the main centre for training in black theology, Bethge tried hard to inform the leadership of the Evangelical Church in Germany, encouraging them to send protest messages to the regime.[21]

Countess Marion Dönhoff, a prominent German journalist, visited South Africa during the first half of 1976, perhaps anticipating momentous events, and subsequently wrote what Bethge regarded as the best article on South Africa he had read in a German journal in recent years.[22] This prepared him to under-

---

18. See *The Trial of Beyers Naudé: Christian Witness and the Rule of Law*, ed. International Commission of Jurists, Geneva (London: Search Press, 1975).

19. The newspaper of the South African Council of Churches.

20. Letter to the author, 23 March 1974

21. Letter to the author, 21 March 1975.

22. Letter to the author, 18 May 1976; I have been unable to trace any further information about this article.

stand the traumatic Soweto uprising in June 1976. Writing from Union Theological Seminary in New York a few months later, Bethge, while still decrying the lack of substantial knowledge about the background and the facts of the situation, noted that 'the way South Africa has come into the news in Germany just in this last year is breathtaking'.[23] South Africa, and the friends they had made there, were now constantly in the minds of the Bethges as the news of what was happening in the aftermath of the uprising flashed around the world. Certainly the news, as they noted in several letters, was not encouraging as the situation continued to deteriorate over the next few years. In a letter in June 1980, Renate Bethge remarked:

> Things must be very tense around you. It always seems to be as you write, that as soon as some things are improved so that there could be some hope, all the frustration and anger which had to be kept down through long years is exploding, which prevents things to become better altogether.[24]

These were the years in which, despite the government's attempt at 'reforming' its policies, repression and resistance became increasingly intense. This was also the context in which Bishop Desmond Tutu, now General Secretary of the SACC, and Dr Allan Boesak, a minister of the black Dutch Reformed Mission Church, emerged to prominence as church leaders engaged in the struggle. Boesak, it may be noted, acknowledged the influence of Bonhoeffer in shaping his theology and resistance to apartheid when speaking at the Fifth International Bonhoeffer Congress in Amsterdam in 1988.[25]

---

23. Undated letter to the author. *c.* September 1976.
24. Letter to the author, 28 June 1980.
25. Allan A. Boesak, 'What Dietrich Bonhoeffer has Meant to Me', in *Bonhoeffer's Ethics: Old Europe and New Frontiers*, pp. 21–9.

Confession and Resistance

Several ecumenical events brought into greater prominence the relation between Christian confession and political action in the struggle against apartheid. These were of considerable interest to Bethge, both in terms of South Africa and in enabling him to rethink the relationship between confession and resistance. The first event was the meeting of the Lutheran World Federation (LWF) in Dar es Salaam in June 1977, which adopted a resolution put forward by South African delegates that the situation in South Africa be declared a *status confessionis*.[26] Then in February 1980 the SACC held a Consultation on Racism at Hammanskraal, near Pretoria, at which the black delegates issued an ultimatum to their respective churches. Calling on 'all white Christians to demonstrate their willingness to purge the church of racism' they went on to declare that

> if after a period of twelve months there is no evidence of repentance shown in concrete action, the black Christians will have no alternative but to witness to the Gospel of Jesus Christ by becoming a confessing church.[27]

While this threat was not implemented as such, it contributed to the birth of the Alliance of Black Reformed Christians in South Africa (ABRECSA) in 1981, led by Allan Boesak. Then, at the World Alliance of Reformed Churches (WARC) meeting in Ottawa the following year, the Alliance declared that a *status confessionis* existed in South Africa and that apartheid was a theological heresy.[28] And it was the black Dutch Reformed

---

26. See *From Federation to Communion: The History of the Lutheran World Federation*, ed. Jen Holger Schjørring, Prasanna Kumari and Norman A. Hjelm (Minneapolis: Fortress Press, 1997), pp. 399–400.

27. *Ecunews*, 27 February 1980, p. 11.

28. 'Racism and South Africa', a statement adopted by the General Council of the WARC, 25 August 1982. Published in *Apartheid is a Heresy*, eds John W. de Gruchy and Charles Villa-Vicencio (Grand Rapids: Eerdmans, 1983), pp. 168–73.

Mission Church, of which Boesak was moderator, that drafted the Belhar Confession of Faith in 1982, which effectively made it a 'confessing church'.[29] This was a historic document. Not only was it the first time since the Reformation period that a Dutch Reformed church had adopted a new confession, but it was also a confession which made ethical commitment to justice central to Christian faith and church unity. In this way, Bethge's earlier concerns about the character of a possible Confessing Church in South Africa were overcome. Indeed, Bethge recognized the significance of this event when he wrote a brief meditation on the Belhar Confession, significantly dedicated to Beyers Naudé, whom Bethge, as a former Barmen-Dahlemite, acknowledged as its pioneer.[30]

Some ten years after his visit to South Africa, at the *Kirchentag* in Hanover in 1983, Bethge and Lutheran theologian Ulrich Duchrow engaged in a public discussion on confession and resistance in the Third Reich and in South Africa. Bethge recalled how for Barth and Bonhoeffer the Barmen Declaration was a confession of Christ against heresy in the church, not an act of political resistance, as it was misrepresented in the Western press.[31] But, *as such*, it was also an implicit act of resistance, even though it never actually dealt with the political issues. Two theological issues undermined the witness of the church in Germany, Bethge argued, issues that he constantly returned to when discussing South Africa. The first was a misuse of Luther's 'two kingdoms' teaching which, he said, was used to great effect by the apartheid political leadership in South Africa who claimed to be Christians. The second was a 'docetic Christology' that

---

29. *A Moment of Truth: The Confession of the Dutch Reformed Mission Church, 1982*, ed. G. D. Cloete and D. J. Smit (Grand Rapids: Eerdmans, 1984).

30. 'Kurze Meditation über das Belhar-Bekenntnis vom Oktober 1982', in *Zwischen Bekenntnis und Anpassung*, ed. Güvan Norden (Cologne: Rheinland-Verlag, 1985), p. 151.

31. 'Südafrika: Das ist mein pervertiertes Gesicht. Gesprach mit Eberhard Bethge und Ulrich Duchrow über Bekenntnis und Widerstand im Dritten Reich und heute in Südafrika 1983', in Eberhard Bethge, *Bekennen und Widerstehen* (Munich: Chr. Kaiser Verlag, 1984), p. 180.

resulted in a Christ unrelated to the concrete situation of today.[32] What was clear in South Africa was the need for a confession of Christ that spoke directly to questions of racism and human rights.[33] Bethge emphatically gave his support to those members of the Dutch Reformed Mission Church who refused to participate in Holy Communion with their white Dutch Reformed colleagues at the World Alliance of Reformed Churches meeting in Ottawa in 1982. To do so, he claimed, would have been cheap reconciliation.[34] He then turned to the theme of solidarity, what this meant with regard to the Jews in the Third Reich, and what this now meant with regard to the victims of apartheid. In conclusion, Bethge stressed the fact that German Protestants had a special responsibility towards South Africa, sharing in its guilt and sharing responsibility for the situation. They could not wash their hands of this legacy.[35]

Bethge's reflections on South Africa had clearly sharpened his understanding of the relation between confession and resistance, and he returned to this theme in his address to the Seattle Assembly in 1984 that celebrated the fiftieth anniversary of the Barmen Declaration. In it he stressed both the distinction and the connection between Christian confession and political resistance. Confession is not resistance, but public witness 'to that Christ who brings God to us in the midst of our lives, to that God who directs our hearts, thoughts, and actions against the false gods and, at the same time, to the victims of those false gods'.[36] Political resistance, by way of contrast, is all about tactics and strategy, effect and success, hiding and concealment, double meanings of acts and actors. Confession and resistance are not and should not be allowed to become identical, for the sake of both the confessors and the resisters. But believing that there is no relation between them 'means finally complicity with crime,

---

32. Bethge, *Bekennen und Widerstehen*, pp. 182–3.
33. Bethge, *Bekennen und Widerstehen*, p. 196.
34. Bethge, *Bekennen und Widerstehen*, p. 189.
35. Bethge, *Bekennen und Widerstehen*, p. 198.
36. Eberhard Bethge, 'The Confessing Church, Then and Now: The Barmen Declaration, 1934 and 1984', in *The Barmen Confession*, p. 219.

means turning confession into alibi words, means victimization of human beings who will bring an unappeasable charge precisely *against confessors*'.[37]

The Bethges met Beyers Naudé again in May 1985 when, following his 'unbanning' they were together at a conference on South Africa held at the Evangelical Academy in Arnoldsheim. This occasion demonstrated yet again Bethge's interest in and commitment to the anti-apartheid struggle. In a letter Bethge mentioned that for two weeks they had been involved in 'a protest march to the SA Embassy to back a petition for the imprisoned 16 in SA waiting for their trial'. But, he added, 'the papers reported only about police actions and not about the reasons for the actions'.[38] The truth was that resistance to apartheid was reaching a climax. President P. W. Botha tried to quell the developing mass action with the declaration of a state of emergency (the second of two) on 21 July 1985, which lasted until the demise of the regime in 1989. In a letter from their holiday resort in the South Tyrol Dolomites, Renate Bethge showed that even on holiday these events were not far from their thoughts. She wrote:

> Yesterday we heard that 3 white persons were killed at a black funeral, and I believe that these Whites had been there to support justice for blacks. Should it really have come this far, it would be very bad. But Botha indeed does not seem to understand the situation, it seems. Of course, no easy solution offers itself, and one also can understand the fear of the white minority, which of course must increase through this way of handling the problems.[39]

This was the context within which the *Kairos Document* was drafted in 1986 by a group of theologians associated with the Institute for Contextual Theology (ICT), based in Johannesburg. Recognizing that the basic difference between Christians in

---

37. Bethge, 'The Confessing Church, Then and Now', p. 221.
38. Letter to the author, 27 May 1985.
39. Letter to the author, 2 August 1985.

South Africa was not primarily denominational or confessional, but political and economic, the *Kairos Document* perceived that the church itself was a site of the struggle. Thus the *Kairos Document* not only rejected the 'state theology' of those who gave their support to apartheid, but also opposed what it termed the 'church theology' of the mainline multi-racial churches, accusing them of promoting 'cheap reconciliation'.[40] In doing so, the *Kairos Document* called for direct Christian participation in the struggle, including acts of civil disobedience in resistance to government tyranny.

The *Kairos Document* evoked a great deal of interest within church circles in Germany, especially those concerned about South Africa. Bethge, again, was well aware of this development. Indeed, he was invited to present the opening paper and also preach the Sunday sermon at a conference on the *Kairos Document* held in Bad Godesberg near Wachtberg-Villiprott on 5–7 December 1986.[41] It is remarkable that more than thirteen years after he had visited South Africa, he was still regarded by those well informed about current developments as someone who could speak on the subject with sharp, prophetic insight. Bethge, of course, knew his limitations and was surprised by such invitations, but South Africa was so close to his heart that he seldom refused to participate and did everything possible to remain informed. Given his heavy writing, lecturing and travelling schedule, and the fact that he was nearing his eightieth birthday, this was all the more remarkable. But perhaps even more remarkable was the theological depth and insight evident in both his lecture and sermon.

Bethge began his lecture by recalling how, in Berlin in 1933, Karl Barth had challenged the prevailing theology with his

---

40. *The Kairos Document* (Johannesburg: Institute for Contextual Theology, 1986), p. 9, art. 3.1.

41. The conference was sponsored by 'Plädoyer für eine ökumenische Zukunft'. Bethge's lecture was entitled 'Die Erfahrungen von Widerspruch zwischen "Staatstheologie – Kirchentheologie – Prophetischer Theologie" – in unserer gengenwärten Situation: auf dem Weg zu einem Bundesdeutschen Kairos-Papier', Bethge papers.

fundamentally different understanding of God, and then in 1938, after *Kristallnacht*, he had spoken of the need to overcome the *political* heresy of Nazi ideology. The *Kairos Document*, Bethge suggested, had brought these two together, namely, the theology of the First Commandment *and* its political consequences. But what did this mean for Christians in Germany today, he asked? How should the church in Germany respond to the *Kairos Document*? This prompted a third memory of the Nazi period, namely, that of theologians who tried to paralyse the challenge of the Barmen Declaration by raising objections to its 'one-sidedness'. The same danger now presented itself as Germans tried to respond to the challenge of the *Kairos Document*. One danger was to say that the *Kairos Document*, however appropriate as a call to action in South Africa, was theologically flawed from the perspective of good German theology. Another was to think of it as a statement of the 'theological left', of those more influenced by Marx than the Bible. But in fact, the *Kairos Document* was addressing a *status confessionis* on the basis of biblical theology; it was not inviting endless discussion, but praxis.

Of course, criticism of the *Kairos Document* was necessary, but Bethge emphasized that criticism was dangerous if in the name of 'good theology' it failed to recognize its testimony to the God of the Bible. Bethge reminded his listeners that the Barmen Declaration had addressed its own *kairos* in the same way, something recognized also in the witness of Beyers Naudé. This was also Bonhoeffer's understanding of a confession of faith. It was not an attempt to state the whole of Christian dogma, but on the ground of dogma to address a specific issue at a specific time and place. In doing so it drew the boundaries, as at the Reformation, between 'true' and 'false' church.[42] Of course, this was also dangerous because it could demonize those who disagree with us, a danger to which the *Kairos Document* was prone. But again, that was the risk of true confession in identifying heresy and seeking to counter it. Bethge also addressed the criticism that the *Kairos*

---

42. Bethge had in mind Bonhoeffer's lecture to the first class of seminarians at Finkenwalde in 1936, entitled 'Zur Frage nach der Kirchengemeinschaft', published in Bonhoeffer, *Finkenwalde*, pp. 655-91.

Document's theology was pre-determined by its social analysis rather than the Bible, but concluded that all true theology arises out of response to a situation and that this requires an understanding of that context. Genuine theology is never done in a vacuum. The *Kairos Document* represented theology from the perspective of those oppressed by colonialism and apartheid; it was a theology born out of struggle, a theology of the Soweto uprising rather than one emanating from the spheres of political and ecclesiastical power.

So Bethge turned in conclusion to consider the implications of the *Kairos Document* for the German church today. For him the danger could be summed up in two phrases that paralleled the 'state' and 'church' theologies of the *Kairos Document* – a theology of complicity (*Komplizentum*) and a docetic ecclesiology – which he regarded as two sides of the same coin. The first was a theology that gave support to the status quo in Germany, uncritically accepting the prevailing capitalist ideology; the second was an understanding of the church that stressed the 'spiritual' at the cost of the concrete embodiment of the gospel, thereby avoiding dealing with the critical social and political issues. Bethge brought his lecture to an end with a reference to what he had learnt from Bonhoeffer and which he had never forgotten, namely his single-minded concern 'to reclaim the form of Jesus Christ' among us today. Bethge here recalled a passage from Bonhoeffer's *Ethics*: 'either the Church must willingly undergo this transformation, or else she must cease to be the Church of Christ'.[43] The *Kairos Document*, Bethge asserted, strongly affirmed such a concrete reclaiming of the form of Jesus Christ. Bethge lectured at least once more on the *Kairos Document*, but he suspected that his Christological approach, one he had learnt so well from Bonhoeffer, was no longer appreciated.[44]

In a sense, history had turned a complete circle. When Bethge came to South Africa the question was what South Africans could learn from the German *Kirchenkampf* and from the legacy of Bonhoeffer. But over the years the question had become what

---

43. Dietrich Bonhoeffer, *Ethics* (New York: Macmillan, 1965), p. 116.
44. Letter to the author, 15 April 1987.

Germans could and should learn from the church struggle in South Africa, from the testimony of black theologians, the Belhar Confession, and now finally from the *Kairos Document*. Was Bonhoeffer's testimony more real and relevant, better appropriated and better understood in South Africa, than in Germany, perhaps even the Germany of the *Kirchenkampf*? We may recall that in 1959 Bethge had observed the danger of regarding 'thinking of the theology of the church struggle as only an interlude'.[45] Yet now it appeared that the issues facing the church, whether in Germany, the United States, Britain or South Africa, were recurrent ones, albeit in different guises. In addressing the South African situation, Bethge reminded his audiences that Bonhoeffer's legacy was to remember rightly the past in which he struggled to witness to the true meaning of Jesus Christ.

---

45. Bethge, 'The Editing and Publishing of the Bonhoeffer Papers', p. 16.

13

Remembering the Past Rightly

Bethge's long life straddled the years that stretched from before the war through the traumatic post-war era with its division of Germany into East and West, and he was blessed to live ten years into the new united Germany. All of this meant that he was well placed to fulfil a unique pastoral role within German society as a custodian of the memory and moral conscience of those who had tried, albeit in vain, to resist Nazi tyranny. But as Bethge reflected back on those times, he increasingly came to recognize the enormity of the Holocaust or Shoah and its challenge to the church. Thus rightly remembering those who were murdered for their resistance to tyranny was inseparable from rightly remembering the victims of the Holocaust. Remembering both and making the connection between them became his special passion during the last two decades of his life. To remember rightly had various dimensions, but they all centred on the need for an appropriate confession of guilt, the accepting of responsibility, and a corresponding change of attitude, theology and action.

Mediator of Resistance Memories

Regularly invited to speak at commemorative events, Bethge responded to these anniversary celebrations with pastoral sensitivity and prophetic wisdom. He showed consummate skill in reflecting back on key moments during the Third Reich: the Barmen Synod in 1934; *Kristallnacht* in 1938;[1] the 20 July 1944

---

1. In their Advent family newsletter in 1988 Renate Bethge notes that

plot, annually recalled at an ecumenical service at the execution site in Berlin-Plötzenzee; Bonhoeffer's murder at Flossenbürg on 9 April 1945, among others. As Bishop Wolfgang Huber would later say at his funeral, Bethge was 'chaplain to the "July 20th" families'.[2]

Bethge was not only in great demand as a speaker or preacher on such occasions, being as one who had personally experienced many of those events, but he was also extraordinarily gifted in getting to the heart of the matter in a way that brought history to life and made it relevant to the present. He well understood how such rituals helped people deal with the past, how necessary they were for the healing process, and the opportunity they provided to reflect on their contemporary significance. Occasions such as these, together with his sermons, radio talks and media interviews, made a cumulative impact within a widening circle of interested people. All of this, and more, was publicly honoured and recognized when he was awarded the Great Distinguished Services Cross of the Federal Republic of Germany in 1989.

Long life brought with it another responsibility, however. For as the years passed, and as his contemporaries passed on, Bethge became the mediator of memories. And, as one of the longest-lived survivors of Finkenwalde, the *Kirchenkampf* and the resistance, he also had to say regular farewells to old comrades and friends who had shared much of that history with him. It must have been with considerable sadness that he so often had to preach or write memorials on the occasions of their deaths, among them Franz Hildebrandt, Heinz Eduard Tödt, Otto Dudzus and, perhaps most poignantly, Sabine Leibholz, Bonhoeffer's twin sister, who died in July 1999.

'Eberhard spoke in many places for the 50th anniversary of the "crystal night".' Commenting further, she wrote that his lectures 'on this topic were extremely well attended, many young people came'. Bethge's memorial sermon, preached on 6 November 1988 in the Marktkirche, Neuwied, is published in *Bonhoeffer Rundbrief* 62 (August 1990), pp. 1–7.

2. Wolfgang Huber, 'Funeral Sermon for Eberhard Bethge', *International Bonhoeffer Society Newsletter: English Language Section* 73 (June 2000), p. 6, translated by Victoria Barnett.

The year of Bethge's eightieth birthday, 1989, was also one of momentous importance in the history of Germany, signalling the changes that led to the reunification of East and West, and therefore reuniting Bethge's place of birth, for so long part of East Germany, with the places where he had lived and worked since the end of the war. This meant a great deal to Bethge. Even though he had kept contact with friends and family in East Germany, especially his brother, and had regularly visited there over the years, the fact that Germany was reunited brought to an end the division that had begun in those chaotic days of 1945 when he had escaped from prison and was starting his search for the truth about what had happened. And, of course, the eastern regions of Germany were where Bethge's friendship with Bonhoeffer had begun, where Finkenwalde was located, and where they had spent so much time enjoying one another's company.

The reunification of Germany led to the unification of the East German Bonhoeffer Society and the German Section of the International Bonhoeffer Society. In March 1992 a joint conference was held in Eisenach, and Bethge spoke on the legacy of the Confessing Church and its significance for what was now happening in Germany.[3] Would all the hopes for the new Germany and the new world order be realized? Bethge's analysis was sobering as he spoke of the hopes that his generation had had in 1945, and how they had been frustrated so soon. This was why it was so important to remember the witness, and the weaknesses, of the Confessing Church and to reflect on the resistance. What was the role of the church today in the vacuum created by the collapse of Communism, in the pursuit of a just democracy, in developing a peaceful Europe, in relation to Israel? Invariably in responding to such questions, Bethge drew deeply on Bonhoeffer's legacy, but never in an ahistorical way.

With the hindsight of a lifetime's experience, Bethge had a profound sense of historical fate and yet, amidst his sober reflections and the challenge he invariably expressed, one always discerned a clear sense of hope. But hope was not, for him, wish-

---

3. Eberhard Bethge, 'Das Erbe der Bekennende Kirche: Transport über die Wenden', *Bonhoeffer Rundbrief* 38 (May 1992), pp. 7–19.

ful thinking; it implied action that would anticipate a better world. So his remarks were not intended to comfort but to provoke thought and awaken the conscience of his audiences. Speaking on the occasion of the unveiling of the memorial in July 1990 to those of the resistance who died in the Lehrter Strasse 3 prison, Bethge said:

> Today is the beginning of a fresh and necessary phase of working through that history, since only now through the turnaround [*die Wende*: the changes of 1989] is access to important sources being opened. But even more importantly: liberation without memory becomes a dance around the golden calf. The biblical story relates truthfully how the people who were liberated from slavery in Egypt and brought along the difficult path to the promised land became enslaved by the golden calf, and forgot the period of slavery with its sacrifices.

He continued:

> Today we experience the overwhelming caesura of recent months as 'historic'; yet it threatens to become unhistoric if, through this, the history of fifty years ago slides from our consciousness and thought. The responsible formation of consciousness about that past helps keep us now from succumbing to difficulties and losing ourselves.[4]

On 1 November 1993, Bethge addressed the founding meeting of a new association in Germany known as Gegen Vergessen – für Demokratie (Against Forgetting – For Democracy). This association was established to help Germans remember their past history rightly, to combat forgetting, so that the new Germany could build a stronger democratic tradition. Bethge began his address with these words:

> Commemoration renders life human; forgetfulness makes it inhuman. We know of course about the grace of forgetting.

---

4. Eberhard Bethge, 'Gedanktafel – enthülling für die Lehrter Strasse 3', 19 July 1990, text in Bethge papers.

But even when remembrance carries grief and shame, it fills the future with perspectives. And the denial of the past furthers the affairs of death, precisely because it focuses exclusively on the present. The degree of accountability regarding yesterday is the measure of a stable tomorrow.[5]

Referring to the outbreak of neo-Nazism in Germany at that time, Bethge went on to speak about the danger and destructive power of delusion about the past. 'But', he said, 'anyone who accepts the burden of the past, struggling "against forgetting", will experience a healing scarring-over of the wounds. Scarring, however, makes for mature people.'[6] The only way forward was to research the truth, to tell the story honestly and imaginatively to new generations, and to engage in acts of regular 'liturgical' commemoration. That was why it was so important to learn how to mediate memories in a way that spoke to the present. 'There is no life', Bethge declared, 'without its calendar' of such events:

> There are places, stones, graves, documents, dates and gatherings. These are moments for new commitments. What has been identified through research and mediation can lead to new identifications. Things are renounced and others are promised; we say No to some and Yes to others. Commemoration reaches out for a renewed world.[7]

One place that had a particular significance for the Bethges was, of course, the Bonhoeffer family house at Marienburger Allee 43, standing alongside the Schleicher house, no. 42, where Renate had grown up. In 1983, Bethge initiated a project to restore the house and make it a place where Bonhoeffer's legacy could be remembered. His dream came to fulfilment in June 1987 when the 'Bonhoeffer-Haus' was dedicated. In his dedication address, Bethge recalled the significance of the house both as a private home full of family memory, and as a gathering place for those

---

5. Eberhard Bethge, 'Research – Mediation – Commemoration: Steps to Combat Forgetting', in Bethge, *Friendship and Resistance*, p. 105.

6. Bethge, *Friendship and Resistance*, p. 105.

7. Bethge, *Friendship and Resistance*, p. 110.

engaged in the resistance.[8] To enter this house was to experience again the spirit of all that it had meant in the past, and to bring it into the present. This was one of several places that the Bethges helped restore as memorials; another was the Bonhoeffer-Haus in Stettin. Memories, to be effective, need more than words; they needed consecrated places where people can visit and reflect, and contemporary responses that embody the truth they represent.

Mindful of the fact that the changes in Germany were paralleled by equally remarkable changes in apartheid South Africa, and that both called for new initiatives in remembering the past rightly, Bethge was excited by the establishment of the South Africa Truth and Reconciliation Commission (TRC). In many ways the TRC seemed, for Bethge, to provide the model for dealing with the past in a way that led to healing and reconciliation. In so far as he was able, he followed the progress of the TRC and in May 1999 Bethge was present in Berlin when the Bonhoeffer Prize was awarded to the TRC, represented by Desmond Tutu, its chair, and Alex Boraine, the deputy chair. As the citation indicated, the award recognized in the work of the Commission the spirit of Dietrich Bonhoeffer's witness, civil courage and Christian reconciliation in the world.[9] Bethge was personally delighted. His long-standing hope for justice in South Africa was being fulfilled in a way that united it with his hope for a new Germany chastened by its past and renewed by remembering rightly. But this required not only reuniting East and West in a way that was just; more especially it demanded dealing with the Holocaust.

Bethge, Bonhoeffer and the Holocaust

During the last decades of his life Bethge became particularly burdened by memories of the Holocaust. This led him to embark on an intensive study of the issues and a campaign to get his own

---

8. Eberhard Bethge, 'Einweihung Marienburger Allee 43', delivered 1 June 1987, *Bonhoeffer Rundbrief* 25 (October 1987), pp. 4–10.

9. See Christian Gremmels' account of the event, 'Versöhnung braucht Wahrheit', *Bonhoeffer Rundbrief* 59 (June 1999), pp. 7–10.

Church of the Rhineland to reconsider its present attitudes towards Jews and Judaism. It also led him into conversation with many Jews and Holocaust survivors, and to participation in seminars and conferences on the Holocaust and Jewish–Christian relations. In his address to Gegen Vergessen – Für Demokratie, previously mentioned, Bethge spoke of this burden, recounting his own painful experience of being rejected by Jews as a German irrespective of what Bonhoeffer, the resisters or he himself had done, and of the need to come to terms with that rejection. There was, he remarked, no way to escape that burden, no way to get rid of recent history, no way whereby even 'good Germans' could look sideways and point at others as the guilty ones.

As intimated in the Introduction, Bethge's contribution to the German response to the Holocaust, and to the church's attempt to rethink Jewish–Christian relations in the light of it, is one that requires much fuller treatment than can be provided here. All we can do is to provide an overview and locate Bethge's role within the wider context of the debate. But it is clear that nothing challenged him more than this issue in retrieving Bonhoeffer's legacy, in developing his own theology, and above all in thinking about his faith in Christ and his membership of the church. So it was that in entering this emotionally charged and controversial arena, Bethge not only gradually recognized the need to reconsider honestly what Bonhoeffer had said and done with regard to the Jews, but moved beyond Bonhoeffer into unfamiliar territory.

For the first several decades after 1945, the persecution of the Jews, the history of theological and ecclesiastical anti-Semitism and anti-Judaism, and the Holocaust itself received only brief mention in most histories of the German church struggle and the German resistance. In much of the historical literature until the 1970s, the genocide of the European Jews was treated as separate, almost marginal history. This changed with the emergence of Holocaust studies as a distinct field and, more importantly, with the growing documentation of how individuals and institutions had responded to the persecution and murder of the Jews. Such studies were slow in gaining recognition from the Confessing Church and its leaders.

In 1945, the Allied occupation authorities had classified the Confessing Church as one of the few resistance organizations in Nazi Germany. As a result its leaders had a certain status in post-war Germany, and portrayed their battles with the German Christians and their conflicts with Nazi authorities as part of a larger heroic struggle against the Nazi regime. In fact, however, most German Protestant clergy and leaders had been strongly nationalistic, many had been early supporters of the Nazi Party, and with very few exceptions they had been silent about Nazi persecution of political opponents and of the Jews. Church statements on behalf of the Jews were largely confined to support for 'non-Aryan Christians' – Christians who under Nazi racial laws were considered to be of Jewish descent. The Confessing Church was deeply divided, particularly over how to respond to state policies, and the stance of the churches in general had been one of at least public compliance with Nazi policies. Church opposition had been largely focused on the extremist Deutsche Christen and those areas in which state policies presented problems for the church.

Only gradually did more critical studies of the Confessing Church emerge to offer a corrective. In the 1960s, Wolfgang Gerlach wrote a dissertation on the Confessing Church's record with respect to the Jews. It was a damning portrait in which Gerlach published the explicitly anti-Jewish statements of prominent church leaders such as Otto Dibelius, under whom Bethge had served in Berlin, and traced both the Confessing Church's active complicity in and passive silence about the persecution of the Jews. Gerlach's work was so controversial that he had to fight for its acceptance as a dissertation, and only in 1987 was it published in Germany.[10]

Even as this more critical portrait of the Confessing Church emerged, however, Bonhoeffer appeared immune. Gerlach's work singled him out as one of the few Confessing Christians to resist on behalf of the Jews. Most works conflated Bonhoeffer's

---

10. It was published in the United States as *And the Witnesses Were Silent: The Confessing Church and the Jews* (Lincoln, Nebr.: University of Nebraska Press, 2000).

role in the resistance, his clear opposition to Nazism, his work for the Confessing Church, and his execution by the Nazis into a clear narrative of resistance in which it was viewed as self-evident that Bonhoeffer had been driven at least in part by his outrage against Nazi anti-Jewish policies. This was underscored by the fact that his twin sister, Sabine Leibholz, was married to a man of Jewish descent and that a close friend, Franz Hildebrandt, was also affected by Nazi anti-Jewish laws; both, as we have seen, were forced to emigrate to England in the late 1930s.

There were certainly indications, in both Bonhoeffer's writings and actions, that he viewed the Nazi persecution of the Jews with horror. In his 1933 essay *Die Kirche vor der Judenfrage* (The Church Faces the Jewish Question),[11] Bonhoeffer raised the question of how the church should react when state authority had ceased to be legitimate, and concluded that the church might face an obligation not only to help the victims but eventually to resist and undermine the state. In 1935, as we have seen, he had taken his Finkenwalde students, including Bethge, to the Steglitz synod to demonstrate on behalf of a church statement that would have condemned Nazi anti-Jewish laws, and there are other glimpses of such sentiments from his correspondence and from accounts of his students and friends. Outrage at the persecution of the Jews was a clear motive for some of his colleagues in the conspiracy, including his brother-in-law Hans von Dohnanyi.[12]

In the volumes of Bonhoeffer's writings, however, there is little actual documentary proof that Nazi anti-Jewish policies were a driving motive for Bonhoeffer's action. Even Bonhoeffer's famous statement 'Only the one who cries out for the Jews can sing Gregorian chant' may be apocryphal; it was never written down and none of his students, including Bethge, could definitively pinpoint the occasion, or even the year, when he made it. Throughout the 1930s, most of Bonhoeffer's public statements

---

11. English translation titled, 'The Church and the Jewish Question', in Bonhoeffer, *No Rusty Swords*, pp. 217–25.

12. See Winfried Meyer, *Unternehmen Sieben: Eine Rettungsaktion* (Frankfurt am Main: Verlag Anton Hain, 1993).

and writings focused on issues of church independence and the identity of the Confessing Church, while his resistance and prison writings concentrated on the necessity to rethink religious identity as a result of his experience under Nazism. While he was undoubtedly far ahead of other theologians in speaking out on behalf of the Jews, as in the draft document he penned for the Bethel Confession,[13] something later recognized by Barth in a letter to Bethge,[14] his clearest public condemnations of Nazi racial laws focused exclusively on the plight of 'non-Aryan Christians'. And whereas his essay 'The Church and the Jewish Question' was a radical break with Lutheran thinking that opened the door for the church's political resistance against the state, with respect to Judaism it was traditionally supersessionist. Bonhoeffer quoted Luther on Jewish suffering as the punishment for the crucifixion of Christ, and concluded that the ultimate resolution of 'the Jewish question' would be the Jews' conversion to Christianity.[15] Even in his later writings, notably the *Ethics*, there is some ambiguity. While, on the one hand, in his chapter on 'Heritage and Decay', Bonhoeffer strongly asserts the Jewishness of Jesus Christ (that in itself took courage in Nazi Germany),[16] there is much in that same chapter that supports a view of Christendom that could so easily lead to anti-Judaism.[17]

With regard to the Holocaust, then, most early interpreters of Bonhoeffer assumed that his clear and undisputed record of resistance against the Nazi state was based upon his solidarity with the Jewish victims of Nazism. As Bethge himself would later write, his isolated statements on the issue, coupled with his resistance, appeared to the post-war generation 'like an exciting continuity. For Bonhoeffer himself, however, it was hardly ever

---

13. Bonhoeffer, *No Rusty Swords*, pp. 236–8.

14. Barth, *Fragments Grave and Gay*, p. 119.

15. Bonhoeffer, *No Rusty Swords*, p. 222.

16. Bonhoeffer, *Ethics*, p. 105.

17. While Bonhoeffer scholars differ in their interpretation of these passages, there are several pejorative references to Pharisees in *Ethics* that some interpret as anti-Judaic. See, for example, Bonhoeffer, *Ethics*, pp. 309–15.

clear and decisive.'[18] Bethge was far more cautious than many other scholars about drawing conclusions on Bonhoeffer's thinking in this area. Indeed, he tackled head-on the question whether Bonhoeffer had been, in fact, a bystander, one who tried to look the other way rather than confront the issues directly. Undoubtedly there was ambiguity, as he argued in a paper written in 1988 on the occasion of the fiftieth anniversary of 'Crystal Night'.[19] Yet one could not deny that there was also a remarkable continuity in showing solidarity with the persecuted, including the Jews, and that this was a driving force of his life.

Bethge, as we have noted, initially began to address the issue of the Holocaust within the larger context of the necessary German confrontation with the Nazi past. As in other areas, this occurred to a great extent in conversation with colleagues in other countries as well as in Germany, amongst them Martin Stöhr, director of the lay academy at Arnoldsheim and a key figure along with Bethge in Jewish–Christian dialogue in Germany,[20] and Franklin Littell in the United States. Littell's role was particularly important. Already in 1958, Bethge had written the name of Littell on the outline to his Harvard lecture, next to a point he made about rethinking Nazi history. A Methodist minister who had been present in Germany at liberation and remained in the country during the early post-war period, Littell wrote an early work on the German churches under Nazism.[21] He then became interested in Jewish–Christian dialogue in the wake of the Holocaust and would devote his life's work to exploring the failure of Christianity and its churches to withstand Nazism. Eventually he founded the Annual Scholars' Conference on the Holocaust and the German Church Struggle and invited Bethge to participate as a speaker at the first Conference, held in 1970. As a result,

---

18. Bethge, 'One of the Silent Bystanders?', in *Friendship and Resistance*, p. 71.

19. Bethge, 'One of the Silent Bystanders?', in *Friendship and Resistance*, p. 71.

20. See Martin Stöhr, 'Juden, Christen, Deutsche: Anmerken zur Geschichte eines Dialogs', in *Wie eine Flaschenpost*, pp. 311–19.

21. Franklin Littell, *The German Phoenix* (Garden City, NY: Doubleday, 1960).

Bethge came into conversation not only with Christians working on this question, but with Jewish scholars who forced him to reread German church history – and Bonhoeffer's own writings – more critically.[22] It was, as he said on more than one occasion, a painful process, one that brought him into conflict – once again – with his church. In a 1976 essay, 'The Holocaust and Christian Anti-Semitism: Perspectives of a Christian Survivor', Bethge observed that

> there is that identity of mine which, burdened by the Holocaust, longs to be independent from the body to which I belong: my Church organization. . . . But there is that other identity of mine: the churchman who does not want to cut off his links and bonds with that organization which apparently is so scared about its identity. And is it not true that its inherited identity is threatened by the demands of the Holocaust to an extent known only to very few in the churches?[23]

Re-examining his own history in the Confessing Church, Bethge described the phases of his attitudes toward the Jews: of 'indifferent innocence up until 1934', 'blind fighting up to 1945' and, afterward, 'the ongoing phase of painful survival'.[24] While he had indeed fought against the Nazi state, he realized in retrospect that none of his Confessing colleagues, including Bonhoeffer, had listened to or discussed the work of their great German Jewish contemporaries Martin Buber, Franz Rosenzweig, and Leo Baeck. While he and other radical young pastors in the Confessing Church had focused on the plight of 'non-Aryan Christians', there had been no communication, let alone solidarity, with the Jewish religious community. The Barmen confession, the founding document of the Confessing Church, said nothing about the persecution of the Jews. Recalling an

---

22. See Eberhard Bethge, 'The Holocaust and Christian Anti-Semitism: Perspectives of a Christian Survivor', *Union Seminary Quarterly Review* 32:3–4 (1977), p. 148.
23. Bethge, 'The Holocaust and Christian Anti-Semitism', p. 142.
24. Bethge, 'The Holocaust and Christian Anti-Semitism', p. 142.

incident from his university days in which Jewish students were harassed and beaten, Bethge realized that at the time his outrage 'reflected a feeling for the underdog' but not an awareness of the anti-Semitic sentiment that was the source of the incident or of the passivity of onlookers, including Bethge.

Bethge's confrontation with his own past made him realize 'how even in Bonhoeffer's writings a theological anti-Judaism is present'[25] and this led Bethge to seek 'a dignified integration of guilt and new faith'.[26] Like the Barmen Declaration, the German Protestant Church's post-war statements of guilt in Stuttgart and Darmstadt made no mention of the Jews or the Holocaust. A statement adopted by the church synod in Weissensee in 1950 acknowledged 'that by omission and silence we became implicated before the God of mercy in the outrage which has been perpetrated against the Jews by people of our nation',[27] but as Bethge noted, this was still 'a language of distance' that was 'insufficient' to address the profound nature of what had happened.

Bethge decided to take a leading role within his own church. In 1975 the Evangelical Church of Germany published a study, *Jews and Christians*, which was distributed to churches throughout the country. Yet as Bethge noted, the document was intentionally distributed for study, not as an official position of the German Protestant Church, and it had three essential flaws: it did not renounce Christian proselytization of Jews, it failed to address the issue of theodicy, and it failed to address directly the Holocaust and the issue of Christian complicity in that historical event.[28]

Bethge's critique of this document led him to push his own regional church, the Church of the Rhineland, to take a stronger, more binding position. In preparation for the 1980 Rhineland synod Bethge led a commission to address the issue, and he

---

25. Bethge, 'The Holocaust and Christian Anti-Semitism', p. 148.

26. Bethge, 'The Holocaust and Christian Anti-Semitism', p. 153.

27. For the entire text of the Weissensee statement on the Jews, see Matthew Hockenos, *A Church Divided: German Protestants Confront the Nazi Past* (Bloomington, Ind.: Indiana University Press, 2004), appendix 8.

28. Bethge's critique of the document is in 'The Holocaust and Christian Anti-Semitism', pp. 150–3.

invited Jewish leaders to join the commission. Bethge's own hopes were

> that we would start to reread our New Testament sources, together with Jewish experts . . . that we would reread the early Church fathers . . . that we could begin a new defining of our creedal identity and liturgical customs, one which would show that creeds and practices cannot remain untouched by the Holocaust . . . that we could enter anew the debate about the messianic event . . . that I could transfer these hopes to friends in my Church without losing or severing my allegiance to my Church – and at the same time without losing the help of my new Jewish friends.[29]

As a result of Bethge's work, the Rhineland synod in 1980 approved a statement, 'Towards a Renewal of the Relationship of Christians and Jews'. It fell somewhat short of Bethge's expectations and did not manage to surmount the obstacle that confronts all post-Holocaust Christian theology: the challenge of understanding salvation history in a way that does not usurp Jewish understandings of the Judaic faith.[30] Still, as Hannah Holtschneider writes, the statement 'has to be welcomed as the first theological statement that reflects on the Holocaust and defines itself as a contextual approach to Christian-Jewish relations in Germany'.[31]

With the Rhineland synod document, Bethge had come into his own. Although he continued to refer to Bonhoeffer's writings and wrestle with their post-Holocaust implications, the titles of his public speeches and publications on these matters during the 1980s focused on the larger issues. Hence, while they can be viewed as an important part of Bonhoeffer interpretation (and many of them are correctives or amplifications to Bethge's

---

29. Bethge, 'The Holocaust and Christian Anti-Semitism', p. 154.

30. For a detailed discussion of the Rhineland document, see Hannah Holtschneider, *German Protestants Remember the Holocaust: Theology and the Construction of Collective Memory* (Munster: Lit, 2001), pp. 37–62.

31. Holtschneider, *German Protestants Remember*, p. 59.

earlier writings) they represent Bethge's own theology. In particular, an essay on the Holocaust and Protestantism was an
extensive reflection and elaboration on the meaning of theology
and resistance after Bonhoeffer, drawing upon Bonhoeffer's (and
Bethge's) experience and activism, but bringing it into dialogue
with the lessons Bethge had learned in the decades after his
friend's death.[32]

Throughout all this Bethge was an unusual figure in the
German Protestant scene: a self-described 'free Christian
scholar' with a need to be both part of his church and nonetheless
independent of it.[33] His role and his outspokenness brought
admiration from some quarters and condemnation from others.
In 1982 the Jewish philosopher Emil Fackenheim wrote Bethge:

> It must be most extraordinarily hard for a Christian thinker to
> rethink his theology in the light of an event so terrible as the
> Holocaust . . . How much harder must it be for you when it
> involves one who was your friend, and who is thought of as a
> beloved friend even by such as myself who know of him only
> from his writings and reports . . . That you should think of
> dialogue with Jews (not about Jews!) as an unexpected gift
> virtually revives my faith in the enterprise when on many
> occasions I was close to losing it . . .[34]

But Bethge's increasingly critical examination of the past
brought anger from some in Germany. In 1989, after giving a talk
that was critical of the anti-Semitism of some resistance figures,
Bethge replied to one German critic with a long and thoughtful
letter. Noting that the 'old tradition' of Christian anti-Judaism
had converged with the radical anti-Semitism of Nazism, Bethge
wrote:

---

32. Eberhard Bethge, 'Schoah (Holocaust) und Protestantismus', in *Der
Holocaust und die Protestanten: Analysen einer Verstrickung*, ed. Jochen-
Christoph Kaiser and Martin Greschat (Frankfurt am Main: Athenäum,
1988), pp. 1–38.

33. Bethge, 'The Holocaust and Christian Anti-Semitism', p. 142.

34. Letter to Bethge, 12 December 1982, Bethge papers.

we have simply been long, long blind and – without having been radical anti-Semites – nonetheless we were in our language and consciousness the bearers of unholy potential. I see the problem in that even extraordinary resistance fighters were at the same time still sunk in the kind of language and attitudes whose anti-Jewish content could only be made clear decades after 1945 . . . But the problem . . . must be seen and must lead to new insights among Christians.[35]

In the letter, and in virtually all of his speeches, Bethge spoke of 'we'. It was a way of disarming his critics, but it reflected a sincere sense of shared guilt and shared responsibility.

In 1989 Bethge gave a talk, titled 'How Should We Commemorate?', at the German national lay assembly, the Kirchentag, which stressed the three necessary aspects of remembering the past: researching; publicizing and changing the public consciousness through the historical task; and finally commemorating, an act that not only witnesses to the past but 'renews and fulfills engagement' in the present. Commemorating, he said, had to be more than just remembering:

remembering seeks forgiveness as the opium for the uncleansed; commemorating confronts that which cannot be cleansed . . . here it is not a matter of siblings ending a long fight in reconciliation; rather, it is that Cain killed Abel, and that Cain must continue to live with that'.[36]

Bethge's stark conclusion was no doubt reinforced by his encounter with the custodians of Yad Vashem, the Israeli memorial site that commemorates the 'righteous Gentiles' who rescued Jews during the Holocaust.[37] During the 1980s, and

---

35. Letter of 19 March 1989, Bethge papers; the recipient has been kept anonymous.

36. Eberhard Bethge, 'Wie gedenken wir? Gedenktage und -orte. Notwendigkeit und Verlegenheiten', address given on 9 June 1989, text in Bethge papers.

37. See David P. Gushee, *The Righteous Gentiles of the Holocaust: A Christian Interpretation* (Minneapolis: Fortress Press, 1994).

more recently, applications were submitted on behalf of Hans von Dohnanyi and of Dietrich Bonhoeffer; both were turned down (although in 2004 Yad Vashem recognized Hans von Dohnanyi as a righteous Gentile; subsequent applications on behalf of Bonhoeffer have not been successful).[38] Bethge's correspondence indicates his disappointment at Yad Vashem's decision, yet throughout his other writings on the Holocaust there is a constant acknowledgement of the complexity of the history. In 1985, a US journalist interviewed him about the controversy that followed President Ronald Reagan's visit to the concentration camp memorial at Bitberg-Bergen Belsen. Bethge explained how this history felt to Germans:

> You have a wound, and the healing is a long process. In this act of healing there will be a scar. The scar will be seen all the time . . . in a slow process, more or less, the wound will heal. The wound will not disappear. The signs will stay . . .

At the same time, he said, confronting the Holocaust was important for Germans: 'It's opening a door. It is really something you are afraid to come to, that point. But when you come to that point then you know what grace really is.'[39]

Bethge's role in post-Holocaust conversation in Germany is best understood as part of a much longer and as yet incomplete process of evolving Jewish–German and Jewish–Christian dialogue in the wake of the Holocaust. His conclusion ('that Cain killed Abel, and that Cain must continue to live with that') was that some matters could not be 'resolved', at least in his lifetime. This required a new way of living as a Christian and a German in ongoing dialogue with the Jewish victims of the Holocaust. Only in this way was it possible to begin to remember rightly. But it also required rethinking classical Christology, a subject that was

---

38. The correspondence regarding the earlier applications is in the Bethge papers.

39. Interview with Sharon Lehman, 1985; an unedited transcript of the interview, titled 'Response to Bitberg-Bergen Belsen', is in Bethge's private papers.

particularly perplexing and difficult for Bethge. For how could one truly believe in Jesus as the Messiah and Son of God and, at the same time, not be supersessionist in one's understanding of the relationship between Christianity and Judaism? Could Bethge remain true to Christian tradition, especially to the Trinitarian and Christological affirmations of the classic creeds, with a clear conscience?

The more he wrestled with these questions, the more Bethge found it necessary to express his faith in Jesus as the Christ in ways that led away from any Christian triumphalism and exclusiveness. Perhaps his most significant attempt to do so is found in his paper on 'Christology and the First Commandment', presented at the International Conference of Christians and Jews at Oxford in July 1988.[40] Bethge was forced to the conclusion that whatever else the confession of Christ meant, it could not mean a disregard for the First Commandment, the commandment that forbids idolatry. More and more he was convinced that Christian triumphalism, so often associated with the confession of Christ as Lord in pursuing national and ecclesiastical self-interest, was nothing other than a form of idolatry. The question, then, was, how to remain faithful to the first article of the Barmen Declaration – that 'Jesus Christ is the One Word of God whom we must trust and obey' – and to the First Commandment and the *Sh'ma*: 'Hear, O Israel . . . I am the Lord your God . . . you shall have no other gods before me' (Deut. 5.1, 6).

For Bethge, the confession of Christ must mean nothing less than an affirmation of the First Commandment; it was a confession that opposed idolatry. The clue for Bethge, as for Bonhoeffer, was to be found in Luther's 'theology of the cross' or *theologia crucis*, for this had to do with the question of the nature of the God who Christians worship. The God of Jesus Christ is not the triumphalist God who gives legitimacy to Christian

40. Eberhard Bethge, 'Christology and the First Commandment', in *Jews and Christians During and After the Holocaust*, vol. 1 of *Remembering for the Future: Working Papers and Addenda*, ed. Yehuda Bauer, Alice Eckhardt, Franklin Littell, Elisabeth Maxwell, Robert Maxwell and David Patterson (Oxford and New York: Pergamon Press, 1989), pp. 690–701.

crusades, but the God who is on the side of the victims, the oppressed, the poor. Thus every Christological statement raised the question of the God in whom we really believe; had that God had become an idol, or was that God truly the God of Jesus Christ?

In the concluding paragraph to his paper on Christology and the First Commandment, Bethge provides us with a succinct statement of both his commitment to the Christ of Christian tradition and his concern for a Christology without idolatry:

> As to my own position, it has clearly been determined by the traditions in which I was raised; it is founded upon the ancient, more or less clearly formulated Christologies of tradition; it is determined further by my professional responsibility for the protection of Christian teaching and the defence against its perversions; it is formed by the communal internationalization of expressions and forms of the hymnal and the liturgy.

But, he continued,

> As to my ethical-political socialization, this has been effected in a geographical, historical and 'Christian' framework which I cannot escape. Given this enclosure I can only hope that time and again there will be someone there – be this Jew or Gentile – who will warn me against the dangers not only for the faith but also for the persons I oversee, when Christ is transformed into an idol. The same holds for the Church at large. Those who confess belief in Christ need to have at their side, as close as possible, those who daily pray the *Sh'ma Jisrael*.[41]

How strongly he felt about this was revealed in the interview he gave on the occasion of Reagan's visit to Bitberg-Bergen Belsen. The First Commandment must, he said in answer to a question, 'be the meaning of everything else we say about Trinitarian and Christological issues so that Christ does not become a pagan god . . . Christology must never become idolatry.'[42]

---

41. Bethge, 'Christology and the First Commandment', p. 701.
42. Interview with Lehman, 1985.

14

A Remarkably Fulfilled Life

After Eberhard Bethge's retirement in 1976, the Bethges moved to their new home in Wachtberg-Villiprott, near Bonn. This brought them close to Renate's sister Dorothee and her husband, Karl Dietrich Bracher, the noted historian of the Third Reich.[1] As in Rengsdorf, so in Villiprott, the Bethge home became a place of pilgrimage for people interested in Bonhoeffer. Even in retirement, the Bethges shared their hospitality, knowledge and insight as remarkably as they had done in Rengsdorf.[2] Indeed, apart from no longer being responsible for the pastoral college, the Bethge's life and work continued seamlessly. Yet as the years passed, many of the visitors who came to Villiprott from all over the world came not just to talk about Bonhoeffer but to enjoy the company and friendship of the Bethges. Even when the discussion turned to Bonhoeffer, as it invariably did, the focus was often on contemporary issues facing the church and society. Well into retirement, Bethge's theological insights remained clear and incisive, always adding fresh perspective to any conversation.

On the occasion of his seventieth birthday in 1979, Bethge received the Dr Leopold Lucas Prize from the University of Tübingen as well as a Festschrift celebrating his life and achievements. Entitled *Wie eine Flaschenpost*, it documented the extent to which Bethge's contribution was recognized by his friends and

---

1. See for example Karl Dietrich Bracher, *The German Dictatorship: the Origins, Structure and Consequences of National Socialism* (London: Penguin, 1973).

2. See, for example, 'Zu Gast bei Bethges', speeches given at the celebration of Eberhard Bethge's eightieth birthday, 2 September 1989, at the Protestant research institute (FEST) in Heidelberg.

colleagues in Germany, and by the larger ecumenical family that stretched around the world.[3] At the venerable age of three-score years and ten, it might have been assumed that Bethge would have felt satisfied with what he had achieved and that now at last, five years into retirement, he would take time off to enjoy his remaining years. Enjoy them he certainly did, but as we have already seen in the previous two chapters, not through slacking off. Indeed, ten years later, when colleagues and family gathered yet again on the occasion of Bethge's eightieth birthday, they could continue to celebrate a still remarkably active life. At a seminar at the University of Heidelberg to mark the event, Bethge was lauded for the special contribution he had made to theology, church history and Jewish–Christian relations.[4] And another ten years lay ahead. Not only did these twenty years beyond his seventieth birthday enable Bethge to continue doing what he had done previously by way of writing, lecturing, travelling, and enabling others to pursue their own projects, but he also energetically presided over the International Bonhoeffer Society and embarked on the massive project that became the sixteen volumes of the critical edition of the *Dietrich Bonhoeffer Werke*.

Senior Colleague

Although the International Bonhoeffer Society (IBS) had been founded prior to Bethge's retirement, much of its growth occurred afterwards, with the second Congress taking place in Geneva in 1976 shortly before the move from Rengsdorf to Wachtberg-Villiprott. Coinciding with the seventieth anniversary of Bonhoeffer's birth, the Geneva Congress was a poignant occasion, attended as it was by several of Bonhoeffer's family, including his twin sister Sabine and Maria von Wedemeyer, with whom Bethge had retained contact over the years. There were

---

3. *Wie eine Flaschenpost: Ökumenische Briefe und Beiträge für Eberhard Bethge*, ed. Hans Pfeifer, with Heinz Eduard Tödt and Ferdinand Schlingensiepen (Munich: Chr. Kaiser Verlag), 1979.

4. See Tödt, 'Eberhard Bethge als Theologe und Zeitgesichtforscher'.

also several other participants who had been students of Bonhoeffer, or who had known him personally, all of them also close friends of the Bethges.[5]

The keen participation of the Bethges together with the involvement of family and former Bonhoeffer students added immeasurably to the life and significance of the IBS, its various sections and congresses, providing a link with the past and making an invaluable contribution to the contemporary discussion. Over the following years such participation would gradually dwindle, but several of Bonhoeffer's students continued to attend the meetings of the two German Sections, and some also participated in the International Congresses until the late nineteen-eighties. These were held at four-year intervals: Oxford (1980); Hirschluch, East Germany (1984); Amsterdam (1988); New York (1992); Cape Town (1996); Berlin (2000); and Rome (2004). Apart from the last two, the Bethges were always in attendance, giving keynote presentations, and providing the genial guidance that made the events so memorable. The Congresses and other meetings were, at one and the same time, celebrations of friendship that pursued intellectual rigour, and opportunities to foster interest in Bonhoeffer both within and beyond the boundaries of academic theology and the church. After Eberhard's death in 2000, Renate continued to participate in the life of the IBS, attending the Rome Congress in 2004.

In fostering international research on Bonhoeffer, the IBS fulfilled an important role in enabling Bethge to achieve his own goals. This was so at a number of levels. One was the development of an expanding international network of people, including younger scholars, who helped to foster interest in Bonhoeffer through their own research and participation in conferences, seminars and workshops. In Germany itself Bethge received much collegial support from a notable group of scholars. These included Ernst Feil, Christian Gremmels, Hans Pfeifer, Ilse Tödt, and Bethge's old comrade and friend from Finkenwalde, Albrecht Schönherr, as well as Heinz Eduard Tödt and Wolfgang Huber, whose Bonhoeffer seminar at the University of

---

5. See above, Chap. 9, n. 2.

Heidelberg stimulated much research. These scholars provided the core editorial leadership for the new critical edition of the *Dietrich Bonhoeffer Werke*.

The *Dietrich Bonhoeffer Werke* was an enormous undertaking for Bethge, but it was also the fitting culmination to all he had sought to achieve in preserving and handing on Bonhoeffer's literary estate. All of Bonhoeffer's writings, including his books, papers and essays, and his copious correspondence, together with letters he had received and other supporting documents, many of them previously unpublished, were brought together in sixteen volumes, some of them extending to well over a thousand pages. Each of the volumes is introduced with a lengthy essay, concluded with an equally detailed postscript evaluation, and provided with extensive critical documentation and notes. While Bethge himself obviously did not do all the work himself, he was the driving force behind the project, involved in a considerable amount of research, consultation and writing. And everything he did, he did with meticulous care for detail and accuracy. If we keep in mind that this was not all he was doing, not even all he was doing by way of writing and publishing, the completion of the *Werke* at this stage of his life and before his death was an amazing achievement.

Amidst all this the Bethges continued to travel frequently to other countries. Between 1978 and 1993 they visited Poland, Hungary, Ireland, Canada, Japan, Korea, Czechoslovakia and, of course, the United States on many occasions, where Bethge was in regular demand as a lecturer and speaker. And their travels, whether in Europe or overseas, certainly did not end in 1993, even though long-distance travelling became more onerous than before.

The visit to Japan in April 1981 was of particular interest, not least because of the cultural differences that the Bethges experienced.[6] A Japanese Bonhoeffer Society had been in existence since 1978, and a small group of Japanese theologians had begun to attend the International Bonhoeffer Congresses. Professor

---

6. See Renate Bethge, 'Eindrücke in Japan', *Bonhoeffer Rundbrief* 11 (June 1981), pp. 10–18.

Hiroshi Murakami, the president of the Japanese Committee, was particularly active, and it was at his invitation that the Bethges visited Japan. Bethge was interested to discover the relevance of Bonhoeffer's 'non-religious interpretation' of Christianity for the dialogue with Buddhist scholars.[7] Also of relevance was Bonhoeffer's response to militarism and Germany's war guilt, subjects that were burning topics of discussion among the Japanese Christians as they sought to come to terms with their past, not least in relation to Korea. And, for Japanese Christians, as for Christians elsewhere who had been influenced by Bonhoeffer, there was the key question of what it meant to confess Christ in response to his question 'Who is Jesus Christ, for us today?' On the way back to Germany, the Bethges stopped over in South Korea, where they discovered that Bonhoeffer's book *Discipleship* had been banned by the authorities as subversive!

The outreach of the English-speaking section of the IBS, centred in the United States but including members from Canada, South Africa and elsewhere, spread well beyond the confines of scholars and seminaries, attracting a variety of people from different disciplines and walks of life, as well as pastors and priests of different denominations, into the circle of its influence. Without this wide and growing interest in Bonhoeffer, engendered by Bethge's presence and lectures, the possibility of publishing Bonhoeffer's writings in English may not have been financially feasible. Indicative of interest in the Bonhoeffer legacy beyond the confines of the academy and the institutional church was the production of a number of documentary films on Bonhoeffer's life, as well as an opera, and the Bonhoeffer-Triptychon of cantatas based on his poetry. Bethge and other members of the Society acted as consultants for much of this. This made not only Bonhoeffer more widely known, but also Bethge's own role as his friend and interpreter.

Visiting North America was particularly special for the Bethges because it provided an opportunity for them to visit their daughter Sabine, who had settled in Connecticut. As in

---

7. Eberhard Bethge, 'Zu Gast bei japanischen Bonhoeffer-Gesellschaft, April 1981', *Bonhoeffer Rundbrief* 11 (June 1981), pp. 3–10.

Germany, so in North America, the Bethges were surrounded by
a group of scholars whose friendship stretched over the years and
meant a great deal to them. This led to many invitations to visit
seminaries, colleges and churches across the continent, though
the Bethges were always delighted when they could spend time
in New York City with its many cultural attractions and its
reminders of the times Bonhoeffer had spent there. Indeed,
the Bonhoeffer connection with Union Theological Seminary
remained very important and was sustained and developed by
the Bethges. Eberhard was several times a visiting professor, as
well as the Broadway Scholar in Residence, which required that
he preach regularly in the Broadway Presbyterian Church nearby. Union Seminary was also an ideal location in opening doors
and providing possibilities for dialogue with Jewish and other
scholars in the area who were interested in the Holocaust. In
1984 Bethge was awarded the Union Medal for his outstanding
contribution to scholarship. Ten years later, in February 1994, a
Dietrich Bonhoeffer Professorship for Theology and Ethics was
established at Union, funded by generous gifts from both the
United States and Germany.

While the Bethges loved being in New York, they also appreciated the generosity and hospitality of many other smaller
centres around the country. One such place was Lynchburg
College in Virginia, where they were both honoured with doctor-
ates.[8] Staying in Lynchburg, the headquarters of Moral Majority
leader Jerry Falwell, also provided an opportunity for them to
experience the heartbeat of American fundamentalism. The
Bethges were particularly bothered by what they experienced
when they visited Falwell's church because so much that was
referred to as 'American Christianity' reminded them of aspects
of the German Christianity of the 1930s. Eberhard later wrote,

> As we entered the foyer, an usher stepped forward and gave
> me two badges to fasten to my lapel: the one on the left said,

---

8. The Bethge's host, Patrick Kelley, another member of the IBS,
became a good friend and regular visitor to the Bethge home in Wachtberg-
Villiprott.

Jesus First and on the right, one with an American flag . . . I could not help but think myself in Germany in 1933 . . . Of course, Christ, but a German Christ; of course, 'Jesus First', but an American Jesus! And so to the long history of faith and its executors another chapter is being added of a mixed image of Christ, of another syncretism on the American model, undisturbed by any knowledge of that centuries-long and sad history.

Bethge added some remarks that have an uncanny contemporary ring to them:

> The disturbing fact is this new element, the battle for a 'Christian nation' against humanism. The flag has always been in the churches, but now it has come to represent the new threat of binding the political structure to an ideology, which models a whole new educational system, and a new kind of representation in Washington, and a newly interpreted Constitution.[9]

For Bethge, who had a great love for the United States and the democratic vision of its Founding Fathers, and who enjoyed visiting there, these signs were disturbing. He could only hope that they would not develop along the lines he feared they might.

At the Sixth International Bonhoeffer Congress, held at Union Seminary in 1992, Bethge strongly supported the proposal that the next Congress should be in Cape Town. Bethge was not only sure that Cape Town would be able to host the event following the changes that had taken place in the country, coterminous with the changes in eastern Europe, but he was also convinced that it was important for Bonhoeffer studies that the event take place in a context where Bonhoeffer's legacy had become so relevant. But even as he supported this proposal he was aware that in four years' time he might not be well enough to travel the distance. Nevertheless, he kept hoping, and already in 1994 he

---

9. Eberhard Bethge, preface written in September 1985 for a book by Michael Ryan, Bethge papers. The book was apparently never published.

was thinking about the lecture he would give, sensing 'that it might be one of the last public utterances I will make':

> In our present situation I think again and again about the stages and problems of the history of the Bonhoeffer editing and reception. This has come for us to the foreground since we discovered what painful consequences it could have when someone has no knowledge or imagination about the first decades of the history of the edition and reception of the Bonhoeffer-corpus.[10]

This was a striking and telling comment, coming as it did towards the end of his lifetime of work on Bonhoeffer's legacy. It not only reflects Bethge's concern to ensure the faithful representation of that legacy, but also his painful awareness of how Bonhoeffer's life and witness could be abused not only through creative misuse but also through unwarranted mythmaking.

The Bethges kept on hoping to attend the Cape Town Congress, but by December 1995 it became evident that Eberhard's failing eyesight and general health would make it impossible. With great sadness, Renate outlined the reasons, ending with the comment: 'Last but not least it would have been so very interesting to be in South Africa after those long years and after the change.'[11] Nonetheless, the Bethges were deeply interested in everything that took place in Cape Town, and were delighted at the outcome. Eberhard himself contributed *in absentia* an essay to the Congress volume.[12]

'Church Father'

Bethge's role within the wider family circle of the International Bonhoeffer Society was not just that of 'paterfamilias' or custodian of the Bonhoeffer legacy, but also of a theologian in his

---

10. Letter to the author, 5 June 1994.

11. Letter to the author, 16 December 1995.

12. Bethge 'The Nonreligious Scientist and the Confessing Theologian'.

own right. His frequent papers, lectures, addresses and sermons often set the direction for further debate and research. Without this sustained scholarship the Society would certainly not have attracted the people it did, nor would it have continued for the several decades that it has. Indeed, for some Bethge had become a latter-day 'church father'. At least, this is how his old friend Paul Lehmann described him in his contribution to *Wie eine Flaschenpost*:

> So you have now become a church father. From the very beginning, as a hidden place of refuge of the church of God (*latebra Dei ecclesiae*) according to his will and workings, you have been formed as shepherd and teacher of the church (Psalm 139,13). It is no coincidence that Augustine arrived at *veritas catholica* through the death of the close friend of his youth, and was led to *verbum incarnatum*. Nor is it coincidence that the Augustinian Martin Luther became the reformer as he wrestled with the gravity of life and death. So you, dear friend, as the genuine heir of the united Reformation, have been born and called to portray and proclaim the crux and the length and breadth of the Augustinian form of Christ in the *civitas Dei*, that is, in the *true worldliness*, as the meaning and goal of human life. Put differently, you have been called as the guarantor of being Christian in your fatherland and from there far and wide throughout the world – *urbi et orbi* – to witness and to teach that which is essential in the modern world: that the figure of Jesus Christ in and of itself molds us so that it becomes formed in our own form (Galatians 4,19).[13]

Bethge probably laughed with some embarrassment when he read those words, but they were, nonetheless, apposite. He had become an important theologian not so much within the academy as within the life of the church. As the President of the Evangelical Church of the Rhineland, Manfred Kock, later said at his funeral, Bethge made a major contribution to the church as a teacher of pastors, as an interpreter of Bonhoeffer's thought in

---

13. Paul Lehmann, untitled article in *Wie eine Flaschenpost*, p. 89.

a way that had a transforming influence, and as a leader who 'before everything else, helped our Rhenish church to under- stand and deal with the denial of guilt' with regard to the Jews.[14] But, of course, Bethge's influence, though deeply rooted in the Church of the Rhineland, was, as Lehmann said, much wider. The world had become his parish.

If Bethge's stature as a church historian and scholar was demonstrated in what is now regarded as one of the classic biog- raphies of the twentieth century, his ability as a theologian can be judged from the quality of the lectures that were published in the four volumes of his collected papers between 1967 and 1991. The full extent of his many other writings published in other books and journals is evident from the bibliographies in these volumes. These four volumes, collecting some of his most seminal papers over the years from Rengsdorf until well into his retirement, demonstrate his theological stature and provide an excellent overview of the themes that he regarded as of central importance at particular times and places during these decades. In sum, these volumes contain the essence of Bethge's theological insight and help us to see his theological contribution as a whole.

In the first volume, *Ohnmacht und Mündigkeit* (1969), which contains sermons and lectures during the 1960s, the decade of the 'Honest to God debate', Bethge explored historical and theo- logical themes arising out of Bonhoeffer's theology, concentrat- ing on Christianity in a secular 'world come of age'.[15] In the second volume, *Am gegebene Ort* (1979), the breadth of Bethge's concerns is evident as he seeks to interpret Bonhoeffer's legacy for today, reflecting on the *Kirchenkampf* and the significance of Auschwitz, anti-Judaism and anti-Semitism.[16] In the third volume, *Bekennen und Widerstehen* (1984), the selection of articles is more focused. During this period, which included the

---

14. Kock, 'Funeral Eulogy', p. 11.

15. Eberhard Bethge, *Ohnmacht und Mündigkeit: Beiträge zur Zeit- geschichte und Theologie nach Dietrich Bonhoeffer* (Munich: Chr. Kaiser Verlag, 1969).

16. Eberhard Bethge, *Am gegebene Ort: Aufsätze und Reden, 1970–1979* (Munich: Chr. Kaiser Verlag, 1979).

celebration of the fortieth anniversary of the Barmen Declaration, Bethge concentrated on issues relating to confession and resistance, to the meaning of *status confessionis*, pacifism and violence.[17] The fourth volume, *Erstes Gebot und Zeitgeschichte* (1991), as the title suggests, dealt first and primarily with themes relating to Christians and Jews, the *Kirchenkampf* and anti-Semitism, Christology and anti-Judaism. But it also contained other material on Bonhoeffer, as well as other speeches and lectures that both Eberhard and Renate Bethge had given over the past ten years.[18]

As is evident from this brief overview, several major themes dominated Bethge's theological output at various stages over the years. These were determined to a large extent both by his work on Bonhoeffer and by the dominant issues of the time. Undoubtedly as the years passed his focus was increasingly on Jewish–Christian relations and the Holocaust. But he wrote and lectured on a wide variety of other topics: Christians and politics, the church struggle in South Africa, the Stuttgart Confession of Guilt, worship in a secular age, the 'church for others', modern martyrdom, exile, Christology, ministerial formation, Christian resistance, and the pastoral office. As he wrestled with these issues he combined historical and theological reflection in a way that spoke directly to many in his contemporary audience. Though he spent many long hours in careful, painstaking historical research and writing, he never lost sight of his responsibility as a preacher and teacher today. As Gremmels would later say of him:

His voice was loud and clear in the theological debates of these past decades – against racism, against apartheid, against forgetting; the unwritten seventh thesis of the Barmen Declaration; the Rhineland Synod Resolution on Renewal of Christian-Jewish Relations; theology after the Holocaust.

---

17. Eberhard Bethge, *Bekennen und Widerstehen: Aufsätze, Reden, Gespräche* (Munich: Chr. Kaiser Verlag, 1984).

18. Eberhard Bethge, *Erstes Gebot und Zeitgeschichte: Aufsätze und Reden, 1980–1990* (Munich: Chr. Kaiser Verlag, 1991).

Whenever future generations refer to theology in the second half of the twentieth century, Bethge's voice will continue to be heard on these themes.[19]

Despite the many issues that attracted Bethge's attention, there was remarkable continuity in his theological contribution. What held it all together for Bethge was what Bonhoeffer had once suggested to him in his prison letters, a Christological *cantus firmus*.[20] Just as in the music of J. S. Bach polyphony was made possible through a *cantus firmus*, so a firm Christological basis made it possible to hold the fragments of life together, and to explore its rich polyphony. For Bonhoeffer, the key for doing this was to keep on asking the question 'Who is Jesus Christ, for us, today?' This question, Bonhoeffer's 'life's question' as Bethge called it,[21] became central to his own life and work and remained so to the end.

Any attempt to answer the question, as Bethge knew so well, required familiarity with the classic Christologies of the ancient church and how these had been understood through the centuries. But it required something other than an unhistorical, uncritical affirmation of the creeds, as though the context and the issues facing the church today remained the same. Faithfulness to Christ was always 'for today', and therefore a genuine confession of faith was necessarily contextual and contemporary, as it had always been from the beginning. What did it mean to 'confess Christ' here and now, and to do so in a way that corresponded to reality? But whether this had to do with confessing Christ in a secular world, against apartheid, against militarism in Asia, or in dialogue with Jews in the light of the Shoah, it was also personal. Who is Christ *for us*? In a postscript to *Am gegebene Ort*, in one of the few places where Bethge ever wrote of his own

---

19. Christian Gremmels, 'Eulogy for Eberhard Bethge', delivered at Bethge's memorial Service, 25 March 2000, and published in *International Bonhoeffer Society Newsletter: English Language Section* 73 (June 2000), p. 10; translated by Nancy Lukens.

20. Bonhoeffer, *Letters and Papers from Prison*, pp. 393, 437.

21. Bethge, *Bonhoeffer: Exile and Martyr*, p. 149.

personal commitment, he addressed the question 'Who is Jesus of Nazareth for me?' Jesus of Nazareth, he confessed, remained the basis, the measure, and the goal of his life.[22] In sum, he continues, Jesus the essence of truth is revealed as love, enabling us to believe in God; through him we learn to overcome pessimism and respect people, and are bound to God and others; and by him we are set free from hopelessness and fatalism.

Faithful Friend

'Before everything else', wrote his friend and colleague Heinz Eduard Tödt in the Introduction to *Wie eine Flaschenpost*, Bethge was 'publicly known as the interpreter of the theology and life of Dietrich Bonhoeffer.'[23] And in his contribution to the same Festschrift, Hanfried Müller, professor of theology at Humboldt University in Berlin, Bonhoeffer's alma mater, reflected on the fact that Bethge's name had become inseparable from that of Bonhoeffer. Bethge, he wrote, was inevitably and always referred to as 'the friend of Bonhoeffer'.[24] Müller also observed that while there have been many great friendships in the course of history, most of them came to an end when one of the partners died. Not so with Bethge and Bonhoeffer; it might even be said, Müller continued, that Bethge's greatest contribution to the friendship came posthumously.[25] But where did the contribution of the one begin and of the other end? Can we unravel the strands that have been woven by their respective lives? Is it possible, as some have suggested, that through Bethge we hear the voice of Bonhoeffer?

In seeking to answer such questions, we need to remember Tödt's comment that the role of Bethge as interpreter of Bonhoeffer is the one by which he is best known *publicly*. There would never come a time when Bethge was not known publicly as

---

22. Eberhard Bethge, 'Wer ist Jesus von Nazaret für mich?', in Bethge, *Am gegebene Ort*, p. 289.

23. Heinz Eduard Tödt, 'Introduction', in *Wie eine Flaschenpost*, p. 14.

24. Hanfried Müller, 'Würdigung', in *Wie eine Flaschenpost*, p. 168.

25. Müller, 'Würdigung', p. 168.

the 'friend of Bonhoeffer' or referred to as the 'interpreter of Bonhoeffer'. That is how he was inevitably introduced in public. He gladly accepted this description; after all, it was largely of his own making. Bonhoeffer was and remained the dominant figure in the relationship; Bethge, on his own admission, was always the 'country boy' who had been embraced by Bonhoeffer as his friend.

Yet there can be no denying that Bethge was also his own person, far more cultured and astute than his self-description suggests, and there is much to suggest that he was less dependent upon the friendship than was Bonhoeffer. Indeed, there is a sense in which Bonhoeffer needed Bethge's friendship to help him through his own personal struggles, hence Bethge's role as confessor at Finkenwalde. We recall his letter to Bethge in which he thanks him for his patience in helping him to overcome a 'certain volatility' in his character. As a result, Bonhoeffer needed Bethge's friendship in a way that was, perhaps, more exclusive of others than Bethge ever wanted, as in the unfortunate incident involving Gerhard Vibrans. Bonhoeffer had other close friends over the years, but it does seem as though they were usually intense and one at a time, what he referred to as 'singular friendships'. Bethge's personality was more outgoing and inclusive, so that while Bonhoeffer's friendship was pre-eminent and thus very special, he was always a remarkable friend to many others. In fact it was Bethge's warm and outgoing personality that attracted others to him, that first attracted Bonhoeffer – he was someone who had something that Bonhoeffer himself cherished. Certainly, as the post-war years passed, the strength of Bethge's own personality and his ability as a scholar, theologian and pastor became increasingly evident. And the special friend of Bonhoeffer became the special friend of many others.

Towards the end of his life, Bethge reflected at length on the meaning of friendship. He did so in terms of Bonhoeffer's own understanding of friendship, the way in which it had changed over the years as reflected in their relationship, and how it was affected by Bonhoeffer's engagement and Bethge's marriage.[26] In

---

26. Bethge, *Friendship and Resistance*, pp. 80–103.

a deeply moving essay, he referred to Bonhoeffer's poem on 'Friendship' written for him in Tegel Prison. Friendship, Bonhoeffer wrote, is a relationship from which one draws happiness and strength, one of faithfulness in which we are set free.[27] In Bethge, Bonhoeffer had found the companion with whom he could share his concerns and from whom he knew he would receive wise counsel and strength. In Bonhoeffer, Bethge found a friend who encouraged and appreciated his own gifts, who set him free to be himself, and one to whom he could so willingly give his loyalty.

What, then, of the influence that Bethge had upon the reception of Bonhoeffer's life and work after the war? Would Bonhoeffer, a young pastor, relatively unknown except within his circle of friends, colleagues and the emerging ecumenical movement, have become so well known around the world if it had not been for Bethge's labour of friendship? And would Bonhoeffer's theology have been received and interpreted in the way that it has been if Bethge had not provided the direction that he did? Is it an unwarranted exaggeration to say with Paul Oestreicher that 'without Bethge, Bonhoeffer, whose name was to become a household word far beyond the church scene, would hardly be known outside the circle of his family, his students and his friends'?[28] Many would concur. Speaking on the occasion of Bethge's ninetieth birthday, his life-long friend Albrecht Schönherr spoke of the special quality of the friendship between Bethge and Bonhoeffer, but also ventured to suggest that those teaching theology would know little about Bonhoeffer if it were not for Bethge's life's work.[29] Coming from Schönherr, who knew Bonhoeffer before Bethge, and who did so much to further his legacy, these words carry considerable weight.

Bethge would have been the first to say that Bonhoeffer's witness to Christ and the truth was not dependent upon him or

---

27. Bonhoeffer, *Letters and Papers from Prison*, p. 390.

28. Paul Oestreicher, obituary of Eberhard Bethge, *New York Times*, 18 April 2000.

29. Albrecht Schönherr, 'Ein guter Freund: Rede zu Eberhard Bethges 90. Geburtstag', delivered 11 September 1999 in Eisenach; published in *Bonhoeffer Rundbrief* 60 (October 1999), pp. 11–12.

anyone else. The integrity of Bonhoeffer's testimony as one of the twentieth-century Christian martyrs stands firm irrespective of the representation of his friend.[30] Moreover, Bethge never understood his role to be that of an innovator. He was ever and always the faithful custodian and interpreter of Bonhoeffer's legacy – faithful not only to their friendship, but also to the meaning of his friend's life and thought. He sought above all else to pass on Bonhoeffer's legacy to future generations in a way that would have its own integrity and allow Bonhoeffer to continue to speak to them. Bethge did not create the legacy; he interpreted it. Yet, in doing so he inevitably left his own distinct impression upon it. Can an interpreter do otherwise without, in fact, also reducing the legacy to something static?

Bethge's is not the only interpretation of Bonhoeffer's life and work. There have been other biographies of Bonhoeffer and a very large number of dissertations, papers, and books about his theology. Not all of these have agreed with Bethge's interpretation on specific points, though virtually all have acknowledged their indebtedness to him. Bethge welcomed other views even though he may have disagreed with them. While he did not approve the 'creative misuse' of Bonhoeffer, or the ways in which some documentaries portrayed him, he did not believe Bonhoeffer's thought should be placed in a straitjacket, as though there could only be one possible way to understand and appropriate his theology. Nor did he believe that it should simply be appropriated in an uncritical or ahistorical manner.

Yet there can be no doubt that Bethge towered above all others in his Bonhoeffer scholarship, and that his interpretation, especially from the Alden-Tuthill Lectures in Chicago and the biography onwards, has indelibly shaped the way in which Bonhoeffer has been received. This was inevitable – and appropriate. He had already begun to play an important role as the sounding board for Bonhoeffer's theological ideas at Finkenwalde, something that continued until Bonhoeffer's death. No

---

30. On 9 July 1998, a statue of Dietrich Bonhoeffer was unveiled on the West Front of Westminster Abbey in London, along with statues of nine other representative Christian martyrs of the twentieth century.

one better knew the mind of Bonhoeffer; and Bonhoeffer had complete confidence in him as the one who should become his interpreter in case he died. Moreover Bonhoeffer recognized that Bethge would bring to that task the gifts and skills that he had already demonstrated at Finkenwalde and which were appropriate and necessary for the task. After all, he was his 'daring, trusting spirit'. Years later Schönherr wrote of Bethge's remarkable ability to 'generate catalysing thoughts' in Bonhoeffer, while Zimmermann suggested that Bonhoeffer needed Bethge's theologically pragmatic side to counter his own theoretical streak.[31]

Amongst Bethge's skills was his ability to process Bonhoeffer's thoughts, clarify his ideas, and order and communicate them imaginatively. That becomes ever more obvious as we reflect on the correspondence between the two friends both before and during Bonhoeffer's imprisonment. Bethge fulfilled Bonhoeffer's need not only for a close and intimate friend, but also for a colleague with whom he could discuss his views in depth. So even before Bonhoeffer's death, Bethge made an important contribution to the development of Bonhoeffer's thought, and he probably would have continued to do so if Bonhoeffer had lived. If Bonhoeffer had survived, he would undoubtedly have completed much of what remained fragmentary, and he may well have done so in much the same way as Bethge eventually did or, perhaps, differently. Who can tell? But he did not survive, and Bethge did what needed to be done and what only he could do.

During the years of friendship both Bethge's and Bonhoeffer's lives were fragmented by historical circumstances. In Bonhoeffer's case, the fragments were never brought together except in death when, he believed, Christ would make all things complete and nothing would be lost.[32] But his was a lonely, painful death separated from family and friends; and the circumstances surrounding it were unknown to them until much later. In Bethge's case, the fragments gradually and then increasingly

---

31. See Tödt, 'Eberhard Bethge Als Theologe und Zeitgeschichtsforseher', pp. 398–9.
32. Bonhoeffer, *Letters and Papers from Prison*, p. 170.

came together in a life of remarkable fulfilment that ended in the fullness of time, surrounded and celebrated by family, friends and colleagues. Gathering the fragments of Bonhoeffer's life and theology into a coherent, meaningful whole, he brought them to appropriate posthumous fulfilment through his scholarship and his ministry.

Mensch

Bethge was always the 'friend of Bonhoeffer', but far more than the custodian and interpreter of Bonhoeffer's legacy: he was a remarkable person who left his own unique stamp on all that he did. Yes, he was deeply indebted to Bonhoeffer as his theological mentor, but Bonhoeffer also recognized Bethge's own gifts as a theologian, preacher and teacher very early on in their relationship. Had Bethge not already taken a stand for the Confessing Church while a student in Wittenberg even before coming under the influence of Bonhoeffer? But certainly, Bethge became widely known because of his relationship to Bonhoeffer, and in that sense Bonhoeffer made him who he was. Yet he was someone who would undoubtedly have made his mark, undoubtedly differently, even if he had not fulfilled his role as Bonhoeffer's friend. Not only was he a friend to so many others; he was someone who excelled in the art of friendship. And he made a lasting impression on others chiefly because of his great humanity that informed everything else he did. Indeed, his faithfulness to his friend was embodied in the humanity with which he expressed it.

At his ninetieth birthday celebration held in the Godesberg Castle restaurant several months before his death, Bethge himself expressed his gratitude for everything that his life had been. Responding to the speeches of congratulation, standing dignified and tall even in old age, he spoke of his deep satisfaction for all that his life had meant and all that he had been able to accomplish. Avoiding any false humility, yet with a humanity that characterized his own life, Bethge accepted the praise of others for what he had achieved, saying: 'Ich bin stolz' (I am proud).

Not long after, at Bethge's funeral in March 2000, Professor Christian Gremmels, representing the German section of the International Bonhoeffer Society, reflected on how much of Bethge's life was devoted to others, in order that their work should succeed.[33] He also reminded the congregation that despite the many honours he received, Bethge always showed reserve about his own achievements and the role he played, referring to himself simply as 'Pastor Bethge'. He was a pastor at heart, concerned about the church of Jesus Christ, and concerned about other people. But, Gremmels recounted, when asked towards the end of his life what was most important to him, Bethge replied, 'That I was faithful to him.'[34] By 'him' he meant, of course, Bonhoeffer, but he could equally have meant, as Gremmels intimated, the God of the First Commandment, the God of Jesus Christ.

For what motivated Bethge's faithfulness to his friend? Was it the fact that he had made a pledge that he was in duty bound to keep? Surely not. Was it the fact that Bonhoeffer had been his mentor and had left an indelible impression upon him? Certainly that was part of it. There can be no doubt that Bethge became who he was not least because of Bonhoeffer's influence. But there is something more profound at work in Bethge's faithfulness, something intangible that reflected a depth of spirit that gave their friendship a quality not often experienced. Over and above all else, what attracted Bethge to Bonhoeffer was that he represented all that Bethge himself valued most highly. Bonhoeffer was a pastor and theologian of integrity, committed to the truth, to justice, to the plight of the oppressed, to a genuine confession of Christ, the *cantus firmus*. Bethge was faithful to Bonhoeffer because he recognized in Bonhoeffer's person and in his theology an authentic representation of the gospel to which he had dedicated his own life from the moment he decided to become a pastor under the influence of his father. And it was because he believed so strongly in his calling that he gladly engaged in his

---

33. Gremmels, 'Eulogy for Eberhard Bethge', p. 9.
34. Gremmels, 'Eulogy for Eberhard Bethge', p. 10.

life's work on behalf of his friend, and generously 'gave away that which had been given to him'.[35]

Bethge died peacefully at home during his afternoon rest on 18 March 2000. He was ninety years old. His funeral took place on the following Saturday, a cool, rainy day. The service was held in the Marienforster Kirche in Bad Godesberg, a town set on the banks of the Rhine not far from Wachtberg-Villiprott. After the service the large congregation proceeded on foot through the streets of the town to the Burgfriedhof, a cemetery set on the hill leading up to the Godesberg, which gave the town its name. There, not far from the Jewish section, Eberhard Bethge was laid to rest. The gathering that followed in the splendid Redoute, where Beethoven had performed in times past, appropriately celebrated what Bishop Wolfgang Huber described as a fulfilled, accomplished, masterly and well-rounded life. The contrast between Bethge's long life and peaceful death and that of his friend Bonhoeffer, murdered at 39 by the Gestapo, could not have been greater. Appropriately, Huber began his sermon by quoting from Bonhoeffer's poem on the 'Death of Moses', written in prison in September 1944. One stanza reads:

Wondrous deeds with me you have performed,
bitterness to sweetness here transformed.[36]

Bethge had lived to see the 'promised land', hopes realized, tasks complete, bitter memories transformed by the passing of time and the fulfilment of dreams.

Huber's funeral sermon text was from Hebrews 13.9, a text, incidentally, that had been given to both Renate and Eberhard at their confirmation: 'it is well for the heart to be strengthened by grace'. Reflecting on these words, Huber expressed what many others had experienced during the years:

35. Huber, '. . . dass das Herz Fest werde', p. 5.

36. Translation from *A Testament to Freedom: the Essential Writings of Dietrich Bonhoeffer*, ed. Geffrey Kelly and F. Burton Nelson (Harper SanFrancisco, 1990), p. 547.

Seldom have I experienced the grace of God so naturally illuminated in someone's face as in that of Eberhard Bethge. Everyone who met him experienced something of this grace. How generously he gave away that which had been given to him! It is hard to bear the realization that the glow of his humanity will remain only in the memory of it. Yet this unhappiness is surpassed by our gratitude for this great, fulfilled, completed life.[37]

Huber spoke of Bethge's ability as a preacher and teacher, and his interpretation of resistance as a form of public confession. But it was his 'virtuosity at friendship', and what Clifford Green referred to as 'the quality of his humanity that equalled the enormous contribution he made as a scholar and teacher',[38] that made the most lasting impression on all who knew him. He was the epitome of what Bonhoeffer had written from prison: 'The Christian is not a *homo religiosus*, but simply a human being [*Mensch*] as Jesus was a human being'.[39] Yes, Bethge will indeed be remembered as the friend and interpreter of Dietrich Bonhoeffer, his 'daring, trusting spirit'. But he will also be remembered by those who knew him best for what he was in himself, for 'the glow of his humanity'.

---

37. Huber, 'Funeral Sermon for Eberhard Bethge', p. 5.

38. Clifford Green, 'Remarks at Eberhard Bethge's Funeral Reception', *International Bonhoeffer Society Newsletter: English Language Section*, 73 (June 2000), p. 11.

39. Bonhoeffer, *Letters and Papers from Prison*, p. 369.

Index